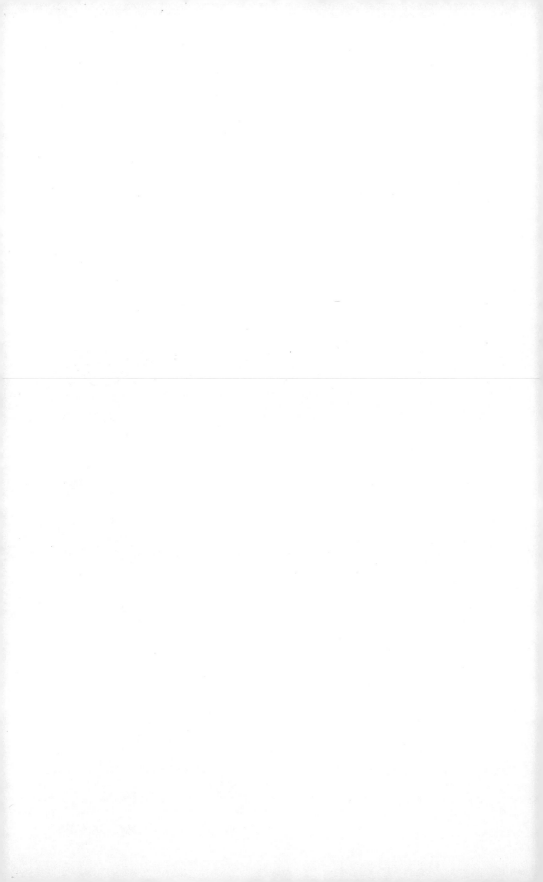

Virtual Economies and Financial Crime

To Bruce, Mum and Dad, with love

Virtual Economies and Financial Crime

Money Laundering in Cyberspace

Clare Chambers-Jones

University of the West of England, UK and General Secretary of the Commonwealth Legal Education Association

Edward Elgar

Cheltenham, UK • Northampton, MA, USA

Published by
Edward Elgar Publishing Limited
The Lypiatts
15 Lansdown Road
Cheltenham
Glos GL50 2JA
UK

Edward Elgar Publishing, Inc.
William Pratt House
9 Dewey Court
Northampton
Massachusetts 01060
USA

A catalogue record for this book
is available from the British Library

Library of Congress Control Number: 2012935286

ISBN 978 1 84980 932 0

Typeset by Servis Filmsetting Ltd, Stockport, Cheshire
Printed and bound by MPG Books Group, UK

Contents

Figures

Tables

Boxes

Acknowledgements

This book was the culmination of an early career research grant from the University of the West of England and I must thank the university and the law department for their belief in my research. I began the research for this book whilst I was in hospital for a trachea replacement and the book itself gave me something to ponder on whilst undergoing hours of recovery. In a sense, the book was my saviour away from health issues.

Secondly, my research would not be where it is today without the unwavering support of my friend and colleague Dr Nic Ryder. Thanks must also be given to my devoted proofreader, my mum, Jill Chambers, who reads everything I write with such diligence and dedication; thank you so much, Mum. Again, thanks to my dad, Chris Chambers, who started my passion for banking and finance when I was just a little girl sitting at the dining room table.

However, the book could not have been completed without the love and support my husband Bruce Jones has given me throughout the last two very difficult years. Thank you, my darling, even though I know you will never read further than this point.

1.   Introduction

You may be forgiven for wondering why virtual worlds are worthy of investigation. You may be forgiven, even more so, for wondering why virtual world economies and financial crime should even be considered in the same breath. However, these are real and worthy subjects for investigation. Why? Because they are real and have real world effects. Do not be confused by the name virtual worlds; these worlds are ever present in society and can have both positive and negative effects. For example, virtual worlds are used by a large demographic of the population. There are 1.4 billion registered accounts (Kzer World Wide 31 August 2011) of people participating in virtual worlds and these people are from all backgrounds, of both genders and racially diverse. More importantly, there is a huge part of this demographic, roughly just under half,[1] who are teenagers or young adults, who will sooner rather than later move into the adult world of work and business and they will want commerce to move as quickly and as diversely as the virtual world games they have grown up with.

Nardo states that, 'The issue of combating economic and financial crime at a global level has become progressively critical in the international arena over the decades which marked the transition from the twentieth century to the twenty-first'.[2] Nardo demonstrates that past work in the area of financial crime in virtual worlds has been largely focused on structure and method approach and not the socio-legal workings of the crime. He states, 'it seems therefore useful to increase the analysis by opening the quest to economic and sociological aspects',[3] and this is where this book is theoretically positioned. Virtual economic crime may appear to be small in comparison with other illicit crimes such as drug trafficking, but it is now emerging that there is a strong connection between organised crime in the real world and economic crime via the internet. 'Illegal markets knowledge is indeed generally very poor', and as such this book aims to add to the research being conducted in this ever growing area. What is widely accepted is that 'the purpose of combating economic and financial

---

[1]   Read Write Web, http://www.readwriteweb.com/, accessed 1 October 2011.
[2]   Nardo (2011).
[3]   Ibid.

crime must confront a multifaceted situation, where numerous and different components interact in a highly complex dynamics'.[4]

Despite the increase in criminal activity via the internet, business and governments can and do take advantage of the advancement of virtual worlds in cost cutting. With the use of the internet becoming more prevalent, uptake for online courses is increasing. More people can attend and effective interaction online is being created. Virtual worlds are also being used as training and educational environments and social places where new economic, political and social theories can be devised within controlled simulations. Furthermore, virtual worlds could also be used as a mechanism for continuing business in times of social hardship or environmental health issues such as swine flu or the recent economic crisis.

This book will explore the realms of the virtual world, exposing its reality and its contributory effects on the real world and real people. In this, the virtual world of Second Life will explored and detailed as a case study on the background concept of financial crime in a virtual world. Financial crime shall encompass any financial crime committed online and which pertains to a broad real world definition of a criminal activity, such as illicit gambling, financial fraud and money laundering. Money laundering shall be focused upon as the main criminal activity within virtual worlds, but this is not to say that it is the only financial crime occurring.

Academics have explored the topic of money laundering and terrorist financing and it has been shown by Levi[5] that despite international efforts, it is hard to show any improvements in reducing risky finance such as money laundering and organised crime. The leap from virtual money laundering to organised crime has become increasingly recognised. Criminals who are committing economic crime are using the internet as a means of gaining, storing and using valuable information.[6] Virtual money laundering can therefore be seen to be even harder to reduce due to the complexities surrounding detection and prosecution, as well as jurisdictional matters.

The purpose of this book as just outlined is to portray the virtual world as being a mere continuum of the real world and therefore worthy of falling under the real world legal remit. The question is how this can be proved so that legislators and law enforcement agencies can create a legislative provision which is not only international but that covers the necessary interlinking crimes within virtual financial crime whilst

---

[4]   Ibid.
[5]   Levi (2010).
[6]   Di Nicola and Scartezzini (2000).

balancing basic human rights. This book is not intended to be the answer to all these issues, but is merely a stepping stone towards growth in acceptance and awareness of the crime as a real issue. Many law enforcement agencies already acknowledge virtual financial crime as a real world crime, but they lack the technological investigatory powers and tools necessary to detect and locate virtual financial crimes taking place. They also lack the necessary legislative provisions to ensure that effective legal measures are in place to ensure prevention, detection and prosecution of virtual world criminals.

Each chapter is designed to demonstrate and build a collective argument that the real world and the virtual are by default governed by some of the same rules and standards that one would expect in a real world situation. Of course, not all rules and laws apply in virtual worlds as they do in virtual worlds. For example, if the virtual world is about fighting each other, then no real world laws apply, unless, that is, there is a detrimental effect on a real world person. Therefore if the virtual world crosses over and touches, influences or affects the real world, then it should be governed by the same standards that the real world expects.

Chapter 2 examines the virtual world of Second Life, given the ubiquitous way in which virtual worlds can evolve and dominate a generation's perception. Second Life is a web-based land which has been developed by Linden Labs. The game requires people to register and become residents of the world 'Second Life'. A player of the game is called an avatar and these can be created in the likeness of any person. Therefore you can be six foot tall and blonde or dark with blue eyes. You can also develop your avatar's personality and personal surroundings. For example, if desired, the avatar could become a successful business person, living in a mansion, who rides around in a sports car all the time. Alternatively, you could be a rugby player or a football star dressed head to foot in Nike clothing and footwear. For big real world brands are also big in the virtual world. Second Life is also governed by Second Life rules and regulations, which is interesting given the cyber jurisdictional debate that occurs in Chapter 6 of this book. Second Life also has its own currency called Linden Dollars. These can be exchanged via the Linden E exchange through PayPal or credit cards for real world money. Linden Dollars can therefore be used to purchase virtual goods within Second Life. The birth of the virtual economy has therefore occurred. What is more important is the economic effects it has on the real economy and how real world criminals take advantage of loopholes in the virtual economy.

Chapter 3 considers the evolution of virtual economies and how law and economics have always played an important part in each other's development and evolution. The chapter also focuses on some of the virtual world economic crimes that have taken place which have affected the real world. It is important to show that it is not simply a matter of detecting money laundering, but that there are a multitude of financial crimes taking place. An example which is used within the chapter is the use of gold farming, which is prolific in Asian countries and is something which can affect the real world economy. The chapter also examines the synergies between the real and the virtual economies, for example the case study of Ginko Financial and Eve Online. Ginko Financial was a successful banking business within Second Life, but due to rule changes specified by Linden Labs, Ginko was unable to meet the demands of the rule changes and as a consequence there was a run on the bank. This was the first run on a virtual bank in history and since its collapse, it has been discovered that it was also a Ponzi scheme. Financial crimes were already taking place before the onset of the bank run. The lack of regulation and clear banking guidance meant that a lot of people lost real money in Ginko's collapse. This book questions whether tighter regulation and control from the real world would have made the virtual investment a safer place for people's real money.

Chapter 4 examines the history of money and the evolution of what we see as being defined as money. The purpose of this chapter is to suggest to the reader that what was once considered overwhelmingly unrealistic and impossible soon becomes reality and accepted as the norm. As society and technology develop, so do people's perceptions and accepted attributed norms and customs. The chapter looks back at how bartering used to be a means of monetary and goods exchange before the use of notes and coins. The use of card payments and electronic, mobile and internet banking are now generally accepted means of monetary interaction, whereas once these were considered to be an exception and not a normally accepted means of transacting. The evolution of money is also charted through the use of regulatory development. The use of regulation to maintain control over an economic system is important not only for the banking system but for society as well. Monetary transactions which are intangible, such as internet payments, are built on trust and the confidence of the transacting parties. Trust and confidence in the real world are built on solid regulatory foundations, where parties know there is legal recourse should any problem arise with a financial transaction. In virtual economies there is no such reassurance and therefore the chapter illustrates the need in the case of a virtual economy which wants to grow, for a real and solid legal infrastructure. Money is important to people and money can be the cause of many legal disputes; therefore it is important to create a foundation on which a stable virtual economy can be built. The chapter also focuses on the many banking and financial regulations that are in place around today's modern banking structure, demonstrating the importance of maintaining an ever closer link with the real world so that when financial crises do occur in either sphere, the effects of the crisis can be maintained and minimised.

Chapter 5 examines case studies of virtual financial crimes. It begins by looking at how virtual money laundering can take place by examining the process of how real world money can be placed in the virtual world. The chapter looks at the technology behind this transactional process, such as PayPal, the virtual wallet and virtual automated telling machines (ATMs), to name but a few mechanisms.

Chapter 5 also moves on to discuss the real world anti-money laundering regulations and examines which are applicable to the virtual world. It is not ideal to have real world regulations bent to fit virtual world financial crime, but it is a starting point and one which is very necessary. The chapter chooses to look at the UK, USA, China and Korea as another starting point for a country analysis. The reason for these countries being selected is because of their interaction with virtual economies and the use of virtual worlds. Though most of the financial crimes that have taken place stem from these countries, that is not to say that other countries are not also prolific in virtual financial crimes, but this is the selection I have chosen to make in this book.

Chapter 6 forms the heart of the book. It looks at laws and virtual worlds and grapples with how to fit virtual financial crimes into an archaic set of real world laws. In places these laws do not even acknowledge the presence of the internet and cyber laws within them. The chapter looks at past judiciary decisions applying the law to virtual world crimes, such as the *Yahoo* and *Zippo* cases examining jurisdictional issues as well as the application of laws within cyberspace and the internet. The chapter further examines the rule of law within virtual worlds and how real world laws can be extrapolated to extend to virtual worlds, as well as more generally to the internet as a whole. A vast discussion on the application of how jurisdiction is measured is also outlined within this chapter.

Chapter 7 is the concluding chapter of this book and paves the way for future research and further questions which must be asked if there is ever going to be a successful and effective virtual economy which commands the trust and confidence of society and law enforcement agencies. Rules and regulations must surely play a part in creating a sound infrastructure in which the virtual economy can grow. Regulating the internet is not about restricting people's freedom of information or impacting on rights of privacy; it is merely about ensuring a safe financial market which could benefit many people in society. We have an opportunity to create a new means of economy which could benefit many people globally. The chance we have is to create a solid platform created out of sensible and realistic laws, providing an opportunity for a virtual economy to grow. International cooperation is essential and Chapter 7 outlines a possible solution to these issues.

2. History of Second Life

> To become a spectator of one's own life is to escape the suffering of life.
> (Oscar Wilde, 1854–1900)

INTRODUCTION

Music, literature, art, performing arts, nature are all forms of escapism into other worlds and as we move towards an increasing technological world, virtual worlds are a new form of escapism that we find ourselves encapsulated within. As Oscar Wilde propounds above, we, as human beings, have used various media as a means of escaping into the unreal to avoid the real. Today these unreal worlds are taking the form of virtual worlds that engage us not only as a single entity but where we interact with others, using, simultaneously, the same medium to escape. What is interesting is that not only is the virtual world a means to escape but the traditional methods of escapism, as listed above, are also featured within the virtual world as a means of escaping the virtual. For instance, there is a thriving English Literature appreciation society within Second Life (SL) (http://literaturealive.blogspot.com/), where users can meet and escape the unreal by discussing the real. Confused?

The aim of this chapter is not to confuse but to highlight the beginning of this virtual world, called SL. From this historical overview and through deliberation of whether virtual worlds have real world effects, we can see how the SL fantasy has permeated reality and has had real world consequences, for the purposes of this book, in relation to the economy and virtual money laundering.

HOW SECOND LIFE STARTED

SL is a virtual world which enables users to live out a second life, in every sense of the word, through a computer program. It is more than just a game. It has an infrastructure similar to that of the real world. It is here where the confusion between the real and virtual begins. SL has a virtual social scene, a virtual economy, virtual crime, virtual employment, virtual

Figure 2.1 Stories without Borders – Second Life

retail. The list goes on as it does in the real world. Today Second Life has hundreds of thousands of users who immerse themselves in this virtual world, for pleasure and/or business.

SL was created by Philip Rosedale in 1999 primarily as a means of developing software to allow users to have full immersion in a virtual world. He drew upon the ideas of Neal Stephenson's novel *Snow Crash*, although Rosedale has said he undertook experiments whilst at university in developing a virtual world. Rosedale considered himself an artist[1] and as such wanted to portray the world as a microcosm. He used computer software instead of paints or materials to build his representation of the world around him. Initially, SL was called Linden World as Rosedale called himself Philip Linden in the virtual world (in-world). However, this morphed quickly into what we know today as SL. In the early days of SL, the game resembled other video games and, although pioneering for its day, was still largely based on the idea that the games developer would create the virtual world in which the users played. Rosedale and his team of developers wanted to change this and so they decided that the users should be able to create their own world. The developers therefore passed over their role to the end user and the uniqueness of SL was born. Terminology within SL is also different: the team of developers that created SL are known as 'Lindens', other unique words and phrases will be explained in due course throughout the book. However, this is not a technical examination of SL, rather an examination of its laws and regulations and how its actions and development can and have affected the real world. It is this cross-over between the real and the virtual which is of interest here. Given this, inevitably some technological aspects will have to be considered, but this will be kept simple and the writer begs forgiveness for the limitations of her technological explanations.

In 2002 Beta testing started and it was opened to the public six months later. During this testing phase taxes were placed on land maintenance, rezzing and maintaining resident-created objects. There was also a teleportation fee and a tax on prims (short for primitives or early residents).[2] Although this initially appeared sensible, since the taxes allowed the Linden developers to extend development, necessary because of the burden placed on the hardware by each extra prim in the virtual world. Later taxation within the virtual world would cause great political ripples of contention (discussed later).

SL went live on 23 June 2003. In October of the same year, many updates

---

[1] Rymaszewski et al. (2008).

[2] Ibid., p. 4.

were introduced. One key update created tools for evading taxes and a new stipend called dwell which rewarded socialising.[3] This met with consternation initially on the part of SL residents, since they believed pointless social gatherings were being rewarded, whilst SL creators of context were being penalised by taxes. This dissent led to a social revolution. The crackdown on prim-tax evaders led to 'drama and dissent'.[4] The revolution did not take long and by December 2003 the revolutionists had won and they introduced a tax based on land ownership. December 2003 also saw the concept of time being introduced into SL (the same as Pacific Standard Time).

So how does SL work?

> SL works as if you were a god. Not an almighty god – more like one of those mythological gods, who tended to specialise in certain areas, get drunk, have sex, fight and (most importantly) cast spells at will. And just like a methodological god, you're also able to fly, and teleport where you like in an instant.[5]

SL looks like earth and resembles the physical world. It has air, water and sea and although you can 'build castles in the sky',[6] you still have gravity, weather and a sun and a moon. Your appearance can be whatever you choose it to be; you can be a cat or a human or a bubble floating in the sky. In SL, your persona is known as an Avatar and SL resident. These avatars create new objects such as clothes, food, tools and cars etc., which are unique to that avatar.

SL consists of interlinked regions that contain the life described above. Each region has an area of 65,536 SL square metres.[7] These regions are geographical as well as administrative so that Universal Unique Identifiers (UUIS) can keep track of what is going on in SL. Such UUIs are, for example, avatar agents, land parcels, group regions, your login sessions, etc.[8]

RULES OF SECOND LIFE

SL is regulated not only by its residents, but also by its creators and by the SL Bar Association.[9] The rules the Linden developers created are different

---

[3]   Ibid., p. 4.
[4]   Ibid., p. 5.
[5]   Ibid., p. 5.
[6]   Ibid., p. 5.
[7]   Ibid., p. 5.
[8]   Ibid., p. 7.
[9]   SL Bar Association website, http://www.slba.info/credentials.hmtl, accessed 20 October 2011.

from those created by the residents of SL and will be dealt with separately. Similarly, this is meant as a brief discussion of the legal aspects of SL, since the law and virtual worlds will be discussed later in Chapter 6.

SL is a community, just not in a conventional sense. However, the residents of SL have created community standards by which to live to. There are also six cardinal sins which have been created and are forbidden. These are:

- *Intolerance* – As in real life being derogatory or demeaning another person's race, ethnicity, religion or sexual orientation is a big no-no.
- *Harassment* – Harassment can take many forms, but the common denominator is that someone is intruded upon. If your actions or words are upsetting someone and they make it plain more than once, stop.
- *Assault* – This includes pushing, shooting, shoving another SL resident in an area marked as safe (safe status is placed as an icon on the top information bar). Making fellow residents miserable by attacking them with scripted objects is forbidden too.
- *Disclosure* – Information about another resident can be freely shared only if it is displayed in the resident's profile, or if you have their consent to share this information. This includes residents' real-life data as well as their conversation in-world and on other official Linden Lab sites – posting or otherwise sharing conversation logs requires prior consent of the people affected.
- *Indecency* – it's simple: if what you want to do can be offensive to other people do it on private land on Mature areas.
- *Disturbing the peace* – Briefly don't be a pest. Every resident is entitled to an enjoyable and peaceful SL. (Rymaszewski et al. 2008, p. 13)

In addition to the self-made regulatory rules by which SL residents live, there is a prolific legal association comprising legal professionals from the real world and faux legal people in the virtual world. To ensure that real legal professionals are recognised, there is a credential-checking service which the SL Bar Association ensures is carried out on new members. This legal association comes together to discuss legal issues affecting their virtual world, to hold lectures and meetings and to discuss legal aspects of the future. By having this legal element of the virtual world, residents are complying with the norms of real society.

CURRENCY

SL economics and money is the central theme of this book. It will be dealt with in much greater detail throughout the book, but this is the central bedrock of the book. SL has its own currency and therefore its

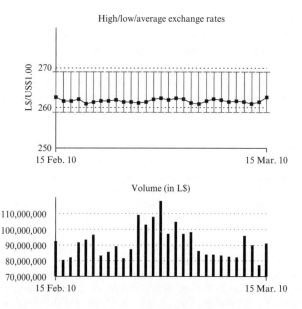

*Figure 2.2   Financial indices for Linden $ (L$), 15 February–15 March
2010*

own economics and financial world within a virtual world. It is when this
virtual economy has an impact on the real world economy and finance
that it becomes interesting. However, before we get to this stage, it is
essential to deal with the currency of SL. SL's own currency is called
the Linden dollar and these are exchangeable for real life dollars. The
exchange rate fluctuates as in real life economies, and is determined by
supply and demand rates. In addition to the normal flow of economics,
the rates are also tweaked by the stipends and bonus contained within SL
and the ratio between new premium and basic accounts started by fresh
SL residents.[10] The economic data for SL is stored and can be viewed
online at http://secondlife.com/statistics/economy-data.php (accessed 15
March 2010).

At the time of writing, the Linden dollar was worth L$249 per
US$1.00.[11]

---

10   Rymaszewski et al. (2008), p.9.
11   SL Index, www.secondlife.com/my.index/market.php, accessed 12 September
2011.

STATISTICS YEAR END 2009

As with any country or community, SL produces end-of-year statistics showing how it has faired during that year. These are not only financial, but cover usage and land acquired. It is important to note that the real world has an effect on the virtual here. The global economic downturn has affected the economic position of SL as well. It has been made clear

Table 2.1   2009 statistics for SL

Financial

- User-to-User transactions in 2009 totalled US$567 million in 2009, growth of 65% over 2008
- The total amount of virtual currency in circulation reached L$6.95 billion, growth of 23% over December 2008
- The US dollar value of L$ in circulation totalled US$26.5 million in December 2009
- Sales of user-generated virtual items on Xstreet SL reached L$1.6 billion or US$6.1 million, growth of 74% over 2008
- The total US dollar value of all Linden dollars traded on the LindeX™ currency exchange in 2009 reached US$115 million in value, 7% growth over 2008
- The total US dollar value of all Linden dollars traded on the Xstreet SL™ currency exchange in 2009 reached US$1.5 million in value, 169% growth over 2008

Usage

- Residents spent 481 million hours in Second Life in 2009, 21% growth over 2008
- User hours lost to downtime as a portion of total user hours were down 66%, to a best-ever low of 0.19% for the whole year
- Monthly repeat logins reached an all-time high of 769,000 in December 2009, 15% growth over December 2008

Land

- Resident-owned regions reached 23,900 in December 2009, up 6% over December 2008
- Total resident-owned land (including Mainland) reached 1.85 billion square metres in December 2009, up 7% over December 2008

Source: Statistics, end of year 2009, Second Life.

Monthly unique users with repeat logins (thousands)

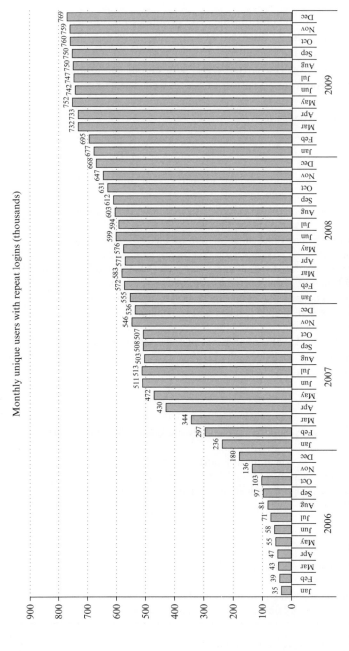

Note: 'Monthly Unique Residents with repeat logins reached 769,000 in December – in December 2009, monthly repeat logins peaked at 769,468. Year to year, December 2009 repeat logins grew 15% from December 2008 while repeat logins and were up 2% over September 2009'. (2009 End of year Second Life wrap up).

Figure 2.3   Monthly unique users with repeat logins

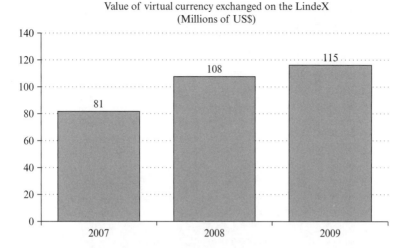

Value of virtual currency exchanged on the LindeX
(Millions of US$)

Note: 'Trading activity on the LindeX reached US$115 million – The volume of exchange on the LindeX, the marketplace for Linden dollars (L$), the Second Life virtual currency, reached US$115 million in 2009. This is 7% growth compared to the previous year'. (2009 End of year Second Life wrap up).

Figure 2.4   Value of virtual currency exchanged on Lindex

that the US as well as the UK economy have both declined since the economic turmoil started in 2007. The SL economy, though, has steadily grown. However, having said this, many residents have suffered through their real and virtual businesses. Despite this, there is money to be made through virtual business (Miller and Stone 2009). 'Spending real money on products that do not exist' is a dream come true for many businesses. People are spending real money on virtual goods, often costing a $1 each, within social networking and gaming sites. The cost of creating the goods is negligible but it is estimated that these products could bring in $1 billion for the US and $5 billion worldwide in 2009 (Miller and Stone, 7 Nov. 2009).

KEY SOCIETAL CHANGES IN THE VIRTUAL WORLD

SL has the status of a real community and as such has a history that charts its development and progress through different eras and stages. Within this next section the historical developments will be charted to show how SL growth affects its policies, rules and economic running. Additionally it

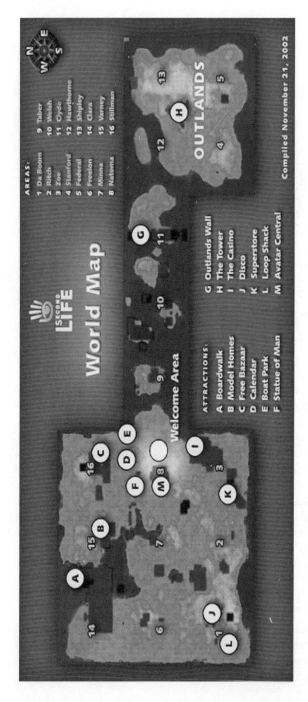

Figure 2.5   Second Life world map

may be useful now to show a map of SL, bearing in mind that it changes daily, if not minute by minute. SL is all about visual stimulation and therefore throughout this book there will be images captured and displayed to give the real essence of the nature of SL.

Philip Linden once said about SL, 'I am not building a game, I am building a new country'.[12] This proposition is not far from the truth. SL's historical, cultural and personal citizen growth demonstrates that it is much more than a game. In fact its history timeline is more akin to reading a history textbook, when studying a new country. Given this, SL's history demonstrates that this virtual world resembles the real world in so many more ways than could be expected from what is, in truth, a computer simulation. This is where the distinction between real and virtual becomes blurred and is what this book is concerned about.

The history of SL has been categorised and charted in seven main eras to date. This will undoubtedly be added to as each year passes and the growth of SL continues.

First Era: 2001 – Early 2003 – Pre-historic, pre–Beta

- Philip Rosedale created a platform to test the possibility of virtual reality.
- It was initially known as LindenWorld and the early avatars were known as Primitars.
- In 2002 LindenWorld was renamed Second Life.
- In March 2002 SL was opened up to non-Lindens, i.e. those outside the group of developers and creators of this virtual world.
- Initially, there were three small tribes that were very close knit and were known as the Alphas and the closed Betas. Joining these groups as by invitation only.
- The land that was created in this first era was shared as common land; no one person 'owned' the land.

Second Era – Summer 2003: Natives vs Colonists

- In April 2003, Beta, which was a closed by-invitation-only group, opened to the public.
- This meant an influx of new residents (as SL users are known, since they do not think of themselves as players of a game but as residents of a new country).

---

12 Rymaszewski et al. (2008), p. 10.

- Most of these new settlers intermingled, but as with any influx of new people, cultural rifts began to appear.
- An area in SL was created, known as the Outlands, and this was the area where any conflicts between residents were encouraged to be settled. Conflict was rife within the Outlands.
- During this period, one conflict was named. The war of Jessie's Wall was a particular battle which is noted in SL's history. Another MMO (Massively Multiplayer) game, World War II online (WWIIOL), joined SL as a means of meeting and using SL building tools to plan tactics in WWIIOL. These new residents were conflict minded and their influx caused a culture shock among the normally placid SL residents. Open battle broke out between these two groups and centred around an area in the Outlands called Jessie's Wall. The wall separated the conflict zone and the peaceful area of the Outlands. The wall was also used as a billboard for anti-war and pro-war statements on the war on Iraq. By having this cross-over between emotions within the virtual world and the real world, SL becomes more than a game and becomes a platform for real world expressions. During the conflict in SL, weapons were created and used, but eventually the battle died down because of the growth of SL. Residents new and old had enough space not to irritate each other with their opposing views.

Second Era: Summer 2003: Revolution!

- 'As society forms, so does upheaval'.[13]
- 2003 saw residents fight against the taxes imposed by the Lindens, which were automatically deducted from the residents' accounts.
- Lindens said that this was a means of preventing overheating of their servers, since residents would not build as many objects within SL. However, residents saw it differently; they saw that they were being taxed for creating and expanding SL.
- As a result of the taxation, what was to come to be known as 'The tea crate rebellion' created the start of the revolution in July 2003. A group called Americana that specialised in replicating tributes to US landmarks was prolific in opposing the taxes. In protest against the taxes, they dropped tea crates across the SL world and set their landmarks on fire. Two groups were formed, the rebels and the redcoats – 'Linden loyalists', in other words. However, 'from conflict, comes

---

[13]   Ibid., p. 315.

community',[14] and so the communities within SL grew and evolved just as real world communities evolve and emerge from conflict with fresh perspectives on their future.

Third Era: Winter 2003: A New Nation is Born

- After the revolution, Lindens decided that they needed to make new policies to govern SL. Although rules had been in place, albeit vaguely, previously, the following three new policy decisions marked the way forward in created a formal regulatory system:

  1. Lindens ended the monthly subscription fee and replaced it with a monthly charge on land purchased.
  2. Lindens adopted a laissez-faire policy on buying and selling the official in-world currency on the open market for real money.
  3. Lindens recognised the residents' legal intellectual property (IP) rights over in-world objects and scripts that they had created.

- *November 14 2003 IP Independence Day*: This was an important day for SL residents; it gave them legally enforceable IP rights over the objects and scripts they had created in-world. This in turn led to a rise in the mercantile class in SL. The policy was initiated by a Stanford law professor, Lawrence Lessig.

Fourth Era: Late 2003 through Early 2004: Expanding the Frontier

- This fourth era saw a rush in December 2003 to buy up land in SL. This was promulgated by the cessation of taxes and monthly sub-scription fees.
- Initially Linden Labs held 'land grabs,'[15] but these were later replaced with the more sophisticated 'land auctions'.
- The first island to be sold was bought by a real world commercial building agency who planned to use the island as a virtual marketing platform. Fizik Baskerville bought the island on 7 January 2004 for US$1,200.
- SL residents were not happy about their country being turned into a commercial venture, but as soon as one piece of land was sold for

---

[14] Ibid., p. 316.
[15] Ibid., p. 317.

this use, other corporations also followed suit. Land barons began to emerge and they in turn made more money by charging residents rent to live on their land.

Fifth Era: Mid 2004 through Mid 2005 – Industrial Revolution

- During this era, various technological advancements took place in the real world which allowed advances within the virtual world. Such advances were the ability to use audio within SL, the ability to customise animations on avatars, the ability to stream quick time video and the ability to export .xml data.
- The new innovations created new industries within SL such as e-commerce, music businesses and advertising and marketing to name but a few.

Sixth Era: Summer 2005–2006: Boom Time

- This was the era of commerce and finance. Linden Labs launched LindeX, which was an internal L$ to US$ commodities market.
- The real world press became excited about this virtual economy and this spurred on money makers, carpetbaggers and entrepreneurs to enter this new financial market.
- This economic development led to real world companies entering the virtual world as a means of making real money. Companies, such as Toyota, Reebok and Warner Bros. (to name but a few), all bought land and used SL as a commercial interest to make real money.

Seventh Era: Late 2006–2007: Conflict and Globalisation

- Conflict
  - This era saw real world laws conflict with virtual world rules. It saw the SL community conflict with the development of the system and outside detractors conflict with the community's angry defenders.[16]
- Legal issues which sought real world rules
  - Real world legal pronouncements were made for virtual issues. Three major legal declarations were made during this time.

---

[16]   Ibid., p. 321.

- Gambling was prohibited
- Extreme forms of sexual content were banned
- Age verification systems were introduced
- Globalisation
  - By mid 2007, 50% of users were from the European Union, whilst 26% were from the US. This demonstrated the global appeal of the virtual world.
  - Because of the globalisation and popularity of the virtual world, Linden Labs released the code to create new versions of SL to others.

From 2007–11 Second Life has evolved quickly amidst the wealth of social media innovations and against the backdrop of the worst economic crisis the world has ever seen. The latter half of 2007 saw Linden Labs create an Architecture Working Group to influence development online, thus enabling residents more opportunity to control their environment. Linden Labs also removed the profile rating system which was used for social reputations, but which was also often abused. Windlight was also introduced in 2007 and allowed much better graphical capabilities for residents.

2008 saw Philip Rosedale step down as CEO and Mark D. Kingdon take over.

In 2009, Linden Labs announced that a Second Life marketplace was being created through the acquisition of OnRex and XStreet. The idea was to merge these two online marketplaces to create a web shopping service for virtual goods. 2009 also saw the creation of Zindra, a special region designed for adult-only content. Linden Labs were beginning to realise that the virtual world they had created had a wider impact on the real world and were slowly integrating real world social norms, constructions and laws into Second Life.

2010 saw another acquisition by Linden Labs of Avatar United, which was a social network for users of multiple virtual worlds to connect. Later that year it was shut down. Continuing this theme, a new Second Life forum was also launched. Mark D. Kingdon stepped down as CEO and Philip Rosedale stepped in as interim CEO. Rod Humble later became CEO of Linden Labs.

2011 saw a resurgence in social networking, with the launch of the new Second Life Community Platform and a new social web page profile. New Mesh technology was launched, allowing all Second Life residents to use the new technology.

SUMMARY

Second Life, just like our own history, has grown and developed through the interconnection to human activity. Linden Labs, just like governments, have devised rules and regulations which allow residents to benefit from the advancement of knowledge and technology. Second Life has been chosen as the case study of the virtual world for this book. Its ability to have a virtual world economy, with its inter-reliance on real world economies, demonstrates the ability of criminals to find loopholes in regulations and legislation and to commit acts of money laundering and other financial crimes. This book will examine money laundering and other financial crimes against the backdrop of Second Life, as well as other virtual worlds. Second Life is continuously evolving and changing and law, as well as our own perceptions, should evolve too.

3. Evolution of virtual economies

> Whoever controls the volume of money in any country is absolute master of all industry and commerce. (President James A. Garfield)

INTRODUCTION

Within this chapter the movement of money and the philosophy behind virtual economies will be discussed. The aim of the chapter is to enable the reader to understand the concepts of virtual economies and the virtual marketplace within virtual worlds. Furthermore, the chapter will advance the position of the book, that the virtual is not as virtual as one may initially think. That the virtual is affected by the real and the real by the virtual demonstrates the continuum of existence that has occurred since human beings evolved. This chapter on virtual economies advocates this theory and will outline the rationale and thinking behind this proposition. In doing this, virtual e-commerce will be discussed alongside the virtual economy and the achievements and benefits the virtual economy has to offer. To this end the economy and marketplace of Second Life will be examined. The chapter will move on to explore the possible macroeconomic impacts of virtual worlds on real world economies. Furthering this theme of synergies between the virtual and the real, an exploration of virtual bank runs and the virtual economic crisis will be examined.

First and foremost, we must turn our attention to the virtual world and its economies, which we will later discuss. In Chapter 2, we discussed the history and development of Second Life. So at this point, we turn to consider what a virtual world is and whether a virtual world, created by a computer software system, can ever be what its namesake makes it out to be, i.e. virtual. If the world is truly virtual, then economic activities or any other activity need not be subject to real world laws. However, if these virtual worlds are not in fact virtual, then the problem of legal culpability and jurisdiction arises. Therefore it is important to establish what is a virtual world. Is a virtual world really virtual? And what activities take place within that world that require real world legal culpability and jurisdiction.

Wang and Mainwaring state that 'money is more than just another kind of data . . . It is a social construct of complex psychological and cultural power. Its use entails connection to wider contexts, not just to "the market" but also to contested structures of personal and public meaning, like social class and political economy'.[1] Money therefore can be seen as a construct of the real world. Its uses allow social progression and social cohesion. It is not surprising therefore, in virtual worlds where users are striving to recreate their real lives in a 'better' and more utopian virtual world, that money has its place.

There has been little research conducted into comparing the virtual and the real world.[2] As we will see, academics like Castronova focus on the pure economic standpoint of the virtual world. Within this chapter, a comparison will be made. One thing that has been discussed by academics is the meaning of virtual worlds. Kock describes a virtual world as being a world created by humans. He says that 'Virtual worlds can be described as technology-created environments that incorporate representatives of real world elements such as human beings, landscapes and other objects'.[3] In other words, Kock is stating that a virtual world is a simulation of the real world, with real world elements within it, but that it is acted out via a computer generated system. It is these real world elements that pose problems for researchers when they examine the virtual worlds. First, if the virtual world is a simulation of the real world, it is not 'virtual' in its truest sense. Secondly, if these real world objects in the virtual world (or in-world if you will) are affected by events in the real world, then they are not 'virtual' either. Rather it is a continuum of the development of e-commerce and the cyber world. It is more akin to a faux representation of the real world and simulates the real world to be a utopia of what real worlds could be. Therefore it is not virtual, but rather faux virtual. Second Life (SL) 'is a good example of a virtual world that attempts to replicate elements of the real world with practical application in mind',[4] and it is for this reason that the SL economy is considered within this chapter.

However, worlds such as SL are termed virtual and this virtual status is at its truest when considering the implications of the actions taken within the virtual world. The implications, whether they are criminal, civil, social or economic, can be seen to have an effect on the real world.

---

[1] Wang and Mainwaring (2008).
[2] Solomon (2010).
[3] Kock (2008), p. 1.
[4] Ibid., p. 3.

The problem therefore comes when the implications, named above, do not have real world consequences. One example is the situation surrounding rape in the virtual world. Whether it is a criminal event in the real world is unclear.[5] If such a serious crime in the real world is ambiguous, to say the least, in the virtual world, then what does the virtual world hold for the more mundane, but no less important world of economics, banking and monetary policy?

Turning our attention to the economy of virtual worlds, and the economy of SL in particular, since its creation SL has been underpinned by its closeness to the real world and its economy is no different. Every economy in the real world is influenced by policy makers and government alike. In SL, the virtual economy is affected by the developers for, as mentioned above, there is no government controlling the virtual world. Sipress points out one of the most recent changes to the economy of SL following decisions taken by the developers, Linden Labs. 'Second life's economy has been surging since Linden Lab made the unusual decision three years ago to grant users intellectual property rights. Thousands of people have created homes and business on virtual land leased from the site and are peddling virtual items as varied as yachts and ice cream'.[6] Sipress therefore points to the turning point in SL's economic history (chapter 2), when intellectual property rights were granted to SL residents, since when economic activities have thrived. We can therefore determine that there is an economically active world taking place within Second Life and this has been demonstrated by recent figures disseminated from SL itself and its own stock exchange, but more of that to come later. What must be considered here is the very nature of what a virtual world is. We have established that within the world called SL there is an economy and that trade does take place. The trade is facilitated through the in-world currency, Linden Dollars. The name itself derives from the real world word, dollars.

What Is a Virtual World?

According to Castronova, a virtual world is a computer program with three defining features: interactivity, physicality and persistence. Before examining these three elements, let us define the words virtual and world, separately.

Virtual, as an adjective, is defined as:

---

5   Lynn (2007); MacKinnon (2007); Bugeja (2010).
6   Sipress (2006).

- Virtual (a): being actually such in almost every respect; 'a practical failure'; 'the once elegant temple lay in virtual ruin'
- Virtual (b): existing in essence or effect though not in actual fact; 'a virtual dependence on charity'; 'a virtual revolution'; 'virtual reality'.[7]

Or as:

- Virtual (a) having the essence or effect but not the appearance or form of.[8]

The word comes from the medieval Latin term *virtualis* or *virtus*, meaning virtue.
  Virtue is defined as:

- Virtue (a) the quality or practice of moral excellence or righteousness;
- Virtue (b) the particular moral excellence;
- Virtue (c) any of the cardinal virtues; justice, temperate, and fortitude;
- Virtue (e) an affective active, or inherent power or force.

Virtue comes from Old French *Vertu* and Latin *Vertus* meaning manliness and courage (Vir – man).[9]
  These definitions give us a clue as to why the name was chosen for the virtual world. The first definition, virtual as 'being actually such in almost every respect', goes along with the line of thinking in this book. The world created online is as close to reality as possible. It simulates the real world and demonstrates its desire to be as close as possible to the real thing, while incorporating everyday aspects into the virtual world. It is more of a utopia than a virtual reality. The second definition, that virtual is 'existing in essence or effect though not in actual fact', also agrees with the assertion that the virtual world exists as a world, but in reality, or in actual fact, it is not a real world. The third definition still does not pose a problem for this theory to work. Virtual is 'having the essence or effect but not the appearance or form of'. In a virtual world, there is no form other than pixels on the computer screen, but it has the essence and the effect of a real world.
  From the definitions above, we can determine that a virtual world is one that exhibits all the characteristics of a real world, the only difference being that the virtual world has no physical form. If this is the case, then it is hard to see why there are no legal ramifications for actions in-world. This, however, is the point to be addressed in Chapter 6.

---

[7] www.wordnetweb.princeton.edu/perl/webwn, accessed 29 April 2010.
[8] *Collins English Dictionary.*
[9] *Collins English Dictionary.*

Returning to Castronova's idea of what a virtual world is, this differs somewhat from the literal definition of what a virtual world is. In so far as the author believes that Castronova's elements can be taken on board and can demonstrate that the virtual world created is not actually virtual but a continuum of the real world, but placed in a virtual platform, if this is so, and this is what the chapter argues, then the virtual should be subject to real world laws.

The word 'economy' has its roots in the Greek word, 'oikonomos'. This can be broken down into 'oiko' meaning home or the clan (if broken down further in its roots) and 'nomos', meaning the rules or administration. Therefore, as Solomon iterates, when we speak of economies we are talking about community management.[10] Economics is a perfect example of how virtual economies are actually highly influenced and driven by economic factors in the real world. This is because the two worlds have a single common denominator: being human. The question is whether anything that is created, played and thought about by humans can ever be truly virtual. As mentioned above, Castronova examines three elements of what constitutes a virtual world. The first can be expanded to include the idea that the game can be accessed remotely by a large number of people, with 'the command inputs of one person affecting the command inputs of other people'. In other words, creating and developing a society within the computer game. This interactivity can be further expanded to demonstrate the idea that the 'command inputs' are given by real world people, and have effects in-world and in the real world on other input commands. Therefore, put simply, the real world is affected by actions in-world, outlining the idea that the virtual is not so virtual.

The second element of Castronova's virtual world is physicality, that 'people can access the programme through an interface that simulates a first-person physical environment on their computer screen; the environment is generally ruled by natural laws of Earth'. By having this synergy with the real world, these virtual worlds are taking on the appearance of being a continuum of the real world and not being as virtual as their name suggests.

The final and third element is that of persistence. This is the idea that the computer remembers the closing play of a person or people, whether anyone is using it or not.[11] Nothing alters unless the users of that virtual world make it happen. This demonstrates that the world needs people to make it work; it needs real world influences to ensure that in-world

---

10   Solomon (2010).
11   Castronova (2001).

occurrences happen. In other words, the virtual world cannot operate without real world influences.

Having examined the definitions of what constitutes a virtual world, it can be logically deduced that a virtual world is all but real apart from its lack of physical form. Therefore, if it has real world effects and is all but real, apart from physical form, could it not be right to say that there needs to be a 'rule of law' operating within the world?

LAW, ECONOMICS AND HISTORY

Virtual economics is a tricky area to pin down. Many academics[12] have considered the economics point of view from a commodity, profit and loss standpoint. Few have considered economics as the economy, i.e. the money, the transactions, the value of goods, the crisis emanating from the economy, of a virtual world. This section of the chapter examines these ideas. It is not meant to be an examination of economics and the calculations of the profits and net gains of the virtual world, which will be considered a little later in the chapter. For now, what is being considered is the monetary policy of virtual worlds. In other words, how can a computer pixel be attributed a real world value and how can this be controlled, given that once withdrawn from the virtual world, it has real world effects?

The reason why we turn to history once again is that history informs us of how things in-world and in the real world have come to be. The idea is that we only have economics, and in turn currency, because it has been accepted over time that this is what happens. In society, we have placed a value on various commodities and we exchange money to get the goods.[13] But the question is how we got to the idea that coins and paper have a value and that these can be exchanged for goods. Now indeed, we consider a plastic card as the means of paying for goods, since this card holds our wealth, or means, to do so.

Let us travel back in time. Where did the idea of money come from? The idea of money dates back to about 4000–5000 BC. Remember please, if you will, that the idea of a virtual currency can be traced back to this early period. After all, what is virtual, this book is arguing, is a continuum of the real. What was considered other-worldly in 4000 BC is now out of date for us and what is virtual money now could be, and most likely will be, considered out of date in several thousand years time. The basic form

---

12 For example, Castronova (2001; 2002).
13 Forbes (2008).

of trade was called bartering, a system where you swap something of yours for something that you want in return. This works for a time, but what happens when you want something and the person does not want to trade your goods for it? This led to the idea of having a common commodity which could be traded for goods, such as grain, rice, honey etc. It is this common feature that we can see in elements of virtual money today. The common feature allows for a fixed and standard measure for goods to be traded and purchased by; it also allows for the common commodity to store its value and also act as a medium of exchange.[14] This is where the concept of money was born; this method provided a common measure, accepted by all, for the exchange of goods. It is important to labour this point, since trade 'cannot happen if there is not an agreement amongst everyone that a particular currency has value'. People of SL accept that Linden $ are currency and that they have an agreed value. They use these Linden $ as a means of bartering and obtaining goods that they would not be able to obtain unless this system of 'money' was in place.

In 3000 BC, collective protection of currency began. The idea was to collect together the currency and share the cost of an army to protect the currency and therefore guard against loss. Along the banks of the Nile, granaries for grain appeared which kept the grain for local people. This is where the name bank comes from, i.e., the storage of currency first occurred along the river banks. The first accountants began logging what came into the collective store and what was removed. Having grain as a mode of currency was fine until there was a drought and grain was in scarce supply and this happened to the ancient Egyptians around 2200 BC. This was the first banking crisis in the world.

As the grain became scarcer, it also became more valuable. After 200–300 years of problems associated with the lack of grain, metal became the chosen common commodity for currency. 'This is important because it finally moves currency to something that is more abstract'.[15]

However, practically speaking, moving large amounts of metal around to conduct transactions posed various physical problems and so countries such as Sweden and China converted the metal currency to paper money. These sums of currency were held in banks. By converting the currency from grain to metal and in turn from metal to paper, another layer is added to our currency continuum, from the real to the abstract.

What happened next, and forgive me, the leap is rather a large one, amounted to a rather interesting turn of events for bankers and currency

---

14   Ibid.
15   Ibid.

globally. This was the creation of the reserve or central bank in an individual country. Created by John Law (1671–1729), who at the age of 29 shot a man in a duel for the hand of a lady and was tried and convicted of murder. He was sent to jail, but escaped to France soon after. Law was an early economist and observed that it would be better for nations to control the flow of currency and to do this he observed, it would be prudent to issue more IOUs than the banks had metal for, should the need arise to issue to the depositors. Law came up with the idea that if a nation had a reserve bank which guaranteed the money, each individual bank could lend more than it had in its reserves. However, this could not have happened without support from the government as the central bank could only be controlled by the law of the land and therefore the government. Law managed to convince the government to undertake this task and created what is known today as 'fractional reserve banking', whereby the banks only hold a fraction of their obligation at any one time. This notion is fine as long as the people of the nation trust their government and therefore the banks. If a society loses trust and confidence in the government and/or the banks, then bank runs can occur, i.e. a situation where everyone decides to take their money out of the bank at the same time, and thus the bank, holding only a fraction of its obligation, is unable to provide each person with their money.

The modern day (from the 1920s) history of the reserve bank and international and national collaboration is a story for another time. For now, what we can see is threefold. First, for currency to be in place, it must be a commonly accepted medium. Secondly, currency has moved from the real to the abstract in the real world and therefore the creation of virtual money is no less real than the creation of paper as a means of representing metal coins; it is just rather new to us all. Finally, and most importantly, someone must be in control of the flow of money into and out of the banks and the nation. This is not the case for the virtual banks at the moment and it is this which is causing problems in the virtual world currently. As Sipress points out: 'Courts are trying to figure out how to apply laws from real life, which we've grown accustomed to, to the new world. The Law is struggling to keep up'.[16] The legal position of virtual worlds, whether in the criminal law or civil law, is ambiguous and unclear. There is no dispute that the virtual world contain elements such as politics, crime and economics, but the law which governs and controls is unclear. A more in-depth discussion of this can be found in Chapter 4.

Under the rule of law, as Lord Bingham suggests, all persons and authorities within the state, whether public or private, should be bound by and

---

[16]   Sipress (2006).

entitled to the benefit of laws publicly and prospectively promulgated and publicly administered in the courts.[17] In general, therefore, it means that no one is above the law and that a state's citizens are bound by the rules, and that if they break them they shall be tried fairly by a fair legal system. Lord Bingham clarifies the rule of law through seven further points:

1. that law must be accessible and so far as possible intelligible, clear and predictable.
2. that questions of legal right and liability should ordinarily be resolved by application of the law and not the exercise of discretion.
3. that the laws of the land should apply equally to all, save to the extent that objective differences justify differentiation.
4. that means must be provided for resolving, without prohibitive cost or inordinate delay, bona fide civil disputes which the parties themselves are unable to resolve.
5. that ministers and public officers at all levels must exercise the powers conferred on them reasonably, in good faith, for the purpose for which the powers were conferred and without exceeding the limits of such powers.
6. that adjudicative procedures provided by the state should be fair. The rule of law would seem to require no less.
7. that the existing principle of the rule of law requires compliance by the state with its obligations in international law, the law which whether deriving from treaty or international custom and practice governs the conduct of nations.

We can say for certain that none of these is being carried out in any clarity of distinction within virtual worlds and it is this which is holding back their economies and development. It is only with the adoption of such rules within the virtual worlds that commerce can begin to have a real positive effect on the real world. What is required is for the rule of law of real world countries to be adopted in these virtual worlds. The legal jurisdiction of virtual worlds is a topic for discussion elsewhere, but whether the jurisdiction is adopted according to the location of the server or whether there is a new international rule of law drafted, agreed on and implemented, it is clear that the legal situation must be clarified.

VIRTUAL ECONOMIES AND MARKETS

Within virtual worlds (and not just SL), there are thriving economies, with their own markets and currency. At the present time, most of these virtual worlds and currencies are separate. They are bifurcated only by the lack

---

[17]   Lord Bingham Text Transcript, Law Society for Hereford and Worcester, Tuesday 15 April 2010.

of open standards, whereby virtual money, avatars and commerce can be exchanged between worlds. An open standard would allow for free movement of goods and trade between these virtual worlds and would pave the way for a definite need for a higher jurisdictional basis. If we assume that the regulatory position at the moment within virtual worlds is that rules are issued by the game developers, and not by a court in a real world, then we can assume that when open standards arrive in virtual worlds, there will be a need for one governing body. The technology is present in these worlds to facilitate open standards;[18] what is lacking is a clear legal position. Therefore, although the economies are thriving in each individual world, they are also stuck within those worlds. If we embrace the idea of having e-commerce developed via virtual world economies, then the legal position of the economy needs to be established. This section of the chapter will examine the SL economy and explore the virtual economies phenomenon and the challenges it faces.

In SL, as mentioned above, the economy really started to thrive once the legal position of ownership rights was clarified, thus giving credence to the argument that once there is a clear legal position within the virtual world, it allows users more freedom and security to fully immerse themselves within the game.[19] Furthermore, it is also important for the economic position to be clear within these worlds. As Castronova indicates, 'economists believe that it is the practical actions of people, and not abstract arguments, [are those] that determine the social value of things',[20] and affect the economy. Catronova believes that, 'virtual worlds may also be the future of e-commerce'.[21] It is therefore important for legal and economic scholars alike to understand the already complex and multi-layered economy of virtual worlds.

As of 12 September 2011, the exchange rate for Linden $ was 249 L$/ EUR.[22]

THE ECONOMY IN SECOND LIFE: LINDEN MONETARY POLICY

'When it comes to money SL and your first life are very similar'.[23] As previously mentioned, SL resembles in most ways the real world. If you

---

[18] Virtual World News (2009).
[19] Sipress (2006).
[20] Castronova (2001).
[21] Ibid.
[22] www.secondlife.com/my/index/market.php., accessed 12 September 2011.
[23] Robbins and Bell (2007), p. 155.

want a new pair of shoes, then in the real world you need to have money to buy those shoes; it is the same in SL. The currency in SL is called Linden dollars or L$ as an abbreviation. This currency only has value in-world, but it can be exchanged at an exchange for real world currency. This is very unusual in virtual worlds, but it is beginning to be the trend for the future. This is because, as we shall see later on, e-commerce has been very successful in-world and in the real world. The in-world exchange is called the LindeX. Therefore, you can say that SL has money in the world. You can use the in-world money to make more in-world money and then cash it out and pay for real world goods with it. LindeX is run and monitored by Linden Labs, and although it is not a government or financial services organisation, it deals with the exchange of money flowing through SL. This poses further queries for the governance of such amounts of money by game developers and not government. In a sense, this is an unregulated monetary exchange. There is no recourse or rule of law governing the exchange of money.

So the question that needs to be asked at this stage is: how do you get real money into the virtual world? This is relatively easy; all you need is either a credit card or a Paypal account. You just select the amount you want to transfer and, like a normal transaction, you can purchase the Linden $. This is done through the LindeX, as in the real world on the stock market. You will then have an amount of Linden $ in your account (top right of the screen) that you can spend or invest as you wish in-world. Linden Labs will charge any user an amount to carry out the transaction to transfer Linden $ to real world currency. Therefore, to cash out of the in-world monetary system will cost you money and will make more money for Linden Labs. However, the price of a transaction is market dependent. It is all about supply and demand. If someone sells a large amount of Lindens for a low price, the price of Lindens goes down. You have three options when you are cashing out your money. You can have it paid into a PayPal account, have a domestic cheque if you are in the USA or have an international cheque if you are outside the USA. It may take a few days for the money to be transferred. It is not such a quick process to get your money out as it is to put your money in. This method of cashing out poses problems for money laundering, which will be discussed later in the book, but if you have the money paid out as a cheque, domestic or international, or through a PayPal account, the anti-money laundering checks for these methods do not allow for checks on money laundering. More of this later.

Another way of purchasing Linden $ is via in-world transactions. During your time in-world, you can press the purchase Linden $ button and purchase the amount you require whilst in-world. The account details you provided when setting up an account are used to debit your credit card or PayPal account by the required amount. SL economy is known for its free market agenda. However, controls are placed on how many Linden $ you can trade in any given transaction. This, is meant to protect Linden $ from fraud, although whether it is completely successful is uncertain, but more of that to come.

The economy of SL has not been far from controversy since its conception and continuous growth. In January 2008, Linden Labs implemented a not so free market banking policy after the financial crisis around the collapse of Ginko Financial. Linden Labs issued a 'new policy' dictum indicating their increasing incursion into the governance of laws and policies over the virtual world. The new policy indicates that no one other than a regulated bank in the real world can now operate a bank within the virtual world.[24] The policy states: 'we are implementing this policy after reviewing resident complaints, banking activities and the law, and we're doing it to protect our residents and the integrity of our economy'.[25] Linden Labs stated succinctly the risk these unregulated banks posed to the SL economy: 'These banks have bought unique and substantial risks to SL, and we feel it's our duty to step in. Usually we don't step in the middle of resident-to-resident conduct'.[26] This highlights the importance of clarifying the legal and regulatory situation surrounding not only the economy but the rest of the in-world society. Linden Labs acknowledges this by stating; 'As these activities grow, they become more likely to lead to destabilisation of the virtual economy. At least as important, the legal and regulatory framework of these non-chartered, unregistered banks is unclear'.[27] However, Linden Labs is not prepared and nor should it be, to become the bank or lender of last resort. After all, it is nothing more than a successful games developer. It is not a bank, but its role, in-world, is ambiguous and unclear at best. It plays at being the law, providing governance and being the financial regulator, but does nothing when there are consequences of residents' actions. What it does is to issue guidance and in-world rules, such as: 'Under its new banking rules, SL says only chartered banks will be allowed, though it isn't clear any real banks will operate in the virtual play world'.[28] However, whether in-world rules can ever amount to the sort of strong and robust economic and financial framework which is needed to control the amount of money flowing in and out of the world

---

[24]   Linden Labs (2008).
[25]   Ibid.
[26]   Ibid.
[27]   Ibid.
[28]   Sidel (2008).

is contentious. Readers and commentators must not forget that SL is a virtual world and ultimately a game. But it is a game which has real world effects. The lines drawn between the two are unclear and blurred. It is no wonder that regulators and governments alike are baffled by how to regulate and control this medium of monetary exchange. Yet it is clear that some degree of control and structure will need to be put into place quickly, given the growth of SL's economy. As Linden Labs outlines: 'The whole SL adventure encourages user freedom, but it's got so many users, and so much money is flowing in, that you have to face that the community needs some degree of control'.[29]

GOLD FARMING

Gold farming is a new form of online employment currently gripping China and other Asian countries, as the fastest growing new occupation. Heeks claims that 'it employs hundreds of people and earns hundreds of million of dollars annually'.[30] Gold farming is said to be the production of virtual goods and services for players of online games and this production and selling of goods can be open to abuse by money launderers and financial criminals. Gold farmers are usually employed as part of a group and controlled by a conglomerate of people. The gold farmers make thousands of different virtual goods and services, which are then sold within online games. The selling of these goods produces an income in online currency. With many online worlds now having their own currency, as SL does, and currency exchanges, virtual money can then be exchanged for real world money. Gold farming is now such a large enterprise, it has been designated as having its own economic sub-sector.[31] However, there has been little academic research into it and very little legislative discussion regarding this new economic phenomenon. Heeks is but one of a very small minority who are investigating this economic sub-stratum.

Gold farming can be traced back to 1997 and the introduction of 'real money trading' (RMT), where it can be seen that the first trades for real money were undertaken for goods and services within virtual worlds. RMT was something of a northern hemisphere phenomenon and did not really penetrate China and Asia until 2001/2, when it has been suggested

---

29 Semuels (2008).
30 Heeks (2008).
31 Ibid.

that US traders saw the opportunity to outsource trading to lower-income venues such as Mexico and Asia.

Gold farmers make money by sitting and playing online games, and by making and selling online goods and services. This is done in three ways. Firstly, and most simply, is by selling in-game currency. This is very much the same as a real world currency exchange, where you can buy and sell money at different rates and if done correctly, you can make money on the exchanges. Secondly, gold farming can be what is known as 'power levelling', which is where a gold farming firm is given the user name and password of a player who wants to achieve a certain level in the game but does not want to do it themselves. Money is then paid to the gold farmer, who plays as the user and attains an agreed level or status within the game. The third way is by selling in-game items for virtual money. The gold farmer buys or creates goods and services which are then sold on for profit in-game. The money is then exchanged for real world money.

Within the above three scenarios, there is the obvious potential to launder money through the gold farming mechanisms. For example, a gold farming firm which employs outsourced lower paid employees could be using criminal money to fund gold farming activities. Once the money has gone through the virtual game and been exchanged back into real world currency through a bank or PayPal, then the money appears to be legitimate.

There is little control over or monitoring of gold farming. However, Korea has in theory[32] banned virtual currency trading.[33] Conversely, it is reported that the Chinese government has invested heavily in gold farming, since it appears to be the new trend of online employment, enabling more people to earn a living, albeit on a modest scale.[34] Gold farming can benefit many in society where employment is hard to come by, but gold farming can also, as iterated above, be thwarted by fraudsters and criminals. There is little that can be done in terms of a response. For example, if there is fraudulent or criminal activity, the activities can be reported to the game developers. In some cases, where gold farmers are found to be making money, then they can be downgraded, which is known as nerfing. Accounts can be banned; the game developers can patch the hole in the game which allows this activity. In more serious cases, the IP address of the gold farmer can be banned and blocked. Similarly, channels

---

32   Ibid.
33   Yoon (2004).
34   Jin (2006).

used for marketing and sales can be blocked. Finally, legal action can be taken against gold farmers if it is thought that the case is able to be proved.[35]

It can, therefore, clearly be deduced that gold farming is not a legal activity or one which is condoned within the gaming industry and it contravenes the terms and conditions the MMORPG developers have set out. Users must sign and agree to End User Licence Agreements (EULA) and also the Terms of Service (TOS) and Terms of User (TOU). These agreements typically set out the prohibition on conducting activities such as gold farming or those similar to gold farming. Governments are divided in their views of the legality of gold farming. The Chinese government has clearly defended the rights of the gold farmers to make money and to earn a living in employment, yet the US is strongly against the use of gold farming, specifically because it opens up yet another avenue for money laundering and financial crime. As we shall see later in the book, tracing and locating end users who commit money laundering or financial crimes is nearly impossible and prosecution through many different jurisdictions poses many problems and again is nearly impossible. To thwart the criminals, a joined-up approach must be taken and a combined code on money transfers through online games must be adopted.

QQ COINS

Virtual World currencies can pose problems for real currencies in the real world. This is only too true in China. In 2002 an internet company called Tencent issued QQ coins. The use of the coins spread, mainly because of the frustration of the Chinese people with the lack of credit card facilities available to them. Use of the coins spread from being traded for only virtual goods within virtual worlds to being used as a commodity in the real world and as such to being used outside the game environment. QQ coins were also used for illicit gambling and laundering activities. The Chinese government was so concerned about the widespread use of QQ coins that in June 2007 the Central Bank barred the practice because of concerns that their use could have an impact on the national currency.

China also decided that the purchase and trade of virtual goods should also be subject to taxation and in 2008 commenced taxing virtual goods at between 3–20%.[36] However, it is not just China who has decided that the

---

35   Heeks (2008).
36   Solomon (2010).

economies of the virtual worlds should be subject to taxation laws.[37] In the US, virtual goods may be taxable depending on the state concerned and is the matter of debate for the Inland Revenue Service. The problem that China, Sweden, South Korea and the US face is not that there is guidance, but that people must disclose their trading on virtual worlds.[38] It is yet again the virtual world's anonymity which poses problems of governance for the authorities.

OPENLIFE

OpenLife is another virtual world which is similar in its set-up and creation to Second Life. It was founded in November 2007 by Australian Steve Sima (avatar: Sakai Openlife). Steve is also the Openlifegrid.com project leader and company president at 3DX. The OpenLife grid is accessible using the Openlife R17 viewer. OpenLife launched its currency, credits, available from PayPal and credit cards, at the end of 2009.[39] Both OpenLife and Second Life advocate the use of credits or Linden $ by users/residents trading to purchase goods or to start their own business in these worlds. The question that should be asked is what can virtual world economies offer the real business world.

E-COMMERCE IN VIRTUAL WORLDS: WHERE REAL MEETS VIRTUAL

There is little point in having an in-world currency such as Linden $ if there is nothing to buy and sell or to make money from. The in-world profits that can be made are immense. Or you can make just a small amount of money. Either way, virtual world trading is the new form of e-commerce. As Castronova points out, 'there are many similarities between Earth economies and their virtual counterparts',[40] and making money through trade is just one of these similarities. However, there are differences too. Virtual world economies are 'all very normal and mundane'.[41] They have work, business, societies, commodities just as we do on Earth. However, Castronova continues to state that, 'given further

---

[37]   Inside Social Games (2008).
[38]   Software Interrupted (2009).
[39]   Engage Digital (2009).
[40]   Castronova (2002), p. 3.
[41]   Ibid.

thought . . . virtual economies may be anything but normal'.[42] By this he means that in the real world, governments control the prices of goods, through supply and demand and price control. In cyberspace, this is one of the major differences. There is no price control since there is no controlling body. There is no government and thus no 'rule of law'. These differences are OK as long as the virtual and the real do not interact, but we have seen already from the beginning of this book that this is not the case. The virtual and the real are more akin to a continuum of each other rather than being separate entities. Therefore, 'As economic and social activity gradually migrate from Earth to cyberspace, these differences may begin to have an impact on the lives of large parts of the population'.[43] Thus to have a clear position on the legal structure and its ramifications, it is essential to further the already successful e-commerce business taking place in world.

The business taking place in SL is not just a game, as some people think, rather it is an important facet of business and can also, as we shall see later, have an impact on criminal activity, if not regulated correctly. 'When people enter a virtual world, perhaps they are just playing a game, so why should [economics] matter. On the other hand, we can say the same thing when people play the stock market, a game that certainly does matter'.[44] Virtual economics therefore must be taken seriously, not only because it crosses into the real world, but because it is not so virtual after all.

Linden Labs, the developers of SL, have always thought of the economy and the economic position of SL when making decisions and as part of this, e-commerce has not been far from their thoughts. Kock outlines this position and says; 'The designers of SL seem to have had support for e-collaboration and e-commerce in the back of their minds when they developed the initial set of features and rules that regulate user interaction'.[45]

Various companies have set up businesses or showcase their brand in SL. Box 3.1 lists some of these companies as of 2010.

Apart from real world companies and organisations that use their brands in-world, there are also in-world companies offering services (see Box 3.2).

In SL, business is taken seriously and within the world there is a page

---

[42] Ibid., p. 4.
[43] Ibid.
[44] Ibid., p. 12.
[45] Kock (2008), p. 5.

BOX 3.1   SECOND LIFE LISTED TRADING
           COMPANIES 2010

- ABN AMRO: ABN AMBR 238, 15, 22 (pg)
- Accenture (Italy)
- AccuWeather: Weather HUD
- Adidas: Adidas 104, 183, 55 (pg) **(closed)**
- Aegon: Aegon 123, 132, 46 (mature)
- Ajax Football Club (Amsterdam): Ajax Arena 128, 189, 23 (pg)
- Alcatel Lucent: Alcatel Lucent 124, 129, 47 (pg)
- Altima Island Nissan Altima Island 122, 180, 28 (pg)
- AMD: AMD Dev Central 124,151, 31(pg)
- American Apparel: Lerappa 138, 92, 24 (mature) **(closed)**
- AOL Pointe: AOL Pointe 128, 128, 0 (pg) **(closed)**
- Armani
- Autodesk: Autodesk 128, 125, 54 (mature)
- Ben & Jerry's: Ben & Jerry's 109, 160, 27 (pg)
- BMW: BMW New World 195, 66, 23 (pg)
- BMW (Efficient Dynamics) BMW New World 2 (pg)
- BNP Paribas: BNP Paribas 128, 128, 22 (mature)
- Boots UK (No 7) Avalon 154, 221, 24
- Calvin Klein, IN2U fragrance promotion: Avalon 21, 146, 25 (pg)
- Cecile: Ginza
- Circuit City: IBM 10 136, 38, 22 (pg)
- Cisco Systems: Cisco Systems 128, 127, 30 (mature)
- Citroen Brasil: MLBR Copacbana 149, 229, 22 (pg)
- Coca-Cola: Vending Machine Competition
- Coldwell Banker
- Comcast: Comcast 17, 231, 23
- The Connected Home: The Connected Home (mature)
- Congrex
- Crowne Plaza: Place To Meet 116, 123, 21 (mature)
- Dell Computer, Main Island: Dell Island 43, 162, 24 (mature)
- Domino's Pizza UK: One Manchester 48, 192, 25
- Europ Assistance: Europ Assistance 45, 167, 31 (mature)
- Fox Atomic: Fox Atomic 128,128, 0 (mature)
- Fujitsu Siemens: Fujitsu Siemens 157, 106, 72
- HermanMiller: Avalon 68, 127, 25 (pg)

- H&R Block: HR Block 113, 48, 37 (pg)
- Gax Technologies, Luxembourg: Luxembourg Business 195, 129, 21 (pg)
- Head Resourcing, Scotland
- IBM
- IBM Business Center: IBM Business Center 128, 128, 0 (mature)
- IBM Sandbox: IBM 121, 154, 33 (pg)
- IBM 1 Virtual Universities Community Theater I: IBM 1 128, 128, 23 (mature)
- IBM 2: IBM 2 128, 128, 22 (mature)
- IBM 3: IBM 3 243, 105, 23 (mature)
- IBM4 IBM05/Recruitment Project: IBM 4 130, 183, 22 (mature)
- IBM 6: IBM 6 128, 126, 22 (mature)
- IBM 7 Greater IBM Connection: (pg)
- IBM 8 SOA Hub: IBM 8 104, 106, 23 (mature)
- IBM 9: IBM 9 128, 129, 22 (mature)
- IBM 10 Theater M, Circuit City: IBM 10 139, 42, 22 (pg)
- ING, Our Virtual Holland: Virtual Holland 119, 133, 22 (pg)
- Intel
- Intel Ignites OCC Intel Ignites OCC 128, 128, 0 (mature)
- Intel Software Network:
- Intel
- Intel 1
- Intel 4
- Intel 7
- Intel 8
- iVillage: Sheep Island 42, 150, 25 (mature)
- Jean Paul Gaultier: Caricavatars 147, 170, 27 (mature)
- Kelly Services: Kelly Services 128, 128, 0
- Keytrade Bank (Belgium) Keytrade Bank (mature)
- Kraft Foods: Phil's Supermarket 108, 96, 28 (pg)
- Lacoste: Launching mid May
- Level 3: Level 3 Island 127, 129, 25
- Major League Baseball: Baseball 214, 129, 27 (mature)
- Mazda Motor Europe: Nagara Island
- Mercedes-Benz: Mercedes Island 128, 128, 0 (pg)
- Microsoft Visual Studio Island: Microsoft Visual Studio Island 128, 128, 0 (pg)

- MovieTickets: MovieTickets 128, 80, 23 (pg)
- NBA: NBA Jam Session 128, 128, 0 (pg)
- Nissan: Nissan 19, 129, 26 (pg)
- One Manchester (launching soon)
- Orange
- PA Consulting: PA Consulting 116, 119, 27 (pg)
- Packaging & Converting Essentials: Sede di Marte 217, 50, 38 (mature)
- Perfect Card
- Peugeot: Peugeot Island 187, 224, 23 (mature)
- Philips Design
- Pontiac Main Island: Pontiac 179, 96, 24 (pg)
- Randstad Holding: Randstad 38, 104, 49 (pg)
- Reebok: Reebok 111, 100, 97 (pg)
- Reuters: Reuters 127, 98, 25 (mature)
- Samsung: Softbank Slim Japan 128, 8, 25 (pg)
- SAP Network: Silicon Island 208, 45, 28 (pg)
- Saxo: Saxo Bank 154, 190, 54 (mature)
- Sears: IBM 10 95, 32, 23 (pg)
- Semper International: Human Resource Island 196, 112, 27
- SonyBMG: Media Island 108, 111, 21 (mature)
- Sony Ericsson: Sony Ericsson 94, 151, 27 (mature)
- Sprint: Sprint Center 175, 141, 41 (pg)
- STA Travel: STA Travel 11, 126, 30 (mature)
- Starwood Hotels: Aloft Island 68, 69, 27 (mature) (Aloft has been donated to TakingIT Global)
- Sun Microsystems: Sun Pavilion 182, 144, 55 (mature)
- Sundance Channel: Sundance Channel 49, 177, 38
- Suruga Bank (Japan): Suruga Bank (pg)
- TAM: Airline Brazil: opening soon
- Telecom Italia: Telecom Italia (pg)
- Telstra Big Pond: The Pond 127, 135, 41 (pg)
- TELUS: Shinda 187, 72, 22 (pg)
- Thompson NetG: Thompson 182, 123, 35 (pg)
- TMP Worldwide
- Toyota: Scion City 44, 40, 23 (pg)
- UGS: UGS Innovation Connection 168, 157, 22
- Unitrin Direct Auto Insurance Burns 145, 71, 67 (pg)
- Vivox
- Vodafone: Vodafone Island 128, 128, 0 (mature)

- Warner Brothers: Warner Brothers 126, 126, 30
- Wipro Technologies (India): WiPro Innovation Island 128, 128, 0
- Wirecard Bank AG (Germany): Wirecard, 128, 128, 0 (pg)
- Xerox: Xerox 128, 128, 0 (access controlled)
- Xerox Innovation Island: Xerox Innovation Island 128, 128, 0 (access controlled)

*List as of 4 May 2010.

devoted to business papers and archives of research. It can be found under: http://wiki.secondlife.com/wiki/Recent_Business_Articles and outlines some of the articles written on business in Second Life. Its achievements are also documented and can be located at: http://secondlife.com/news/.

Doing business in SL is big news and many users of SL blog about their activities online. One such user is Pooky Amsterdam, known in the real world as Veronica Butler-Borror. She lists ten reasons why it is good to do business in SL (see Box 3.3).

Other online magazines also highlight the goings-on in the business world. One such editorial is the Second Life Entrepreneur (http://www.slentre.com/). This editorial has a presence not only in SL, but also on the online blogging network, Twitter. Most of the large organizations which are present in SL also have a presence on other social networking and blogging sites, such as Facebook (www.facebook.com) or Twitter (www.twitter.co.uk). SL Entrepreneur covers topics from the Entrepreneur of the year Awards 2009 (http://www.slentre.com/sl-entrepreneur-2009-and-the-nominees-are/) and the winner of those awards (http://www.slentre.com/slentrepreneur-of-the-year-2009-and-the-winner-is/) to traffic reports (http://www.slentre.com/category/second-life-traffic-report/) to more general business news (http://www.slentre.com/category/sl-business/), all of which represent the citizens within SL and assimilate real world news agencies.

The winner of the Entrepreneur 2009 award provided an interview for SLENTRE. Swaffette Firefly, Second Life fashion designer and entrepreneur, was nominated as SLENTRE's 2009 SLentrepreneur of the Year by the 2008 winner, Mimi Juneau.

BOX 3.2 OCCUPATIONS AND SERVICES OFFERED IN SECOND LIFE

- party and wedding planner
- pet manufacturer
- tattooist
- nightclub owner
- automotive manufacturer
- fashion designer
- aerospace engineer
- custom avatar designer
- jewellery maker
- architect
- XML coder
- freelance scripter
- game developer
- fine artist
- machinima set designer
- tour guide
- dancer
- musician
- custom animation creator
- theme park developer
- real estate speculator
- vacation resort owner
- advertiser
- bodyguard
- magazine
- publisher
- private detective
- writer
- gamer
- landscaper
- publicist
- special effects designer
- gunsmith
- hug maker

Source: Second Life, 'Business Opportunities', http://secondlife.com/whatis/ businesses.php, accessed 4 May 2010.

BOX 3.3   TEN GOOD REASONS TO DO BUSINESS IN SECOND LIFE

1. You can virtually meet people from anywhere in the world easily and inexpensively
2. Your Avatar can be an extension of yourself and increase personal investment for you and the business community you are addressing
3. VoIP puts you in the same room with those you need to speak with
4. You can share any documents you need to
5. You can work in real time on those shared documents
6. Any 3D product or place can be re-created cost-effectively and to scale for business decision making
7. You save on time and travel expense by just logging in from your computer
8. You can establish a secure environment by restricting access to your location
9. Training and Education done in virtual worlds returns great results
10. Video created in Virtual Worlds (known as Machinima) or cinema done on machine will get your message to the public through regular distribution channels (e.g. YouTube). In addition, it will be available as video content on your web site, plus be something you can include in your video emails.

Source: Butler-Borror, V., 'The Business Benefits of Second Life', Its all Virtual, http://allvirtual.wordpress.com/2010/03/23/business-benefits-of-second-life/, accessed 4 May 2010.

SYNERGIES WITH REAL ECONOMIES

The argument iterated within this book is that although money which is used for crime is positioned in the virtual world, the concept of that money is very much real. The money entering the world is real. Therefore it is real. In other words, given that real money is being used to perpetrate real world crimes, the law should keep pace with this changing evolution of the use of money in virtual worlds and as such it should be able to convict

BOX 3.4   INTERVIEW WITH SLENTRE'S 2009 SLENTREPRENEUR OF THE YEAR, 2009

How long have you been in SL? Why did you come?
I came to Second Life in the summer of 2004 – I was an infant teacher but as soon as the summer break came I was looking for ways to create online which had become a hobby of mine – I had been creating on a vrml based 3d world when a friend from there introduced me to Second Life and from that minute, I was hooked.

What Second Life business activities do you engage in?
My business, SF Design, has been supplying clothes to the men and women of Second Life since Autumn 2004. Because I noted a lack of men's clothing when I entered Second Life, the men's fashion line has been my priority, but the female line and shoes and boots soon followed. Designing, marketing and customer care takes up all my time in SL now.

What is your RL profession?
I was an infant teacher for 22 years and left for a variety of reasons in 2007 – a deciding factor was Second Life. The business was demanding more and more of my time – not just creating, but customer care and marketing. After 3 years of building, I really didn't want to lose the business – I knew it needed my full time attention.

Discuss your SL business, business model, profit margin, who are your primary clients, monthly expenses, etc.
I had no business experience before coming to Second Life and I'm still learning. Luckily, I have a business partner (Jamir Jimenez) who helps me with the daily running of over 80 satellite stores – making sure we are up to date on rent, checking out prospective places, checking sales, leaving me able to concentrate on customers and designing.

I've had considerable help from friends and colleagues in Second Life who have helped me consider things like marketing more carefully. I'm always keen to hear customer feedback – even if it's negative – because it's helped me develop and improve my fashion line.

We have always aimed to keep prices reasonable even though hours of work go into the clothes. I've always hand placed prims – not used a skirt machine or script – and always make my own alpha masks for the designs. I think this is important to keep the company brand unique.

I started creating primarily to fulfill the needs of the people of SL so as their needs have changed so have our fashion lines – with more emphasis on the business and high street fashion lines. We have tried to keep up with the ever-changing face of Second Life in other ways too – embracing flexi and sculpties into our designs and always trying to bring something new. I'm very wary of saying we were the first to do anything as SL is so vast it's almost impossible to know, but we certainly were one of the first to use the skirt layer for men's jackets back in 2005. And more recently, the back flap to get rid of that tight issue with jackets.

We have a wide range of clientele with many wedding groups coming to us for formal wear (we work closely with a few wedding planners), club owners coming to us for outfits for their dancers and businesses coming to us for business wear.

I employ my PA Jamir Jimenez, my shop floor manager Melinda Jensen and several models and I own 2 sims and a large part of a mainland sim – so overhead is high, including advertising, wages, land tier, satellite rentals, magazine ads and fashion shows. Profit fluctuates depending on the time of the year. This spring and summer was a hard one for many of us designers and I often wondered if SF Design would survive. But we updated our store, brought out many new lines and high quality free items to attract new customers and this winter is looking good so far.

Is your business growing?
It's definitely growing in stock and growing in execution – sales fluctuate greatly in Second Life. Summers tend to be slow and last summer was particularly bad – however, things are very much back on track this season and we're happy we seem to be reaching a lot of new customers as well as returning ones.

Does your SL business impact or influence your RL?
Very much so. Especially when I was teaching, it was very hard to do both well. I was trying to sort out customers from overnight IMs before going to work and I take my hat off to all the amazing

designers who are balancing SL work around their real life jobs as it's not easy. Second Life business is 24 /7 – because of all the different time zones involved, it means you have customers round the clock. I also have a family who like to see me occasionally! It's important I find time for them. I try to keep Sundays for 'real life' but often end up having to come in for some reason.

Any RL skills translate into SL business?
Unfortunately when I was at school there were no computers or graphics lessons – sounds archaic, doesn't it! But I've always loved art and been involved in drawing and creating in some way or form. I developed an interest in using the computer to create when I started teaching ICT to children.

What is the most promising industry for new business in SL?
That's a difficult one, but I'd say anything that is innovative and has room for development and which takes into consideration the people who use and play in Second Life.

What types of businesses shouldn't come into SL and why not?
I know a lot of people panicked when the biab (business in a box) enterprises started – and I can sympathize when I see you can buy just about anything on xstreet – templates, shadows, creases and textures. So there has been a huge influx of 'designers' and stores. But the more I work here the more I feel there is a place for everyone – it really makes you consider your own business: how can you improve it and keep your customers. Competition is healthy. The only businesses I totally disagree with being here are those built on ripped and stolen content.

What is your opinion on RL business in SL. How will it affect the community?
I must admit I thought 'that's the end then' when I heard that real life fashion designers were entering Second Life. But surely, the important thing is to know your market – how can you address your customers needs if you don't know the customers? And the best way to know them is to spend time with them – doing what they do. Some of these RL businesses came and went quickly. They didn't succeed because they didn't know their customers or Second Life. The ones that survive are the ones that do that.

What are the biggest mistakes SL entrepreneurs make?
Some 'wannabe' SL entrepreneurs make the mistake of thinking this is an easy or quick way to make money – it's not. It means hard work, time and effort – the same as any real life business. Again, it's important to remember your customers. There's no point in making a new product if it's not what the customers want.

Any predictions about the future for SL? New technology? Growth? New potential uses?
I'm continually amazed by the development of content in SL by the 'players' and I don't see it stopping any time soon. It's especially great to see artists and musicians using it to reach a wider audience, language schools and education using SL, charity fund raising and more recently, I heard a US hospital was using it to teach their staff how to evacuate in case of fire. I don't see this ending any time soon. Hopefully we'll see more and more exciting developments – it's all up to us; that's the most exciting thing.

What does having a Second Life give you?
Freedom to develop talents in a way I never thought possible, to learn every day, to meet people from all over the world and to be in control of my own business – it's wonderful!

Is there an element of fantasy or escape?
Definitely. That's where it started – an escape from RL work and stress to a place where I could be what I felt like. A place to explore, relax in and create. Now I sometimes need to escape from SL! But it's still a wonderful learning platform for me and I've met some great people.

Will SL change the landscape of business as we know it today? Will it change any landscape – cultural, social, etc?
I think SL is already changing the landscape of business in the same way the internet and technology is changing it. It means more competition, which encourages change and development. In these days of recession, it has provided an opportunity to develop skills – which in the RL business world would be hampered by high overheads, restrictions and regulations.

It gives us opportunities to move out of our comfort zones and explore new ventures.

Source: Slentre, SLEentrepreneur Profile, Swafette Firefly, Owner and Founder of SF Designs. 6 January 2010, http://www.slentre.com/slentrepreneur-profile-swaffette-firefly-owner-and-founder-sf-designs/, accessed 5 May 2010.

wrongdoers. Despite the world where the crime is initiated being virtual, it is human interaction and cultural development which makes the virtual world real. As Castronova puts it: 'If virtual worlds do, in fact grow, as a human phenomenon, there may be some implication for Earth economies'.[46] Further more Castronova opines that, 'If economic activities migrate into virtual economies, where there are no earth jurisdictions'. . .[47] In the next section the book will explore the real world effects of virtual economic crimes.

VIRTUAL BANK RUNS AND TROUBLES: CASE STUDIES GINKO FINANCIAL AND EVE ONLINE

'So now, Linden Lab has deemed that only banks in the real world can open a bank in SL. And so, folks who deposited money in the virtual banks want their money back, and some have closed'.[48] The reason for this is the financial crises that have occurred within virtual worlds. Virtual economies, like real world economies, have suffered the fate of financial scandal and crisis. Two of the most recent and most well-known are charted here.

Ginko Financial

Ginko Financial was a large investment bank within Second Life. It has been described as 'unregulated, unaudited, and a magnet for controversy'.[49] However, in its day Ginko Financial was a very popular and successful business. It offered investors large returns on their money in return for investing their money in the virtual bank. Linden Labs made

---

[46] Castronova (2002), p. 28.
[47] Ibid., p. 30.
[48] Edu Games Blog (2008).
[49] Reuters (2006).

policy changes to gambling and financial matters in-world which subsequently made investors want to withdraw their money. Ginko Financial could not deal with this demand on investments and there was a run on the bank. This eventually led to many investors losing their money. It has since been discovered that the investment bank was actually a Ponzi scheme, whereby new investors' money is used to pay old investors, thus leaving no money for the new investors to reclaim. Because of this, Linden Labs made any bank which was not regulated or chartered in the real world illegal in SL.

As Sidel states, 'The banking crisis at SL surfaced during the summer, when Linden banned gambling on the site, citing conflicting regulations around the world. That caused a run on Ginko Financial. A SL bank that has invested heavily in the virtual world's gambling operations, Ginko capped withdrawals and ultimately issues bonds to customers instead. The bank went out of business in August'.[50] Sidel continues: 'The collapse led to an outcry from depositors at SL banks'.[51] Linden Labs responded by allowing only chartered banks to have bank status in the virtual world. However, Linden Labs insists it cannot and will not act as a banking regulator. 'If this is real money, there is an argument you need to follow real law'.[52]

However, Duranske points out that 'A lot of people forget, Second Life *is* governed by US law and the laws of California, it just so happens that these laws haven't been enforced'.[53] This lack of enforcement and confusion over whether there could be a legal safety net for investors causes many problems for the virtual world economy's ability to grow and furthers the argument that the virtual world is not so virtual and should be regulated via real world laws. An advocate for not incorporating real world laws is Bloomfield who says: 'I am really hoping that RL (real life) regulation does not come to SL because right now SL has the chance to sort out what type of oversight and regulation it wants'.[54] He further opines that, 'If the RL authorities or Linden Lab do start meddling with business affairs, it could ruin a golden opportunity for real innovation and creativity, a chance to recreate a world in a new image'.[55]

The Ginko Financial scandal undoubtedly changed the face of in-world banks and financial institutions and just as in the real world, it is scandal

---

[50] Sidel (2008).
[51] Ibid.
[52] Ibid.
[53] Gardiner (2007).
[54] Ibid.
[55] Ibid.

which pushes through policy changes and regulatory reform. In this case, it is Linden Labs that has altered policy by allowing only real world banks and financial institutions to act as such in the virtual world, but it has not produced much-needed clarity on the legal jurisdictional issues.

Eve Online

A games developer and one of Iceland's top companies set up a virtual world called Eve Online. What happened to Eve Online during 2009–10 demonstrates the similarities with real world banks. Eve Online is very successful. In 2009 it had 300,000 players paying $15 a month to use the platform for interacting on the site. The virtual world has a free 'anything goes' market and allows users to buy goods and support their role within the world. 'Eve has 66 market places for some 5,000 items with more than one million transactions per day'.[56] Eve created a virtual bank, Ebank. The currency is called interstellar credits (ISK) and is traded for goods within the world. However, when some players did not have enough ISKs to purchase goods, an entrepreneur in Eve created a bank that would accept depositions and lend to players who would pledge their in-world assets as collateral.[57] Given the interplay of human nature and banking, the bank was a success and accumulated 8.9 trillion ISK in deposits and 13,000 accounts belonging to 6,000 users.[58] The top executive of the Ebank made off with the deposits of the bank and sold them for real cash to gamers on the black market exchange on Eve. He has since been kicked off the game and the bank has shut down. The bank, along with its board, is trying to sort out the crisis that has ensued. Depositors have withdrawn 5.5 trillion ISK from the bank.

Reports are unclear as to the amount that the executive embezzled, but it has been suggested that 10% of the overall bank deposits were taken by him. What is important though is that there is no final regulator nor lender of last resort to offer safeguards to depositors.

When this incident was reported globally, news agencies called it the start of the 'Virtual version of the credit crunch'.[59] In fact, it is supposed that the executive stole the money to pay medical bills and to put down a deposit on a house, both consequences of real world effects. The executive has been thrown out of the game due to the terms and conditions of

---

56   Cox (2009).
57   Ibid.
58   Ibid.
59   BBC News, 'Billions Stolen in Online Robbery', 3 July 2009, http://news.bbc.co.uk/2/hi/technology/8132547.stm, accessed 26 April 2010.

Eve Online and steps are being taken to recapture some of the money, but the issue of law and jurisdiction arises, since the legal situation is unclear.

When real world items are affected by in-world actions, users call on real world enforcement agencies to govern the world. There is, therefore, confusion over whether it is a virtual world where the rules are governed by the developers of the game or whether, because real world aspects are being affected, real world repercussions (laws) should occur. Cox illustrates this succinctly, 'as in the real economy, the customers [are] tempted to appeal to a higher authority'.[60] What is unclear is what this higher authority is: the developers or the rule of law?

VIRTUAL ECONOMIC CRISIS

'Virtual reality investors have been hit hard by the real life financial crisis'.[61] 'Property prices have crashed 84% in SL'.[62] 'Space trading game Eve Online has suffered a virtual version of the credit crunch'.[63] These are just a few of the headlines outlining the financial crisis that is occurring in virtual worlds. It shows that the real world financial crisis has also permeated across the internet ether to affect the virtual world economy. However, many still believe that the virtual world holds the answers to many real world problems. It was reported recently that the internet is immune from physical disasters or acts of God. But this is not really fair. Even the omnipresent internet has its faults and can falter, as we saw with the closure of Second Life in April 2010 for site reconstruction.[64]

Having said this, it is important to understand the synergies and the correlation between the real and the virtual worlds and how this new platform of virtual commerce can have a positive affect on the real world economy, and this, as we all know, is greatly needed at the present time. The internet can traverse many of the complex and diverse problems that businesses encounter daily. Perhaps the internet and virtual worlds could solve some of these. Yet it cannot properly do so, for at the present time, the legal situation surrounding in-world actions is unclear. Clarity is greatly needed for further steps towards future collaboration to be taken.

---

[60] Cox (2009).
[61] Technology, 'Credit Crunch hits Second Life', 30 December 2008. http://www.stuff.co.nz.technology/777892, accessed 15 March 2010.
[62] Technology (2008).
[63] BBC News, 'Billions Stolen in Online Robbery', 3 July 2009.
[64] Korolov (2010).

SUMMARY

Within this chapter we have discussed the evolution of the virtual world economy and how it is similar to the real world whilst having significant differences, such as lack of monetary control and where the users are the issuers of the money. However, it has been noted that virtual world economies are present and pose similar issues to the real, such as financial crimes, scandals and extensive growth. As Yamaguchi explains: 'our current situation has gone far beyond our imagination in those days. What we observe today may be a sign of our future. Virtual worlds can potentially be our new frontier'.[65] If this is so and virtual world economies can demonstrate effective monetary policy lessons, then the need for regulation is ever greater.

Before regulation is tackled effectively, there must be cohesion in the manner in which virtual worlds are seen. There are presently two bifurcating views, one that the virtual economy is just that – it is virtual and has nothing to do with the real world and the real world economy. The other view is that the virtual world and economy are not so virtual, and are just part of the real world.

What is clear from the above is that virtual world economies have an impact on the real world. It could therefore be argued that it is wrong to say they are virtual. Rather they are in fact a continuum of the real world in a new technological sphere.

As the bifurcation continues and uncertainty remains, virtual world economies are becoming a place which can harbour criminal activity. Little if any regulation is present and cross-border jurisdiction is cumbersome and rife with difficulties at its very best. The lack of certain jurisdiction is coupled with the difficulty in tracing and locating cyber criminals. Within this lack of governance and control, there is a lack of real world controls such as price control, taxable assets and income control. The real world is therefore losing out on an element of commerce which really is part of the real world. To ensure that virtual world economies can play a positive part in the real world, as Yamaguchi argued above, a coherent and robust legal system must be in place. For as we know money is integral to everyday living and there is a need to protect people's rights.

---

[65] Yamaguchi (2004).

4. Money and culture: its history and evolution. A virtual reality

> Dishonest money dwindles away, but he who gathers money little by little makes it grow. (Proverbs 13: 11)

INTRODUCTION

Within this chapter the history of money and its place in society will be discussed along with the place of money's rules and regulations. The aim of the chapter will therefore be to examine the proposition that throughout history money has been a continuously changing phenomenon. In other words, in relation to money, the chapter will show that in what we now consider to be virtual or un-real may, if we take history as a guide, be considered the norm in the future. It is this development and social development of human psychology that will be explored alongside the lack of rules and regulations of money and finance in a virtual world. Human culture, society and psychology is an important asset in the development and growth of money and finance and innovation can only be stifled by lack of awareness of this innovation. The chapter is therefore posing a question which will be examined in Chapter 6 which is if the virtual money and economy is considered as real, how can the real world laws be used to control and govern activities which use virtual money? For this to happen, human minds need to grapple with the concept of money in its virtual form and devise laws to transgress the virtual platform and intersect bifurcating jurisdictions. The chapter therefore is divided into several parts. First, the chapter will examine the history of money from the barter system to the acceptance of metal as a means of wealth to the production of paper notes and on to the modern day world of plastic cards and chip and pin.

The chapter will then move on to consider the rules and regulations in place in modern day finance and how these have evolved through time. Evolution plays an important part in the chapter as history can give us important clues as to how to manage the future in terms of regulation. Something may be considered outdated and irrelevant, but consideration of how it developed and progressed can offer insight into how future innovations will evolve, especially in terms of financial regulation of the virtual world.

The next part of the chapter will consider the financial crisis of 2007 to the present. By exploring the financial crisis we can see how the virtual economy can mirror occurrences in the real world, demonstrating the continuum of the real into the virtual, but beyond this, providing an escape for the real, causing a new (virtual) real economy to be created. Taken theoretically as far as it can go, if the real economy transposed itself to the virtual and was accepted as a norm of society, then this would become the new real. However, this is a long way off and not something which needs to be considered in full at this present stage, no matter how interesting it may be. The chapter then moves on to to discussing the functions of money in society and how it is parallel to those functions developing in the virtual world. The chapter at this point then considers the development of society around money and these functions. Throughout this discussion the author will be relating this to the theory that the virtual and the real world are continuums of each other and pointing out how treating the worlds differently in terms of legal structure could cause problems in terms of economic crimes being committed.

The chapter then moves on to consider the nature of money and the internet, given that the internet is the platform for the virtual worlds. This section demonstrates how money is freely and openly used as a means of commerce and is accepted as a norm of society. This section of the chapter will consider the statistics of online e-commerce to demonstrate the expansive and rapid growth over a relatively small period in history, causing the creation of an online economy.

The chapter will conclude with a consideration of the virtual world's economy and culture given the above discussion and will lead into the next chapter on financial and economic crime in the virtual worlds.

HISTORY OF MONEY

Why is looking at history so important when this book is about the future? As any banking scholar will know, history plays an important part in predicting the future, especially when it comes to finance and banks. This is why this section of the book is devoted to outlining the historical development of the simple bank in British culture. By examining how and why the bank was created and how it developed, we can see how the transposition from the innovative and new to the norm can take place. The cultural psychological shift in acceptance not only allows the banking industry to grow but also allows society to flourish as well. As any good historian will tell you, social and cultural growth is spurred on by the economic capacity of that society at any given time. In addition to charting the emergence and growth of the bank, this section will also look at the development of regulation in conjunction with this growth, thus demonstrating the retrospective regulating that comes with innovative growth in the banking sector. Therefore, taking the stance above, that history teaches us lessons, we can predict that virtual finance and economies will be regulated, but only after their initial growth which is unregulated.

In this section of the chapter it is important to recognise the impact of the development of society and its role within society as a means of promoting the simple bank. Finance is something which is very personal to us and we have set beliefs and perceptions about what a bank is and how money affects our lives. This has been born out of social and historical developments. Banks and finance have changed dramatically over their history. Banks originally were created as businesses which facilitated the depositing and borrowing of money so that people could manage their business affairs. Over time banks have widened their application and have become an essential part of life. We can now chart a new movement in banks and finance history, whereby finance and money are moving into the realms of the internet and virtual economies.

Over time many famous sayings have come about in relation to money. For example, 'money makes the world go round' and 'the love of money is the root of all evil'. Money certainly is integral to society's evolution and nowadays, to its survival. Without money and an economic system in place within a country, then society can fall into anarchy and social devastation may occur. The question therefore is: how did money become so important? We can trace money back to the old form of bartering and this can be linked to an age when there were no written records. 'The direct exchange of services and resources for mutual advantage is intrinsic to the symbiotic relationship between plants, insects and animals, so that it should not be surprising that barter in some form or other is as old as man himself'.[1] Barter is where each party exchanges goods or services for something tangible. It is therefore a tangible exchange on both sides. This is different from the current form of exchange that uses money in the form of notes or coins or electronic transfers that are intangible forms of the exchange. Barter therefore is not the same form of property transfer as when money is used for an exchange, but we can say that barter was used as the first method of goods transfer and we can see in history that once monetary systems were in place, they ran alongside the barter system.

---

[1]   Davies (2002), p. 9.

Because of its ancient beginnings, there is little historical evidence of bartering in its truest sense recorded and historians and economists use barter as a crude system of exchange. Bartering and primitive money systems are therefore linked, but are not the same because in monetary systems the use of a coin or note is intangible and used as the exchange for something tangible. Many definitions of what money is have been proffered. Einzig purports that money can be defined as 'a unit or object conforming to a reasonable degree to some standard of uniformity, which is employed for reckoning or making large proposition of the payment customary in the community concerned, and which is accepted in payment largely with the intention of employing it for making payments'.[2]

As we can recollect from Chapter 3, money was an evolution from trading grain for a sheep or some wool for some wood. Money became a means of buying goods when you did not want to trade something tangible for it. We shall not repeat this process here, but we shall pick up at the point in history where money is first held by a primitive banking house. What must be remembered from Chapter 3 is that what was once considered other-worldly and unreal is soon accepted as real and tangible.

The first banks in the UK emerged on the banks of the River Thames in London after the 1640s and in 1663 the first pound coin was designed and made.[3] The culture of the banking industry at this time demonstrated the social position the banks held within society.[4] Banks were initially a means of collecting and distributing money on a large scale for trade. During the seventeenth century banks were in reality groups of men who worked along the banks of the River Thames, taking money and buying grain, which travelled on boats up the river to the capital city. From here grain was purchased from the sellers on the boats and could also be bought by others. It was a meeting point for trade.

Banks during this time were very different from what we consider to be banks nowadays. First, there were very few banks, the people who worked in banks were highly thought of in the community and the only people who did business with the banks were the very rich, the government and the royals. As such, the culture was prestigious; it was not a business for all society. Today's banking culture could not be more different.[5] Although some people (7% of the population)[6] do not have a bank account, 93% of the United Kingdom population do. It is this increase in the uptake

---

[2]   Einzig (1966), p. 317.
[3]   Davies (2002), p. 243.
[4]   Chambers (2010a).
[5]   Chambers (2004).
[6]   Kempson and Whyley (1998).

of facilities offered by banks which has created a 'people's bank' banking culture. Within this evolution there are several main factors that can be seen to construct this modern culture of the banking industry.

The first factor is that banks within the United Kingdom evolved from the rise of the goldsmith banker (1633 till 1673).[7] The significance of the goldsmith as the catalyst for banks is that even at this very early stage banks were not originally intended for everyone in society; they were for those who were wealthy.[8] This can be demonstrated by the fact that in 1660 goldsmith notes were used for the first time as banknotes and wealthy people were beginning to use goldsmiths as borrowers as well as depositors. This was not a facility that would have been offered to everybody. It is difficult to depict the true originator of the banker, whether it be goldsmith or Lombard, but it is true to say that the origins of banking were instigated jointly between the two. Galbraith (1975)[9] denotes the ambiguous beginnings of bankers. He claims that banks are:

> An exceedingly old idea. Banking has a substantial existence in Roman times, then declined during the Middle Ages as trade became more hazardous and lending came into conflict with the religious objection to usury. With the Renaissance it revived as trade revived and religious scruples yielded in normal fashion to pecuniary advantage. So far as any business can be given ethnic association, banking belongs to the Italians.[10]

As banking is such an established and old idea it is difficult to say exactly when and how the culture changed but certain events in history from this date on led to the creation of the modern banking industry culture that exists today.

History depicts the rapid tendency of growth that the banking industry exhibits today.[11] The goldsmith banks were the forerunners of the banking industry that we know today. Private banks were derived from these goldsmith banks and these too showed the rapid growth that was necessary for the development of the banking industry. 'In 1801 one could count sixty-eight private banks which were their direct descendants'.[12] This rapid growth was necessary as more and more people of the upper classes were using banks as a means to organise their monetary affairs. With an increasing number of people using the banking industry, more banks were

---

[7] Davies (2002).
[8] Ibid.
[9] Galbraith (1975), p. 18.
[10] Ibid., p. 18.
[11] Orsingher (1967), p. 39.
[12] Ibid., p. 40.

opened and this led to a greater public awareness of banks and their facilities, which meant that more people wished to do business with the banks. The cyclical effect of supply and demand has dominated the growth of the banking culture and has guided the creation of banking competition, where banks vie for people's custom. Davies[13] states that:

> The development of financial intermediaries enabled rich persons to find profitable outlets for their surplus funds in London which attracted money in increasing amounts not only from the Continent but also internally. Provincial writers were loud in their condemnation of London's power in drawing to itself the liquid wealth of the country. The growing size and wealth of the city stimulated the growth of a vast market in coal and food making available capital for further investment in agricultural improvements in a virtuous spiral.[14]

Another important factor in the development of banks was noted by Orsingher,[15] who believes that during the reign of the goldsmith banker there was no public debt within the United Kingdom. In today's modern society, public debt is on the increase, but it is relatively unsurprising that during the early period there was no public debt, since the only people that did business with the banks were those who could afford to. The banks were selective in their choice of customers and as such banks were considered to be a facility used only by a few upper middle and upper class people. The banks' original aims therefore were not to accommodate the needs of all society but to make money out of deposit and borrowing facilities offered to a select few. The banking industry and those few who oversaw the banking business were not concerned with social responsibility nor whether they were acting in an ethically sound manner, but with whether they made money. It is this business ethos which dominated the banking industry until very recently (twentieth century) and thus the culture has had to alter dramatically to keep up with the public preconception that in today's society a bank is a facility that should be available to everyone. As such, in 2000, the United Kingdom had £127.4bn of public debt.[16]

Another important step forward in creating the modern banking society that we have today was the creation of the Bank of England by the enactment of The Bank of England Act 1694.[17] The Act was the

---

13   Davies (2002).
14   Ibid., p. 248.
15   Orsingher (1967), p. 40.
16   Consumer Affairs Directorate (2001), p. 7.
17   The Bank of England and the legislation that enabled its creation was based on the foundation of the Bank of Amsterdam in 1609.

beginning of bringing banking to the majority of society. However this was to be a long and arduous process. At this stage in banking history, the Bank of England's purpose was to 'act as the Government's banker and debt-manager', and to undertake more conventional banking business as we know it today such as accepting deposits and discounting bills. The creation of the Bank of England really was an important step towards the modern banking culture, since it provided a backbone and regulatory mechanism which the industry had not seen before. It is noted that:

> The history of the Bank is naturally one of interest, but also of continuing relevance to the Bank today. Events and circumstances over the past three hundred years have shaped and influenced the role and responsibilities of the Bank. They have moulded the culture and traditions, as well as the expertise, of the Bank which are relevant to its reputation and effectiveness as a central bank in the early years of the 21st Century.[18]

The Industrial Revolution further helped to increase the number of banks within the United Kingdom, which in turn led to the cyclical effect of people taking the opportunity to use their facilities.[19] The Industrial Revolution did not just increase the number of banking houses but it also helped to promote the cultural attitude that banks were not just a business for the upper classes but that ordinary people such as businessmen could use them. Banking, however, was still a very limited facility, but it was this mild change in public conception that enabled the idea that banks could be used by more of society to grow alongside the banking industry.[20]

The banking industry had a cyclical effect on factors around it. If the Industrial Revolution had not occurred, then the banks might not have become more widely accepted as a facility that could be used by society. If banks had not grown to such a degree, the Industrial Revolution might not have been able to take place. Henceforth, factors affecting society are closely linked to the banking industry and the creation of the culture today. Even at the early stage of the Industrial Revolution, it can be seen that the notion of a bank being able to offer assistance to a wider selection of society was emerging.[21]

---

[18] Bank of England website, www.bankofengland.org.uk, 5 December 2011, p. 43.
[19] Chambers (2010a).
[20] Ibid.
[21] Ibid.

However, it is still important to note that although banks were now a more common feature of industrial society, they were still not a common facility for everyone. Indeed, it was still mainly the upper and the business (otherwise known as the merchant) classes, who used the banks at this time. This was reflected in the common name for banks at the time, 'merchant banks'. Banks were therefore strictly businesses to help other businesses to carry out business functions. There was nothing in their beginnings to suggest that this was to become a common feature of society or indeed that it would be thought of as an essential tool of western society. Banks still did not think about whether they had ethical or moral obligations to their customers or whether they should behave responsibly towards society as a whole. For this concept is a modern idea born out of the notion that banks are for everybody and they must serve society's needs just like a utility company such as gas or water. It is this confusion of roles which demonstrates the difficult time ahead for the regulators of the banking industry.

It was not until as late as 1810 that the first savings bank was created and it was also not until this date that the banking industry and legislators really contemplated the notion that ordinary people might begin to use the banks' facilities.[22] The Rothwell Savings Bank, initiated by Henry Duncan, was the first of its kind to encourage the poor to save and it was later imitated in France as well as Holland due to its success in Britain. This was an important step forward for the cultural evolution of the banking industry as it drew on the idea planted in society during the Industrial Revolution and that had slowly grown during this period, that banks could be used by ordinary people.[23]

Although the evolution of the banking industry up to this point and the culture associated with it did form the basis of the modern banking industry culture of today, there are several other factors which influenced the culture just as much and as such should be considered, since they are also present in the development of virtual economies. These are:

- Bank Failure
- Growth of the Savings Bank
- Societal Influences
- Regulation.[24]

---

[22] Davies (2002).
[23] Galbraith (1975).
[24] Chambers (2010a).

Bank Failure

From 1873 until the present day there have been six main banking crises which created an apathetic mood within society and the banking industry. The crises have caused regulation to be put in place and have led to a mistrust of the banking industry that had not existed prior to the bank failures. Before each crisis, society was unaware of the fact that a bank could fail and lose their money. It was hard on society and was the first gap to appear between the public and the banking industry. This gap in modern society is now very large. Public support for the banking industry is at an all time low (see later in the chapter). Thus bank failures have been an important part in forming modern banking culture. The main banking crises were as follows.

A banking crisis in England (1825–6) saw 60 banks fail in only one year.[25] The legislators did not know how to regulate against this occurring again. As a consequence of this crisis, legislation was enacted to regulate the industry. The Bank Charter 1844 Act tried to regulate and control the banks' deposit and borrowing facilities.[26] '. . . the 1844 Act gave the Bank the note issue and the nation a sound currency . . . linking the bank's notes to its gold reserves placed a limitation on the Bank's ability to develop its commercial business'.[27]

Another banking crisis, this time in the United States in 1857, made its effects felt as far away as Britain and Germany. The banking industry this time recovered fairly quickly.[28] A great depression in Britain in the period 1873–86 gripped the financial climate and affected many ordinary people and saw public support wane.[29] The Great Depression was experienced in 1931–3 throughout Europe and the United States in which there were many banking collapses as well as over 30% unemployment.[30] A secondary-banking crisis followed in the UK in 1973 and lasted until 1976, affecting much of the decade economically and socially.[31] The present day financial crisis of 2007 will be discussed later in the chapter in relation to the regulatory effects of the crisis.

---

[25] Galbraith (1975), p. 20.
[26] Ibid.
[27] Ibid.
[28] Ibid., p. 30.
[29] Ibid.
[30] Ibid., p. 34.
[31] Ibid., p. 35.

The Growth of the Savings Bank

The growth of the savings bank did much for the creation of the culture of banking in today's society. The savings bank allowed ordinary people to save as much or as little as they wanted and created a huge uptake of people who had accounts and who entered financial society for the first time. Several important factors depict how the savings bank altered the perception of society towards saving.

1847 saw the creation of building societies in Britain, but initially they were only temporary associations.[32] In 1861 the Post Office Savings Bank was founded in Britain. The creation of the Post Office showed that society as a whole was progressing towards a more monetary-led culture which compass not only the upper and middle classes but also some of the poor.[33] In 1947 The Woolwich become the first permanent building society in Britain which did not terminate their contracts when its members purchased their houses.[34] In 1970 building society deposits surpassed those of the London clearing banks. Building societies achieved tremendous success with their personal savings accounts and thus took a growing share of the market. Their success is deemed to be associated with their branch network and the public consensus at the time that banks were for people with money or for businesses. It was therefore building societies, and not strictly banks, which brought the financial society to the majority of people. From this point banks were beginning to be used by the majority of the people in the United Kingdom. The face of the modern financial industry was starting to emerge.[35]

In 1986 British building societies were given new banking powers, which allowed them more freedom to change their status to a public limited company if they so wished. In retrospect, this was the first step for many of the building societies towards becoming banks through demutualisation.[36]

Societal Influences

The two world wars and the General Strike of 1926 had a profound effect on twentieth century banking culture. These factors created not only apathy towards the financial industry on the part of society but also saw support for the financial sector go into decline. Many ordinary people

---

[32] Chambers (2010a).
[33] Ibid.
[34] Galbraith (1975), p. 35.
[35] Chambers (2010a).
[36] Ibid.

who placed their trust and savings in the banking industry were let down by factors that were out of their control and the banking industries' control.[37]

Throughout this chapter there has been discussion of the social acceptance of banks and money as a means of facilitating improvements in living standards. Without these changes in social perceptions, money and banks would not have been able to thrive. As we can see, what was once considered odd or weird or not acceptable has been accepted as the norm as social attitudes have changed and technology has advanced. Societal acceptance of new methods of banking and new forms of money is important in the development of the virtual economy. There will be more discussion of this issue later in the chapter when the growth of the internet as a means of e-commerce will be explored.

Regulation

Regulation was to become an important factor in influencing the culture of the banking industry. Since the mid 1970s there has been a plethora of banking legislation and codes, which have tried to maintain market and consumer confidence in the banking industry. Regulation has become one of the main aspects of the banking culture and as such more of society is aware of the other aspects of the banks' business such as their corporate social responsibility (hereafter CSR). The notion of CSR stems from the changing culture of the banking industry, whereby banks are now seen as a service for the public rather than a facility to be used by the elite. The following factors are some of the most important changes in regulation which affected the perception of the banking industry within society.[38]

The Banking Act of 1979 increased the regulatory powers of the Bank of England, which was intended to rectify the weakness produced by the secondary financial crisis in 1973, but failed to go far enough to regulate and monitor the banking industry's business practices. This led to further mistrust and apathy within society towards the industry.[39] From 1986 onwards there was an economic boom in Britain which coincided with the London Stock Exchange opening up to new competitors and a new system of automated operation being introduced. This was the beginning of increased growth within the banking industry and also led to an increase in consumers, as well as the numerous scandals and crises that occurred because of the

---

[37] Ibid.
[38] Ibid.
[39] Galbraith (1975).

growth and lack of effective regulation. If the regulators could not regulate the banks' activities in the past, it would now soon become impossible.[40]

Recent legislation demonstrates the manner in which the culture of the banking industry leans towards regulation as a method of control and monitoring. From 1986 to 2000 a plethora of Acts were passed, not to mention other codes and self-regulatory schemes that were put in place. The aims of these Acts are clear: they were created for specific purposes, but their effects on the banking culture are not so well defined.[41]

Financial Services Act 1986

Up until 1986 the financial sectors in the United Kingdom had a limited range of effective legislation regulating the industry, which was unstructured and not comprehensive. The Prevention of Fraud (Investment) Act 1958 was the main regulatory piece of legislation for the financial service sector and was shown to be highly inappropriate for regulating the banking industry due to several financial scandals, laying aside the fact that it was nearly 30 years old. Furthermore, at this time, the financial sector was largely self-regulating, a state of affairs which appeared to be losing support due to the number of financial scandals taking place.[42]

Due to this, in 1981 the government of the time[43] invited Professor Gower to 'conduct a review of the protection of investors'.[44] Although he had published the first part of his report on 18 January 1984,[45] the government published a White Paper in January 1985[46] before Professor Gower could complete his work. The White Paper adopted the majority of what was contained in Professor Gower's report 'but it differed in the institutional structure which it advocated'.[47]

The White Paper's recommendations were enacted in the Financial Services Act 1986 which was regarded as ensuring and maintaining confidence in the financial markets. The Act was a mixture of self-regulation and statutory intervention and created two tiers of regulators.[48]

---

[40] Ibid.
[41] Chambers (2010a).
[42] Such as the Barings Bank and the Maxwell scandals.
[43] The Conservative Government 1979–97.
[44] House of Commons, Financial Services and Markets, Bill No. 121, 1998–9.
[45] House of Commons 1984, Cm 9125.
[46] Department of Trade and Industry 1985, Cm 9432.
[47] Department of Trade and Industry 1985, Cm 9432.
[48] Chambers (2010a).

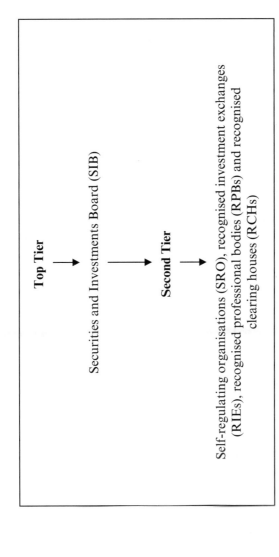

Figure 4.1 Two tiers of regulators

The self-regulatory bodies were set up to regulate and monitor the financial service sector within the United Kingdom and it was this aspect of the legislation which led to its downfall. The Act was primarily set up to control investment business only.

The regulatory system set up by the Financial Services Act 1986 has been subject to persistent criticism since it first came into operation. Those in the financial sector have been critical of the cost it imposes on the industry, and find the changing regulations expensive to comply with. Outside critics feel that the self-regulatory structure appears to favour the industry rather than the investors, and whilst the system is expensive, its costs are not proportional to the degree of investment protection which it provides.[49] However, as a result of numerous financial scandals[50] and the inadequacies of self-regulation, the 1986 legislation was reformed in July 1998 with the eventual passage of the Financial Services and Markets Act 2000.

Bank of England Act 1998

Traditionally the Bank of England undertook the regulation of the banking industry. However, under the newly proposed legislation, this power would be handed over to the FSA by way of the Bank of England Act 1998.[51] The Bank of England's response to this was 'studiously guarded'.[52]

The Bank stated that: 'what matters is not the Bank's position but the whole structure of financial regulation and what is best for depositor, investor and policy-holder protection, on the one hand, and for systematic ability, on the other'.[53] It was apparent that the Bank of England was strongly opposed to the loss of its regulatory powers, nor was it impressed that it had not been consulted about the decision to strip the Bank of England of its traditional supervisory powers.[54] It is conceivable that this was purposefully done in order to allow the Bank no time to object. It is

---

[49]   House of Commons, Bill 121 1998–9, p. 7.

[50]   Maxwell Pension Fund Scandal; see Treasury Select Committee, 'The Mis-selling of Personal Pensions', 12 November 1998, HC 712-II 1997-8. See Treasury Select Committee, Memorandum submitted by the Department of Trade and Industry and HM Treasury, April 2002. For the collapse of Barings Bank and the BCCI scandal.

[51]   Part 3 Bank of England Act 1998.

[52]   House of Commons, Bill 121, 1998–9, p. 23.

[53]   Bank of England Website, www.bankofengland.org.uk, 5 December 2008.

[54]   *The Financial Times*, 21 May 1997.

also perhaps too much of a coincidence that at the same time the Bank of England was relieved of its regulatory powers, it was awarded a degree of independence and responsibility for setting interest rates.[55] This, it has been argued, was an offering to the Bank of England to prevent it complaining too greatly regarding the demise of its regulatory control, but it was also considered to be an economic decision which would be beneficial to the Bank.

Financial Services and Markets Act 2000

The Financial Services and Markets Act 2000 received Royal Assent on Wednesday 14 June 2000, its purpose being to provide a single legal framework for the FSA, replacing the different frameworks under which the various regulators currently operate.[56] The FSA in effect replaces the SIB, although it was not a straight swap as 'the old SIB was only' a regulator of regulators'.[57] Under this system, any company wishing to deal in investment advice must apply directly to the FSA for authorisation.[58] It has been claimed that the FSA will be the broadest regulator in the world.[59] As such, it possesses the statutory authority to impose either criminal or civil sanctions to chastise any occurrences of market abuse.[60]

The Financial Services and Markets Act 2000 introduced four statutory objectives that the FSA was to work by. These were to maintain market confidence,[61] to ensure consumer protection,[62] to educate consumers[63] and to prevent and reduce financial crime.[64] It was hoped that by having these statutory objectives the financial services industry would be regulated in a more formal manner than it had been previously. These four statutory objectives represent an important alteration in banking culture. The FSA at this stage is aware of the financial problems that are being experienced

---

[55]   Part 2 Bank of England Act 1998.
[56]   Chambers (2010a).
[57]   Alcock (1998), p. 371.
[58]   The FSA inherits the regulatory responsibility of the self-regulating organisations, recognised professional bodies, the Insurance Directorate of the Treasury, the Building Societies Commission, Friendly Societies Commission and Registry of Friendly Societies. (*Current Law Statutes* (1998), vol. 1, pp. 11–40).
[59]   Alcock (1998), p. 371.
[60]   Part 8 of the Financial Services and Markets Act (FSMA) 2000.
[61]   S3 FSMA 2000.
[62]   S4 FSMA 2000.
[63]   S5 FSMA 2000.
[64]   S6 FSMA 2000.

by people in society and these objectives are aimed at helping these people. History has shown how if society loses support for, or confidence in the market, then the banking industry will suffer. History has illustrated that if customers do not feel that their money is safe in a bank, the banking industry will suffer. History also shows that it is only a wider knowledge and education of the banking industry which leads to growth within the industry. Finally, history has also illustrated that society mistrusts a banking system that demonstrates, through scandals and crises, that it cannot fully control and regulate financial fraud. All these objectives are therefore impacting on the culture which has developed over history and which has caused there to be a gap between public perception and the banking industry.

The Electronic Communication Act 2000

The Electronic Communication Act 2000 was set up to: '. . . make provision[s] to facilitate the use of electronic communication and electronic data storage . . . [also it] is designed primarily to facilitate the use of electronic commerce in the United Kingdom by building confidence in electronic commerce and the technology underlying it by providing for approved encryption services, recognition of electronic signatures and removing legal obstacles to the use of electronic communications and storage information in place of paper'. This was the first piece of legislation which allowed the internet to flourish and grow in terms of finance and virtual economies.

With the enactment of the Electronic Communication Act 2000 it was hoped by the banking industry that their online and telephone banking facilities would now be considered a more viable option by even more customers due to the safeguards put in place by this Act. Internet and phone banking are now very popular methods of conducting banking and it is contested that without this piece of legislation the banking industry would have had a much harder time in convincing customers to take up the new modern practices of banking. The legislation has therefore gone some way to try to regulate for a modern and ever changing banking industry. However, the regulators have in this piece of legislation only tackled the technological aspects of banking and not the ethical, moral or societal elements.[65]

---

[65]   Chambers (2010a).

The Regulation of Investigatory Powers Act 2000

The Regulation of Investigatory Powers Act 2000 was introduced in response to enormous advances in technology and the enactment of the Human Rights Act 1998. Its purpose is to maintain law enforcement over such new technologies as the internet. To this extent it is relevant to modern banking practices. If more and more people are using modern technology to interface with their financial service providers, then there must be adequate legislation to protect their interests.[66]

Yet again, though, the legislators have demonstrated their ability to consider only the advances in technology and not the ever growing proportion of people who are in financial difficulty or financial exclusion.[67] Their mindset is one of profit maximisation and not social responsibility. It could be argued that this is the correct path to follow. The legislation does help both the banking industry and those people who conduct their banking business via these modern facilities. Also it is beneficial for business and corporate entities and if we refer back to the origins of banks, they were primarily set up for business.[68] However, it is argued that with the widening scope for ordinary people to use banks and their facilities, the bank is no longer primarily a merchant bank but also a people's bank and thus there should also be legislation to regulate the activities of the banks in relation to this aspect. The bank is now two dimensional. It is a banking industry for business as well as for the people.[69]

As iterated above, the new 2000 legislation came into force as a consequence of a change in government. In 1997 Labour came to power and its main aim was to transform and reform the regulation of the financial sector. It brought in the FSA as its principal regulator and set new standards for the industry, recognising the change and growth of the industry in new technologies. During the beginning of Labour's time in power, the UK economy flourished and the golden age of finance was booming. However, in the latter part of their term, problems linked with regulation and the banking sector started to emerge. In 2007 a financial crisis hit the United Kingdom – an unprecedented catastrophe. The causes and consequences of this crisis, will be explored later in the chapter. As a regulatory consequence of the crisis, various pieces of legislation have been enacted to try to minimise the effects of the crisis on the banking system, not just

---

[66] Ibid.
[67] Chambers and Shufflebottom (2010a, 2010b).
[68] Ibid.
[69] Chambers (2010a).

within the UK but also globally. A further complication of the economic crisis was the change of government in 2010 and as such the regulation enacted was greatly affected by the general election and manifesto promises.

THE BANKING ACT 2009

The Banking Act 2009 was the first piece of legislation after the crisis hit in 2007. Legislation prior to the Act came in the form of the Banking Acts 1979 and 1987, which were enacted as a direct consequence of the banking crisis. The Banking Act 1987 was repealed by the Financial Services and Markets Act 2000. In 1998, s21 of the Bank of England Act 1998 transferred to the FSA the supervision powers previously held by the Bank of England under the Banking Act 1987. The 1987 Act needed to be replaced because it did not stop a plethora of financial scandals from occurring during the period between the 1970s and the late 1990s. Here, once again, regulation follows crisis; and yet regulation continues to fail to prevent crisis.

Before the new Act came into force and before the FSMA, both the Banking Acts of 1979 and 1987 imposed on the Bank of England not only the power but also the duty to supervise the banks authorised by it to carry on deposit-taking business in the UK.[70] However the Bank of England Act 1998, Part III transferred the Bank of England's powers and responsibilities for the supervision of the banking sector and wholesale money market institutions to the FSA.[71] These changes had far reaching consequences. Arora concluded that the 'the changes announced . . . will have an unprecedented effect on the powers of the Bank of England'.[72] The secondary banking crisis of the 1970s was preceded by a 'period of UK financial liberalisation, a number of smaller or "secondary" banks rapidly expanded their lending to property companies in the early 1970s'.[73] The growth was

---

[70]   For a more detailed commentary on how the Bank of England regulated the banking sector, see Singh (2007) and more specifically for its role under the Banking Act 1987, see Arora (1988).

[71]   Bank of England Act 1998, s21. The Act transferred to the FSA the Bank of England's supervision powers under the Banking Act 1987, the Banking Coordination (Second Council Directive) Regulations, s101(4) of the Building Societies Act 1985, s43 of the Financial Services Act 1986 and the Investment Services Regulations 1995.

[72]   Arora (1988).

[73]   Dale (1995), at p. 327.

however short-lived when the government decided to limit its financial policy in the early 1970s. This limiting of financial regulation meant the passing of the 1979 Banking Act.

However, this 1979 Act was not to be enough of a deterrent to stop the secondary banking crisis nor the financial scandals that were to occur only five years later. In 1984 Johnson Matthey Bank collapsed. This highlighted the inadequacies of banking regulation under the Banking Act 1979.[74] This bank began to have financial problems in 1984 after it decided to lend to a small number of customers who faced financial problems.[75] The Bank of England became aware of the difficulties in 1984 when it was informed that the bank needed extensive financing to prevent its collapse. The Bank of England decided that this bank could not be allowed to collapse and it formulated a financial rescue package of £245m.

The regulatory approach at this time was so-called 'light-touch'. It was not by any means robust enough to withstand the failure of the bank's collapse. This light-touch approach led to the bank being able to breach the Banking Act 1979's safeguards, and obscured the Bank of England's view of their internal troubles. Ellinger et al. took the view that 'if JMB had been subjected to the more stringent supervision applied to licensed deposit-takers, its financial difficulties would have been discovered earlier'.[76] They added: 'following the JMB affair, the question of bank supervision was reviewed by a Committee set up by the Chancellor 1984 and chaired by the governor of the Bank of England'.[77] It is important to note that this collapse led to the enactment of the Banking Act 1987.

The Banking Act 1987 first came to light in 1985 when a White Paper (Cmnd 9695) was introduced. The Banking Act 1987's main focus was on the supervision and regulation of banking activities and the protection of depositors' interest. It did not deal with customer–bankers' transactions, consumer protection or with technological advancements.[78] Arora stated at the time that the Banking Act 1987 considerably reinforced the powers of the Bank of England to advise, supervise and control the banking sector. There was much hope for the Banking Act 1987. The 1987 Act contained many detailed provisions, all designed to control the banking industry.

The Banking Act 1987 abolished the two tier system and created a harmonised focus of supervisions on insitutions lending money in the

---

[74] Ellinger et al. (2006), p. 33.
[75] Dale (1995), p. 327.
[76] Ellinger et al. (2006), p. 33.
[77] Ibid.
[78] Arora (1988), 8–10.

markets. The new legislation also provided powers for the Bank of England to request institutions to commission reports from reporting accountants on their prudential returns, as well as on their systems and controls. The 1987 Act gave the Bank of England wider investigatory powers. This entailed more scope to interact with overseas banking supervisors and to investigate the controllers or shareholders of the banks. However, the 1987 Act did not stand the test for which it was designed and in the early 1990s Barings Bank and the Bank of Credit and Commerce International (BCCI) collapsed. The collapse of each of these banks was thought to be because of mismanagement by senior management. Because of these failures the Bank of England took over the supervisory role in 1998, as mentioned above. With the enactment of FSMA 2000, the 1987 Act was repealed. The banking and financial regulations from the 1970s to the late 1990s was piecemeal, flimsy and not robust enough to keep pace with the financial markets and systems that were evolving. The new Act 2009 will now be examined to determine whether it is merely another reactive piece of legislation responding to the economic situation we find ourselves in now or whether it really does have the teeth to ensure a clean and effective market.

The Act

The Banking Bill was introduced into the House of Commons on 7 October 2008, with a second reading on 14 October 2008. The Bill had a very quick session in Parliament as it appeared that there was an obvious feeling of urgency to rush the Bill through both Houses. The Bill is 240 clauses long and it was based on three consultation documents. These were Financial stability and depositor protection: strengthening the framework;[79] Financial stability and depositor protection: further consultation;[80] and Financial stability and depositor protection: special resolution regime.[81]

The research paper accompanying the Bill states clearly the problem with regulating financial crises in the future. 'Every crisis offers the hope that the worst is now past; but such hope lasts only till the next crisis.

---

[79]   TPA, CM 7308, 30 January 2008, available at: www.hm-treasury.gov.uk/media/3/5/banking_stability_pu477.pdf, retrieved 1 February 2008.

[80]   TPA, Cm 7436, 1 July 2008, available at: www.bankofengland.co.uk/publications/other/financialstabilitydepositorprotection080701.pdf, retrieved 10 July 2008.

[81]   TPA, Cm 7459, 22 July 2008, available at: www.official-documents.gov.uk/document/cm74/7459/7459.pdf, retrieved 23July 2008.

Policy makers across the world have appeared variously resolute, united, divided, bewildered and helpless.'[82] It is a fruitless task to draft legislation for financial crises.

The Bill also states that it is just one part of the multifaceted strategy that the government is enacting to help ease the financial crisis.[83]

The Banking Act 2009 received Royal Assent on 12 February 2009 and came into effect on 21 February. The Act strengthens the UK's statutory framework for financial stability and depositor protection.

The reforms that the Act brings in are: the special resolution regime; the bank administration procedure; the new bank insolvency procedure; inter-bank payments systems; financial services compensation scheme; and strengthening the role of the Bank of England. Many of the reforms have been welcomed by industry. Guy Sears (Wholesale Director of the Investment Management Association) said: 'The IMA supports the need for an explicit framework of powers to protect depositors and address bank failures. The Banking Act is a welcome step forwards. We are grateful for the open and constructive approach with which the Treasury engaged with us on the very complex technical impacts of the legislation. We remain committed to the future work of the expert liaison group.'[84]

The Banking Act 2009 extends the powers of The Banking (Special Provisions) Act 2008, which was enacted to allow the Treasury to rescue Northern Rock via nationalisation of the ailing bank.[85] The 2008 Act gave the Treasury extraordinary law making powers.

The aim of the new legislation is not to prevent banks from failing, but to allow them to fail in an organised manner that will not disrupt the industry or consumers as a whole (The Banking Act Explanatory Notes).

As stated above, the 2009 Act establishes a permanent special resolution regime.[86] This reform contains five objectives[87] and sets out three

---

[82] Research Paper, 08/77, Banking Bill, Bill 147 of 2007–08, 10 October 2008.

[83] Ibid.

[84] HM Treasury, Newsroom and Speeches, 'New Banking Act Comes into Effect', 23 February 2009, http://www.hm-treasury.gov.uk/press_16_09.htm, retrieved 23 February 2009.

[85] Tomasic (2008).

[86] The Banking Act 2009, s1, provides that the special resolution regime for banks is to address the situation where all or part of the business of a bank has encountered, or is likely to encounter, financial difficulties.

[87] The Banking Act 2009, ss4(4)–(8), (1) protect and enhance the stability of the financial systems of the United Kingdom; (2) protect and enhance public confidence in the stability of the banking systems of the United Kingdom; (3) protect depositors; (4) protect public funds; (5) avoid interfering with property rights in

stabilisation options for the use of the special resolution regime:[88] (1) transfer to a private sector purchaser;[89] (2) transfer to a bridge bank;[90] and (3) transfer to temporary public sector ownership.[91] In creating the special resolution regime the Banking Act builds on the tripartite framework to enhance the Authorities' (the Bank of England, the Financial Services Authority and the Treasury) ability to deal with crises in the banking system, to protect depositors and to maintain financial stability.[92]

The 2009 Act also established new bank insolvency (s90(1)) and administration (ss136–137(a)–(b)) procedures, to provide for the orderly wind-up of or transfer of business from a failing bank. These sections were provided to prevent the insolvency legislation (The Insolvency Act 1986) from further interfering with any future failing bank rescues. Furthermore, the 2009 Act makes changes to the compensation scheme which protects depositors' deposits by establishing contingency funding ('pre-funding') (Banking Act, s170) and makes it possible to provide support covertly.[93]

The 2009 Act reveals a change in philosophy by the government and regulators alike.[94] Banks should be allowed to fail, because it is part of the cyclical nature of the economic system. It has been acknowledged that regulators cannot regulate against every possible crisis.[95] Regulation is reactive to the current crisis being experienced. Therefore you cannot regulate for future crisis. What can be done is to regulate in order to minimise the effects of possible crisis.

Therefore the reforms can be said to allow institutions to fail in an organised manner that will not disrupt the industry or consumers as a whole (The Banking Act 2009, Explanatory Notes). It could be said that banking failures are integral to the development and progression in banking regulation. They form a vital part of reforming the regulatory

---

contravention of a Convention right (within the meaning of the Human Rights Act 1998).

[88] The Banking Act 2009, s1(3).

[89] Ibid., s11.

[90] Ibid., s12.

[91] Ibid., s13.

[92] HM Treasury, Newsroom and Speeches, 'New Banking Act Comes into Effect', 23 February 2009.

[93] BBC News, 'Banking Act comes into Effect', 21 February 2009, http://news.bbc.co.uk/1/hi/business/7902350.stm, retrieved 21 February 2009.

[94] *The Economist*, 'Barbarians at the vault', 15 May 2008, see: http://www.economist.com/opinion/PrinterFriendly.cfm?story_id=11376185, retrieved 18 February 2009.

[95] House of Commons Treasury Committee, 'The Run on the Rock, Fifth Report of Session', volume 1, London, 2008, p. 73.

machinery.[96] Furthermore, a system that never fails has been argued to be unattainable[97] and that, as argued above, financial crises can never be eradicated.[98]

Overall the main purpose of the Act is to enable the Bank of England to intervene more quickly to help troubled banks and protect investors. The Bank of England will be able to give hidden support to stricken banks, with the aim of maintaining financial stability. However, critics of the Act say it throws a cloak of secrecy around the banking world, which could be detrimental to consumers.[99] The Act allows for certain decisions to be exempt from the Freedom of Information laws and therefore if a bank is in danger of collapsing, this information could be withheld from its customers and the media under this clause. As we saw in the Northern Rock case, although customers were given assurances that their savings would be safe, there was still a run on the 'Rock'. It takes a couple of weeks to recoup losses from a failed bank and customers may not be willing to take this chance despite assurances. What the Act aims to do is to give the bank time to react internally before the media and its customers become aware of the banks' troubles. This clause causes controversy. Peter Thal-Larsen propounded that the Act will basically allow the financial authorities to take early action to move savers' deposits from a failing bank before tackling other problems without causing widespread panic. 'The idea is that, if there is a bank that gets into trouble, to insulate it and make the wider impact of that less, but I don't think they can actually stop banks from getting into trouble in the future'.[100]

There is still a dichotomy here. The FSA and the respective financial legislation is meant to be transparent and customer focused. By withholding information so that the banks can act quickly without bank runs, you are not allowing customers to choose what to do with their own savings in a timely fashion. This cloak of secrecy goes against the FSA ethos. Conversely, by withholding this information and throwing the cloak of secrecy around the banks' shoulders, you may be able to inhibit the panic

---

[96] Havranek (2000), p. 76.

[97] McCreevy C., European Commissioner for the Internal Market and Services, 7th Annual European Financial Services Conference, Financial Markets and Economic Recovery, 27 January 2009, Brussels. See: http://www.forum-europe.com/7th_Annual_European_Financial, retrieved February 24 2009.

[98] Sir Nigel Wicks, Chairman Euroclear, 7th Annual European Financial Services Conference, Financial Markets and Economic Recovery, 27th January 2009, Brussels.

[99] BBC News, 'Banking Act comes into Effect', 21 February 2009.

[100] Ibid.

that we saw in the Northern Rock case. Another point of view that could be entertained here is that with consumer confidence at an all time low, having a clause like this only heightens mistrust of the banks. Consumers may feel even more isolated and excluded from being the master of their own monetary destiny. This in turn will extrapolate the problems of consumer and market confidence and awareness and breach the FSA statutory objectives, to protect the confidence of consumers (s5 FSMA 2000); to ensure market confidence (s3 FSMA 2000); and ensure public awareness (s4 FSMA 2000). It will be interesting to see in days to come if banks do fail again and this clause is used by the industry and government, whether the already beleaguered consumer will stand up and use the statutory objectives which are meant to give them rights for their intended purpose.

Consequences

As previously stated the banking sector has changed irrevocably and the Banking Act enacted because of the financial crisis is unlike anything seen before. A return to simplistic banking, a more conservative approach[101] has been proffered as the way forward, yet it is questionable whether it will be successful. Indeed, it is questionable as to whether any piece of legislation can regulate against crisis. Moreover, economic crisis can be seen as an integral part of the economic cycle. There are times of economic boom and economic bust. What regulators should do is to ensure there are no extremes to this cycle.[102] 'Bubbles, excess and calamity are part of the package of Western finance'.[103] Not to acknowledge this and to believe that a return to a simplistic form of banking would prevent further economic crisis is 'absolute madness'.[104] You cannot 'turn back the clock' and expect crisis never to occur again.[105]

Looking at history can help to focus the regulation of the future, but 'banking has changed, the world has changed – finance moves much faster now and . . . it is impossible now to go back to that era'.[106] Regulation must accept this and move forwards. The Banking Act does not totally do this, nor does it look to history in much detail. In fact, having been

---

[101] BBC News, 'Brown: Banks Should Be "Servants"', 22 February 2009, http://news.bbc.co.uk/1/hi/uk/7903985.stm, retrieved 22 February 2008.
[102] *The Economist*, 'Barbarians at the Vault', 15 May 2008.
[103] Ibid.
[104] BBC News, 'Brown: Banks Should Be "Servants"', 22 February 2009.
[105] Ibid.
[106] Ibid.

rushed through Parliament, the Act is lacklustre but well intentioned. Furthermore, 'Critics of the Act say it throws a clock of secrecy around the banking world, which could be detrimental for consumers'.[107]

As we can see from the Banking Act 2009 regulation, it is reactive. It only concentrates on a solution to a situation; it is not a cure for a future problem. 'The safest forecast in banking is that the next crisis will not be rooted in America's mortgage market'.[108] This is because regulation has been enacted to stop the mortgage market failing in this manner again.

This is not to say that the crisis did not call for a change in regulation and philosophy.[109] It did; but it must be embraced with caution. The economic crisis that is occurring presently is a once in a lifetime event. Alan Greenspan, Chairman of America's Federal Reserve, 'calls the collapse a one in a half century, probably one in a century type of event. Financial Markets promised prosperity; instead they have brought hardship'.[110] This time of financial crisis was unprecedented. The regulation that comes into force must accept that this crisis is an extreme of the cycle of economics that most likely, will not be seen again in our lifetimes.

The Economist has said that if there was ever a time to make a radical change in the financial sector it is now. The UK government has acted. How successful it will be, only time and the next crisis will tell. What is questionable now is whether it is wise to throw the shackles over the sector.[111] To clamp down entirely would be a retrograde step. 'Attempts to regulate finance to make it safe often lead to dangerous distortions as clever financiers work their way around the rules'.[112] It is still unclear as to the effects of the new Act. Whether it will clamp down or whether it will secretly shield the banking sector no one yet knows.

'The aim should be neither to banish finance nor to punish it, but to create a system that supports economic growth through the best mix of state imposed stability and private initiatives. Modern finance is flawed, unstable and prone to excess'.[113] This is the story of our time. However, a more thoughtful reflection on this situation than that of *The Economist* is that, no, we can never regulate for all financial crisis, but what is required is a mechanism to stop or lessen the extremes of the financial cycle occurring. Finance will always have areas of boom and bust and no matter

---

[107] Ibid.
[108] *The Economist*, 'Barbarians at the Vault', 15 May 2008.
[109] Ibid.
[110] Ibid.
[111] Ibid.
[112] Ibid.
[113] Ibid.

what legislation is passed, these will occur, but what legislators should work towards is lessening the extremes.

If there was a simple way to regulate against crisises it would already be the foundation stone of financial regulation.[114] As stated previously, reactive regulation can only hope to stop the current economic crisis, not any future crisis. Economics and finance are pro-cyclical. The lessons we must take from this is that there will always be crises, but it is how we deal with them that counts. We must not also forget the good times when considering all the economic doom and gloom. 'After 20 years of growth, the flaws of modern finance are painfully clear. [But] do not forget its strength'.[115] We can surely learn from our history, both good and bad.

Financial Services Act 2010

Another major piece of legislation which was enacted as a direct result of the financial crisis and in response to the demands of society is the Financial Services Act 2010. On 19 November 2009, the government introduced the Financial Services Bill.[116] This Bill drew from on the response to the White Paper and is built on the Banking (Special Provisions) Act 2008 and the Banking Act 2009. The Act, which received Royal Assent on 8 April 2010, is the third piece of legislation that seeks to contribute towards the government's financial recovery plan.[117] This law is not meant to be a panacea for economic recovery but is meant to supplement already existing legislation. The Act increases the duties and the powers of the FSA in various respects relating to consumer awareness, protection of consumers, recovery plans for banks and remuneration policies. This Act has granted the FSA more power so that they can act in such a way as to monitor and control the financial market without having the chaos that followed the collapse of Northern Rock.[118]

When Labour came to power in 1997, financial reforms were at the forefront of the legislative mindset, due to the inadequacies of the Financial Services Act 1986.[119] People's confidence in the financial services sector had suffered under the previous Conservative government due to several

---

[114]   *The Economist*, 'Greed & Mash; and Fear', 22 January 2009.
[115]   *The Economist*, 'Barbarians at the Vault', 15th May 2008.
[116]   House of Commons, Research Paper, Financial Services Bill, Bill No. 6 of 2009–10, 27 November 2009.
[117]   Chambers (2010b).
[118]   For an excellent discussion of the collapse of Northern Rock, see Singh and LaBrosse (2010).
[119]   See, for example, MacNeil (1999).

major financial scandals. This resulted in the creation of the FSA, or 'super regulator', under the initial guidance of Howard Davies.[120] The FMSA 2000 was heralded by the government as a groundbreaking piece of legislation designed to thwart financial criminals, protect consumers and to maintain London's reputation as a global financial centre. Uniquely, the FSA was granted four statutory objectives. These were: to maintain market confidence; to promote public awareness;[121] to protect the consumer; to reduce financial crime.[122] The 2010 Act now provides that the FSA has the statutory objective 'to ensure financial stability' (s1). The FSMA 2000 created a single joined-up regulator which provided for the first time in financial regulatory history a robust regulatory backbone for the industry.

In 2007, due to the worsening economic climate in the United States of America (US), a ripple effect could be felt across the global financial market.[123] The first victim of the crisis in the UK was the well-documented collapse of Northern Rock,[124] as a result of which the experienced its first run on a bank since Victorian times. The government stepped in and provided a rescue package for this bank, which resulted in its renationalisation. This was not the only bank to be bailed out at the taxpayer's expense. Other banks such as Bradford and Bingley would also follow suit. Investment banks in the UK also suffered and in 2008 Lehman Brothers went into liquidation and collapsed.[125] The bank was not too big to fail and the US government allowed it to fail.

These catastrophic events resulted in the collapse of numerous financial institutions in both the US and UK – too many to mention here. It is important to note that during this time the FSA was not maintaining its statutory objectives, especially those of maintaining market confidence, increasing consumer awareness and consumer protection. A damning report published by the HM Treasury Select Committee openly criticised the FSA for not detecting the risk posed by Northern Rock and its increasing likelihood of collapse.[126] Having said this, no action has occurred and the FSA has not been held accountable for not achieving

---

[120] Lomnicka (1999), p. 482.
[121] For a more detailed discussion about this statutory objective, see Ryder (2001).
[122] Generally, see Ryder (2008).
[123] Hall (2008), at pp. 19–20.
[124] See generally Tomasic (2008a and 2008b).
[125] For a discussion of its collapse, see Marshall and Herrod (2009).
[126] Treasury Select Committee (TSC), 'The Run on the Rock', HC56-II 2007–08.

its statutory objectives.[127] The Banking (Special Provisions) Act (2008) was passed as a direct response to the failure of Northern Rock. This was added to a year later with the Banking Act 2009, which provided, amongst other things, the Special Resolution Regime, which allows the government, the FSA, the Bank of England and HM Treasury to take action once a bank has failed.[128] This provision does not stop banks from failing, but it ensures that if a bank does fail, it fails in an orderly manner.[129]

The Financial Services Bill 2009

The Financial Services Bill 2009 was designed to deliver significant reforms to the sector by providing stronger regulation in order to make sure that banks and other financial institutions are stronger and safer in the future so as to withstand the economic booms and busts of the cycle.[130] The Chancellor of the Exchequer, Alistair Darling MP, stated that 'the Bill . . . seeks to empower consumers and make sure that, in the future, taxpayers will not be called on to protect banks from the consequences of their actions'.[131] The main provisions of the Bill were to:

- Ensure responsibility and action of the Bank of England, FSA and HM Treasury with respect to financial stability matters;
- Place a duty on the FSA to make rules requiring financial institutions to create and maintain recovery and resolution plans in the event that they become financially vulnerable;
- Require the FSA to make general rules about remuneration policies of regulated firms;
- Expand the company law disclosure regime under which companies disclose details of the remuneration of directors, to include executive remuneration reports;

---

[127]   However, it is important to note that the shareholders of Northern Rock are currently embroiled in litigation against the bank. For a more detailed discussion, see *R. (on the application of SRM Global Master Fund LP) v Treasury Commissioner* [2009] EWCA Civ 788 as discussed in Gray (2009).

[128]   For a detailed commentary on the provisions of the Banking Act 2009, see McKnight (2009).

[129]   Chambers (2010c).

[130]   See generally, Walker (2010).

[131]   HM Treasury, 'Government Introduced Financial Services Bill', 19 November 2009, http://www.hm-treasury.gov.uk/press_108_09.htm, accessed 22 March 2010.

- Give the FSA a wider authority to prohibit short selling, by removing the existing link that restricts the power of prohibition to cases of possible market abuse;
- Require the FSA to work in international fora to develop international standards of regulation and supervision;
- Enable the FSA to increase its powers of information gathering and punishment as part of the supervisory enhancement programme;
- Enable the FSA to implement some recommendations of the Walker Review on corporate governance;
- Establish a new legal means – collective court actions – by which consumers might get redress in cases where there has been a mass failure of practice which has affected significant numbers of consumers. Practitioner-based consumer redress schemes will be given greater scope for operation, and to
- Prohibit the issuance of unsolicited credit card cheques to individuals and limits the total number which can be issued in a year to three.[132]

After a relatively quick passage through Parliament, the Bill received Royal Assent on 8 April 2010 and the Act's objectives were enacted relatively unchanged following their passage through the Houses.

The Act can be divided into three parts, these being: to change top-level regulatory structure; to enhance the existing powers of the FSA and to create new duties; and finally to impose measures to improve the rights and capabilities of consumers. It has been said that, 'the [bill] Act expands the reach and obligations of the FSA'.[133] Briefly to take each in turn, the Act does not seek to change the top-level regulatory structure, but seeks to improve the overall structure of the regulators, starting by improving the cooperation and relationship between the tripartite authorities. Secondly, the Act provides the FSA with more powers and duties in terms of acting in bank recoveries and failures, executive remuneration, short selling and expanding its disciplinary role.[134] Finally, the Act seeks to ensure consumer protection and capability. It therefore proposes several methods of consumer redress, including class actions and outlawing certain actions of lenders, such as unsolicited credit card cheques being sent to consumers.[135] The Act is largely based on policy and consultation documents such as

---

[132]   Ibid.
[133]   House of Commons, Research Paper, Financial Services Bill, Bill No. 6 of 2009–10, 27 November 2009, p. 1.
[134]   Ibid.
[135]   Ibid.

the Turner Review (2009)[136] and the Walker Review (April 2009). It has provided the FSA with new powers in a broad range of areas which were seen as problematical either before the crisis, during the crisis or because of the crisis within the UK. Whether it was really the areas themselves which were problematic, or the internal workings of the FSA, it is hard to tell. If the latter is at issue and there are problems with the internal mechanisms of the FSA, then a result of the Act giving more power to the FSA may be that more financial regulatory issues could soon come into being. This of course occurred prior to the general election and the change of government, which has now caused all these new proposals to be thrown into confusion, given the new government's desire to strip the FSA of its powers, and to give them back to the Bank of England.

Consumer confidence

The current economic climate is causing financial regulators concern in terms of consumers and social attitudes towards finance and banks. Consumers, it has been recognised, are losing confidence in the financial institutions and authorities' ability to safeguard the financial system.[137]

One of the FSA's statutory objectives is to ensure consumer confidence. If consumer confidence is not maintained, then there are real risks that could be faced by consumers and the industry alike. If there is disengagement by consumers, the industry suffers economically. This has the knock-on effect of lowering consumer confidence even more, thereby perpetuating a cyclical downturn in the economy and consumer confidence. The FSA have stated that: 'there is a risk that, should market participants lose confidence, markets for certain retail and wholesale products could come under pressure, exacerbating already difficult circumstances for firms and consumers'.[138]

Through 2007 and into 2008 consumer confidence was low. Before this time consumers were over-confident in the market and this is demonstrated in the next section, whereby consumers' belief in the property market and not saving may cause consumers to face financial difficulties in the coming months. The FSA recognises this in its Risk Outlook paper, stating that consumers 'could disengage from . . . parts of the industry'.[139]

When consumers receive a shock or have a real or perceived conception of market failure, a ripple effect of market panic subsequently occurs.

---

[136] Chambers (2009).
[137] Financial Services Authority, 'Financial Risk Outlook 2008', p. 28.
[138] Ibid.
[139] Ibid.

This was seen in the pension scandals of the 1990s and the Northern Rock crisis in 2007. The FSA highlight that the panic is sometimes caused by the low financial capabilities of consumers.[140] Therefore this financial risk is closely linked not only with the statutory objective of maintaining market confidence and the subsequent risk, but also with the statutory objective associated with the objective as well.

However, regulation is not always the solution to restore consumer confidence.[141] The FSA have stated that to restore confidence four issues need to be addressed. These being:

1. Investors believe institutions have revealed their exposures;
2. Investors have confidence that recent financial injections into the market are sufficient;
3. That the financial injections will prove to be effective; and
4. That the peak in future credit losses is manageable.[142]

As consumer confidence is low and recession is a likely possibility, the FSA have recognised a real risk. The manner in which they wish to counter the lack of confidence is questionable if they are already recognising that consumers are not sufficiently financially capable of making the right informed decisions. An issue the FSA should therefore be looking into is how to heighten consumer financial capability when consumers are already disengaging from the financial market because of mistrust, low financial capability and market failures, whether real or perceived.

Increase of financial crime
When there is low consumer confidence among consumers who are thought not to be financially capable, as discussed above, financial crime is a risk that the markets do not want to occur.

A financial crime can be seen from two perspectives. First, when people are in an economic crisis, sometimes they resort to crime in the form of card fraud. Secondly, financial crime can also come from large institutions or a person within a large organisation in the financial sector. Each of these crimes would have a detrimental effect on consumer confidence and the financial difficulties that are already perceived as risks by the FSA. 'Increasing financial pressure on firms, employees and consumers could increase the motivation of some to commit financial crime. At the same

---

[140] Ibid., p. 29.
[141] Chambers (2010a).
[142] Financial Services Authority, 'Financial Risk Outlook 2008', p. 28.

time, the consequences of crimes committed under the more benign conditions in previous years may be more likely to come to light when firms are faced with more difficult economic conditions'.[143]

It is important therefore that markets are clean, but when market conditions are volatile there is a greater chance of market abuse.[144] Although the FSA have put in place a plethora of compliance handbooks for firms to comply with, they have recognised that many firms are complacent as to their own internal systems and controls to counter market abuse. This laissez faire approach will only continue when resources are tight in an organisation and are channelled away to other areas of business.

Financial crime can also be exposed through the laundering of money. It has been found that in the UK direct losses have amounted to £13bn in 2005,[145] and the size of illicit drugs markets is said to be £5.3bn in 2003.[146] However, the new Money Laundering Regulations 2007 should make it more difficult to launder money in the UK, if organisations comply with them.

Financial crime does not remain static and the evolution of different types of crime makes it hard to police. Therefore the FSA has stated that firms need to be vigilant at all times to new mechanisms for perpetrating crime. The FSA also recognises that it is not just financial organisations that need to be aware of financial crime. Non-financial organisations are also a target for financial crimes.[147]

The Financial Risk Outlook paper also reported that fraud was another area of financial crime which posed a risk in the eighteen months following publication of the report. The FSA pointed to the loss of personal data from the infrastructural bodies of the UK as being instrumental in personal identity fraud. 'It is estimated that identity fraud costs the UK economy £1.7bn per year'.[148] The FSA links personal identity fraud with consumers' low financial capability, stating that: 'there is a risk that consumers do not have sufficient understanding of how to prevent their data being used for criminal purposes; the growth of online social networking . . . is leading to consumers putting more of their personal data in the public domain'.[149]

---

[143]   Ibid., p. 34.
[144]   Ibid.
[145]   Levi et al. (2007).
[146]   Financial Services Authority, 'Financial Risk Outlook 2008', p. 35.
[147]   Ibid., p. 35–6.
[148]   Home Office Fraud Steering Committee, February 2006.
[149]   Financial Services Authority, 'Financial Risk Outlook 2008', p. 36.

A pervasive theme throughout the FSA's Financial Risk Outlook Paper 2008 is that the FSA believes consumers, industry and government are all party to the economic risks that each of these groups will face in the next eighteen months. No one single factor is causing the majority of the risks, yet it is the cyclical effect of low consumer capability; low consumer confidence; an increase in financial difficulties being faced by consumers; an increase in financial crime; along with the decline in the economy, which is perpetuating each of these risks. The disengagement of consumers in the financial markets is a key concern for the regulators and the FSA Financial Risk Outlook paper tries to highlight solutions to mitigate the chances of increasing the economic downturn. The question is whether the regulators are posing a solution to a problem that can be fixed.

THE FINANCIAL SERVICES ACT 2010 AND THE FSA: FRIEND OR FOE?

Undoubtedly, the Act provides more powers and duties for the FSA. The questions that need to be asked are: do the FSA need more powers to help them regulate the financial markets; will the new powers and duties help economic recovery; and finally, should these powers and duties have already been carried out as oblique elements of the overarching existing statutory objectives of the FSA? As already mentioned, the FSA was criticised by the House of Commons for its role in the collapse of Northern Rock. The FSA has also come under fire and met with consternation for its lack of structure and regulatory vigour throughout the crisis.[150] There have been calls for increased or enhanced powers for the FSA, but perhaps it is questionable whether the regime is working in its present format. This brings us to the third question: should the FSA have already been achieving these new powers because of the existing overarching statutory objectives? The answer is surely, yes. The statutory objectives cover a wide remit and also cover an enormous scope of regulation, under which these new powers and duties could quite easily have already been in existence. What this Act therefore does is to make the powers and duties explicit when they should already have been under consideration by the FSA. This therefore goes some way to proffering an argument for reforming the FSA under the first question stated above. Moving to the second, will these new plans help economic recovery? This depends on the election and the economic

---

[150]   BBC News, 'Rock Report Prompts Reform Calls', 26 January 2008, http://news.bbc.co.uk/1/hi/business/7210897.stm, accessed 20 February 2009.

recovery plan put in place by the new government. What can be said and what was plainly pointed out at the beginning of the research paper and the Bill is that this piece of legislation is not intended to be the panacea for economic recovery, rather it is the first in a long line of regulatory reform in the area. This too will be hampered should there be a change of government. Therefore, it is justifiable to answer the third question in the negative. The new powers and duties bestowed on the FSA will not promote economic recovery, but what they may do is to help restore the public's trust and confidence in the system, if they are aware of this piece of legislation. This again is problematical as coverage of this legislation and the new powers have been overtaken by election news and the apathy of the public towards increasing their financial knowledge. The Act is highly technical and it is dubious whether the ordinary person on the street would understand and recognise its importance.

It is therefore plausible that new powers and duties under this Act are being imposed on the regulator to ensure financial recovery in the UK. However, this is not without its pitfalls. In other words, the new powers and duties should already have been covered by the pre-existing statutory objectives of the FSA. Additionally, the powers and the duties newly imposed will not promote economic recovery and at best will go some way to restore the public's trust and confidence, should the public become aware of the new powers and duties. Furthermore, if the FSA cannot achieve its existing statutory objectives, which it has been criticised during the crisis for not doing, surely it is the FSA itself which needs reforming.

MODERN BANKING PRACTICES

Although a bank is primarily a business and was originally created to act as a monetary provider for business, it has been said that regulation of banking seems to lag behind the modern ethical, moral and socially responsible aspects of banking practices. Society is juxtaposed with the mechanics of banks. Society cannot live without banks, but it is opposed to the internal operational decisions banks have made, especially during the financial crisis.[151] As we have seen throughout history, society needs to support the banking sector for it to flourish. Should society not support it, then the sector normally changes. Such change could be towards a greater move to the internet and virtual economies, where banking costs are lower and the ordinary person is in charge of their money. One of the

---

[151]   Aragandona (2009).

most worrying problems facing the banking industry with the inception of the virtual banks is the lack of a suitable definition of what a modern bank actually is in today's society. This tends to create a nebulous situation for the above practices and the role of regulation governing them. As we have already discussed in the book, virtual world banking and virtual economies are relatively regulation free and without a suitable definition for a tangible real world bank, much work has to be done to secure the position of the virtual bank and economy.

LACK OF A SUITABLE DEFINITION

Cranston believes that the most authoritative definition of a bank is one supplied by the case of *United Dominions Trust Ltd. v Kirkwood* [1966] 2 QB 431,[152] where Lord Denning stated:

> There are usually two characteristics found in bankers today: i) they accept money from and collect cheques for, their customers and place them into their credit; ii) they honour cheques drawn or orders drawn on them by customers when presented for payments and debit their customers accordingly. These two characteristics also carry a third: iii) namely they keep current accounts or something of that nature, in their books in which the credits and debits are entered.

This, however, does not allow for the modern trend of using internet or telephone banking and therefore if one uses this definition of a bank, which is considered to be the most authoritative, the new banking trend is excluded. Cranston, however, notes this inefficiency and opines that 'such analysis would not now be regarded as sufficient'.[153] Although there has been no conclusive definition of a bank or the inclusion of modern banking practices, there have been many cases which have tried to establish a definition. In *Commissioners of the State Savings Bank of Victoria v Permewan, Wright & Co Ltd* (1915) 19 CLR 457[154] Issacs J gave a general definition of a bank. He articulated that: '. . . the essential characteristics of the business of banking are . . . the collection of money by receiving deposits upon loans, repayable when and expressly or impliedly agreed upon, and the utilisation of the money so collected by lending it again in such sums that are required'.

---

[152] 2 QB 431 (CA).
[153] Cranston (1997), p. 4.
[154] 19 CLR 457.

Lewis notes that there is no satisfactory definition of banking, but he does accept that generally banks can be described as collecting and debiting money from accounts. Ellinger and Lomnicka[155] also suggest that there is no all-encompassing definition of banks. They state that: 'as a result of this proliferation, the legislature has not found it necessary to provide a functional definition that distinguishes banks from other financial institutions'.[156]

However, Ellinger and Lomnicka argue that to have an adequate common law definition of a bank there would need to be three stipulations. First, the definition of banking would have to change and modernise from time to time to keep pace with the diverse and changing financial industry. This can be supported by the current trend for traditional banks to move away from over-the-counter banking towards internet and telephone banking. This dichotomy becomes a problem when, as in *Woods v Martins Bank Ltd* [1959] QB 55,[157] the court is called upon to decide whether or not giving investment advice falls under the guise of banking. The Court held that it did, but Salmon J stated: 'The limits of a banker's business cannot be laid down as a matter of law'.

Secondly, they purport that the house where banking is considered to be engaged in, is not necessarily considered so elsewhere. This means that a banking house in one country may not necessarily be considered a banking house within a different country where the beliefs and culture are not the same. Thirdly, Ellinger and Lomnicka believe that if a bank is widely accepted as a bank, then the courts will generally regard it as being so, as in *Re Birkbeck Permanent Benefit Building Society* [1912] 2 Ch 183.[158]

It is therefore clear that what a bank is and what is does is rather fluid in its remit. A virtual bank can and does do all of these things, barring its lack of physical presence. A virtual economy in which a virtual bank sits also fulfils these common law definitions. Is it therefore questionable whether, if challenged, a virtual bank would fall under these legal remits?

CURRENT CHALLENGES BY SOCIETY AND THE FINANCIAL CRISIS

Banking history and its reflective regulation demonstrate that the nature of what a bank is has changed over time. In recent months banks have

---

[155] Ellinger and Lomnicka (1996).
[156] Ibid., p. 11.
[157] QB 55.
[158] 2 Ch 183.

been affected by several issues. In 2007 Northern Rock was on the verge of collapse and an immediate plan of action was put into operation by the government and the PSA. The problems with Northern Rock created a small scale banking crisis, with many customers demanding their money back from the bank. This is typical of the historical banking crisis.The Northern Rock fiasco came to fruition over the period of 14 September to 17 September 2007. This was the first time that the UK had seen a run on the retail banks since Victorian times.[159]

It was concluded that there were systematic failures that directly related to the directors of the company, but also that the tripartite system has significantly failed.[160] In addition to this, the FSA[161] had also failed in its regulatory duty to ensure that Northern Rock would not pose a systematic risk.[162]

The House of Commons took it upon themselves to ensure that this would not happen again and proposed that: [163] the relevant authority be given the power to acquire information relating to individual financial institutions and to take action in relation to an institution in specified circumstances; and to propose a special resolution regime for failing banks to enable the smooth administration of such a bank to be combined with arrangements to ensure that insured depositions were safe and accessible.[164]

Subsequently, the banking sector in the United Kingdom has been pulled into an economic crisis that is unlike any for over a century.[165] The banking industry has been hugely influenced by the sector in the US. The crisis started after a two year period (2004–6) when US interest rates rose from 1% to 5.35%.[166] This meant homeowners struggled and more and more people defaulted on their mortgages. Those in the sub-prime market, where lenders lent to customers with poor or no credit history, began to see their homes repossessed as they defaulted on their mortgages.[167] This occurred from April 2007 up until the end of 2007. The failure of the

---

[159] TSC, 'Run on the Rock', p. 3.

[160] Ibid., pp. 3–4.

[161] BBC News, 'FSA Failed over Northern Rock', 26 January 2008, http://news.bbc.co.uk/1/hi/business/7209300.stm.

[162] TSC, 'Run on the Rock', p. 4.

[163] BBC News, 'Rock Report Prompts Reform Calls', 26 January 2008.

[164] TSC, 'Run on the Rock', p. 3.

[165] *The Guardian*, 'A Financial Crisis Unmatched since the Great Depression, Say Analysts', 18 March, 2008. http://www.guardian.co.uk/business/2008/mar/18/creditcrunch.marketturmoil1.

[166] BBC News, 'Credit Crunch Timeline', http://news.bbc.co.uk/1/hi/business/7521250.stm.

[167] BBC News, 'Sub Prime Crisis Sours US Dream', 5 April 2007, http://news.bbc.co.uk/1/hi/business/6528387.stm.

sub-prime market really impacted on the UK market and with the failure of Northern Rock and the first run on the bank in a century, the market took its first steps towards a steep decline.[168]

It is important to assess how and what led up to the current economic turmoil that is gripping the country at the moment. In July 2007, investment bank Bear Stearns first suffered the effects of the beginning of the credit crisis when it informed investors that they would be unlikely to get much if any of their investments out of their hedge funds. This was because bank to bank lending had faltered because of lack of confidence.[169]

This news was followed in August 2007 by investment bank BNP Paribas who also told its investors that they would not be able to take their money out of funds because the banks could not value the assets within them. This was another indication that the banks were refusing to lend to each other.[170]

The regulators began to step in, with the European Central Bank[171] and US Federal Reserves[172] intervening by adding funds to the ailing banks.

Also in August, in the UK the Bank of England[173] dropped interest rates by half a percentage point to 5.75%. A warning was also issued that the credit crunch, a term never before used in this financial situation, would affect the economic growth of the country. Additionally, UK sub-prime lenders began to withdraw mortgages from customers who had poor or little credit history.

The crisis did not only affect the UK and US but also most other countries within the world. In late August 2008 Germany's regional bank Sachsen Landesbank faced collapse after investing in the sub-prime market.[174]

In September the world saw the rate at which banks lent to each other rise to its highest level since December 1998.

In late September 2007 Northern Rock collapsed[175] and acted as a catalyst for other banks to tumble and admit their struggles. In October 2007 Swiss bank UBS was the world's first top-flight bank to admit to

---

[168]   *Times Online*, 'The Credit Crunch Explained', 14 August 2008, http://www.timesonline.co.uk/tol/money/reader_guides/article4530072.ece.
[169]   BBC News, 'Credit Crunch Timeline'.
[170]   Ibid.
[171]   European Central Bank, http://www.ecb.int/home/html/index.en.html.
[172]   US Federal Reserves, http://www.federalreserve.gov/.
[173]   Bank of England, http://www.bankofengland.co.uk/.
[174]   *International Herald Tribune*, Global Edition of *New York Times*, 'CEO of Germany's Landesbank Sachsen Says He Will Resign', 23 August 2007, http://www.iht.com/articles/ap/2007/08/23/business/EU-FIN-COM-Germany-Sac hsenLB-CEO-Resigns.php.
[175]   BBC News, 'Rush on Northern Rock Continues', 15 September 2007, http://news.bbc.co.uk/1/hi/business/6996136.stm.

significant losses because of their sub-prime investments. This announcement led to the resignation of the Chairman and Chief Executive.[176] Also within that month Citigroup unveiled losses in the sub-prime market.[177] This was one of three announcements where the bank had to write down losses amounting to $40bn in total.[178]

The resignations of the top bankers did not stop there and would not do so in the next year. In October 2007 Merrill Lynch's Chief Executive stepped down because of losses in the sub-prime market. The exposure to $7.9bn of bad debt was too much for the CEO to bear.[179] November 2007 saw the Bank of England announce that the uptake on mortgages was at an all time low, with the Council for Mortgage Lenders (CML) requesting more funds from the government for the financial markets.[180] December 2007 saw the US announce plans to help homeowners who faced foreclosure of their mortgages[181] and the UK's Bank of England cut interests rates to 5.5%.[182] December also saw an unprecedented occurrence where five leading central banks offered billions of dollars in loans to struggling banks. This resulted in a temporary let-up in the stagnation of bank to bank lending, with the banks lowering the level of borrowing to each other and there was a rise in take-up.[183]

The new year did not see a merrier outcome for the banks. It started badly with a run on Scottish Equitable, resulting in a 12 month delay for investors wanting to get their money out of banks.[184] The media and the government both spoke in unison about a harsh time ahead economically for the UK and the world. Each day more and more bad news spewed forth about the economic downturn and the predicament in which consumers found themselves.[185] January also saw global stock markets fall

---

[176] Reuters Video, 'Sudden Exit for UBS CEO', 6 July 2007, http://www. reuters.com/news/video?videoId=59280.

[177] BBC News, 'Credit Crunch Timeline'.

[178] BBC News, 'Citigroup's $9.8bn Sub-prime Loss', 15 January 2008, http:// news.bbc.co.uk/1/hi/business/7188909.stm.

[179] *The Independent*, 'Merrill Lynch CEO Poised to Step Down amid Spiralling Losses', 29 October 2008, http://www.independent.co.uk/news/business/news/ merrill-lynch-ceo-poised-to-step-down-amid-spiralling-losses-398246.html.

[180] BBC News, 'Credit Crunch Timeline'.

[181] Ibid.

[182] Bank of England, http://www.bankofengland.co.uk/.

[183] BBC News, 'Credit Crunch Timeline'.

[184] *The Guardian*, 'Panic Selling Shuts £2bn Fund', 18 January 2008, http:// www.guardian.co.uk/money/2008/jan/18/property.moneyinvestments.

[185] BBC News, 'China Boom "Cushions World Slump"', 9 January 2008, http://news.bbc.co.uk/1/hi/business/7177397.stm.

and for the FT100 this was the biggest fall since the 11 September 2001 attacks on the Twin Towers.[186] The US Fed cut interest rates to 3.5% in the largest slash for 25 years and in February 2008 the UK cuts interest rates to 5.25%, trying to breathe some life back into the market.[187] February and March 2008 also saw mortgage repossessions rise.[188] The G7 stated that world losses on the sub-prime market could result in $400bn losses; $200bn was made available to banks by the Fed; Bear Stearns was acquired by JP Morgan and the UK saw house prices start to fall.[189]

April began with Abbey withdrawing the last mortgage available to customers without a deposit and more and more providers began to withdraw mortgage products. The International Monetary Fund (IMF) stated that the credit crunch could actually cost the world $1trillion.[190] The Bank of England reacted by dropping interest rates to 5%.[191] Confidence was at an all time 30 year low, but the Bank of England announced a £50bn rescue plan.[192] April and May 2008 saw the banks trying to rally round and gather funds from avenues other than the government. The Royal Bank of Scotland tried to raise funds from its shareholders at the same time that they announced a £5.9bn writedown – the largest for any UK bank to date.[193] May also saw the announcement that more than 850 companies had gone into liquidation in the first quarter of 2008.[194] The UBS investment bank announced a $15.5bn rights issue to cover some of its losses. UBS was one of the worst hit investment houses in the credit crunch.[195] Also within the same month in the US, there were significant advancements in investigations in to two credit crunch-related incidents,

[186] BBC News, 'Global Shares Tumble on US Fears', 22 January 2008, http://news.bbc.co.uk/1/hi/business/7199552.stm.
[187] BBC News, 'Fed Slashes Rates in Shock Move', 22 January 2008, http://news.bbc.co.uk/1/hi/business/7202645.stm.
[188] BBC News, 'Home Repossessions Rise to 27,000', 8 February 2008, http://news.bbc.co.uk/1/hi/business/7234254.stm.
[189] BBC News, '$200bn Fed Move over Credit Fears', 7 March 2008, http://news.bbc.co.uk/1/hi/business/7284101.stm.
[190] BBC News, 'Credit Crunch Could Cost $1 Trillion', 8 April 2008, http://news.bbc.co.uk/1/hi/business/7336744.stm.
[191] BBC News, 'Credit Crunch Timeline'.
[192] BBC News, 'Bank of England Plan to Help Out UK Banks', 21 April 2008, http://news.bbc.co.uk/1/hi/business/7351506.stm.
[193] BBC News, 'RBS Sets Out £12bn Rights Issue', 22 April 2008, http://news.bbc.co.uk/1/hi/business/7359940.stm.
[194] BBC News, 'Leap in Companies Administration', 2 May 2008, http://news.bbc.co.uk/1/hi/business/7380531.stm.
[195] BBC News, 'UBS Launches $15.5bn Cash Call', 22 May 2008, http://news.bbc.co.uk/1/hi/business/7414167.stm.

with the FBI arresting 406 people.[196] Meanwhile in the UK, Barclays announced a £4.5bn share issue plan to bolster funds within the bank.[197] July 2008 brought more problems both in the UK and US. In the US, two major financial lenders, Fanny Mae and Freddie Mac, faced problems, and Indymac collapsed. Indymac is the second largest US bank to fail in history.[198]

In the UK the FTSE faced bleak times, dropping to an all time low of 20% lower than its highest point in recent times.[199] August 2008 was rife with bad financial news. HSBC announced that the UK economy was facing recession;[200] the government stated that the economy was at a standstill and the Bradford and Bingley posted large losses.[201] September began with the government announcing a one year rise in stamp duty from £125,000 to £170,000;[202] interest rates were held at 5%;[203] the European Central Bank announced that it was predicting growth to be only 1.2% rather than the previously forecast 1.5%.[204] All this bad news saw the FTSE have its worst week and steepest decline in a week since 2002.[205] The US, in one of the world's largest bailout plans, saved Fannie Mae and Freddie Mac.[206] However, Lehman Brothers investment bank posted losses of $3.9bn and then filed for bankruptcy a few days later.[207] Merrill Lynch, also hit by the credit crunch, agreed to be taken over by Bank of America.[208] The largest insurance company in America, AIG, was also

---

[196] BBC News, 'FBI Hold 406 People on Mortgage Fraud', 19 June 2008, http://news.bbc.co.uk/1/hi/business/7464298.stm; BBC News, 'Bear Stearns Ex-manager Charged', 19 June 2008, http://news.bbc.co.uk/1/hi/business/7463713.stm.

[197] BBC News, 'Barclays Plan £4.5bn Fundraising', 25 June 2008, http://news.bbc.co.uk/1/hi/world/7472666.stm.

[198] BBC News, 'Key US Mortgage lender Collapse', 13 July 2008, http://news.bbc.co.uk/1/hi/business/7503109.stm; BBC News, 'US Moves to Bolster Firms', 14 July 2008, http://news.bbc.co.uk/1/hi/business/7504122.stm.

[199] BBC News, 'Credit Crunch Timeline'.

[200] BBC News, 'Warning as HSBC Profits fall 28%', 4 August 2008, http://news.bbc.co.uk/1/hi/business/7540404.stm.

[201] BBC News, 'Bradford and Bingley Announces losses', 22 August 2008, http://news.bbc.co.uk/1/hi/business/7587360.stm.

[202] BBC News, 'Stamp Duty Axed Below £175,000', 2 September 2008, http://news.bbc.co.uk/1/hi/uk_politics/7592852.stm.

[203] BBC News, 'Credit Crunch Timeline'.

[204] Ibid.

[205] Ibid.

[206] BBC News, 'US Takes Over Key Mortgage Firms', 7 September 2008, http://news.bbc.co.uk/1/hi/business/7602992.stm.

[207] BBC News, 'Lehman Bros Files for Bankruptcy', 16 September 2008, http://news.bbc.co.uk/1/hi/business/7615931.stm.

[208] Ibid.

in trouble in September 2008 and the government came to the rescue, thinking it could not let a giant fail.[209] Meanwhile, in the UK HBOS, the UK's largest mortgage lender, was taken over by Lloyds TSB, creating a giant bank that holds over one third of the UK's saving and mortgage market.[210] European insurance and banking giant Fortis was partially nationalised to ensure that it did not fail.[211]

Continuing with the nationalisation theme, in the UK the Bradford and Bingley was also nationalised.[212] September also saw Iceland in economic trouble, which affected many of UK savers both individuals and businesses.[213] October and November 2008 saw more bad news, markets fell and more and more mortgages were being defaulted on.[214] Both the UK and US governments put in place plans to help out those who were defaulting on their mortgages and the FSA was given powers to ensure the safeguarding of savings up to £50,000 in UK saving banks.[215]

We could add to this historical overview on an almost daily basis. The situation is dire indeed. This economic situation will go down in history as a turning point in economic and banking history. It has made the banks sit up and realise that buoyant lending and what might be described as irresponsible lending has got to stop. The economic situation of a country goes in cycles. There is always a boom and then a bust, but on a world scale the situation is unprecedented and the government will continue to take action. The historical overview of what a bank was compared with what it is now shows the cyclical nature of the banking sector and its effects on society. To say that a bank is not an essential part of the infrastructure of the world is nonsense. Banks are vital; therefore so too is their correct regulation and systematic control.

The economic crisis which is still currently affecting the UK economy will mean that the landscape of both the industry and its regulation will be changed forever. The new regulation outlined above will create a new framework for the industry to work within. As part of this new landscape, reliance on other methods of wealth creation and conducting business will be explored.

[209]   BBC News, 'US Government Rescue Insurer AIG', 17 September 2008, http://news.bbc.co.uk/1/hi/business/7620127.stm.
[210]   BBC News, 'Lloyds TSB Seals £12bn HBOS Deal', 17 September 2008, http://news.bbc.co.uk/1/hi/business/7622180.stm.
[211]   BBC News, 'Deal Agreed for Euro Bank Fortis', 29 September 2008, http://news.bbc.co.uk/1/hi/business/7641132.stm.
[212]   BBC News, 'B&B Nationalisation Confirmed', 29 September 2008, http://news.bbc.co.uk/1/hi/business/7641193.stm.
[213]   BBC News, 'Credit Crunch Timeline'.
[214]   Ibid.
[215]   Ibid.

E-commerce and the use of e-payments and internet monetary transactions are already in place. Society has bought into these new methods of financial transactions and a small percentage of society is interested in virtual banks and virtual economies. The crisis could lead to greater participation in the virtual world economy as a means of wealth creation. If this is so, perceptions of what a virtual bank and virtual economy are will change. Alongside this, there will be an increased need for robust and strong regulation. What this book recommends is early regulation so as to create a safe and secure place to trade, one which will not be influenced by those aspects of banking history depicted above, such as financial scandals and crime and poorly executed regulation. Regulation must not be so rigid as to inhibit growth and innovation, yet regulators must be aware of the inherent dangers that a virtual economy poses, not only for the virtual world but in the real world too.

FUNCTIONS OF MONEY

If we are considering the evolution and the origins of money we must also consider the functions of money and why it is so important in our society. In other words, what are the advantages of having money? Davies outlines the following list of the functions that money provides in society.

Specific functions (mostly micro-economic)

- Unit of account (abstract)
- Common measure of value (abstract)
- Medium of exchange (concrete)
- Means of payment (concrete)
- Standard for deferred payments (abstract)
- Store of value (concrete)

General functions (mostly macroeconomic and abstract)

- Liquid asset
- Framework of the market allocative system (prices)
- A causative factor in the economy
- Controller of the economy.[216]

Therefore money allows us to function in society as a means of payment to obtain the goods we need or want. In a society which is dominated by the

---

[216] Davies (2002), pp. 27–8.

'having of money', if you do not have money, you cannot function properly in that society. If you have money, you can therefore support yourself and get the goods and services you need. If you do not, then you have to rely on others or go without. Money can therefore divide a society into those who do and those who do not have money. The amount of money people have is also important. The more money you have, the more luxuries and non-essentials you can purchase. Money has evolved. We have gone from having enough money to survive on basic goods to a society where the more money you have the more advantages in life you can obtain. This brings out human greed and desire, driving criminals to obtain more money in illegal ways.

MONEY AND THE INTERNET

As we have iterated above, banking has evolved from the barter system to the simple use of coins and paper to using electronic transfers as a means of using money to obtain the goods and services that we require. This part of the chapter therefore makes the leap from this platform of finance and technology to what the future may hold, examining how it is going to affect our society and our lives. In essence, what we are going to be doing is forecasting what the future holds for banking given the already emerging trends and research in this area. In other words, turning the unrealistic, or virtual, to the real.

To begin with it is important to look at the use of the internet in commercial sales because this is where customers have started to get used to using online payment systems as a means of obtaining goods. Some ten or twenty years ago this method of commerce was relatively unheard of, but today as we can see from Tables 4.1 and 4.2, it is pretty much the norm. Customers are happy to use internet shopping channels to purchase goods and services and for their money to be transferred via an electronic system. 'The number of adults who bought or ordered goods or services online within the last 12 months reached 31 million in 2010'.[217]

From this we can see that e-commerce has now become an important commercial trend not only in our social lives but also in our retail business and therefore the economy. Online shopping and e-commerce have been made possible through use of the Internet. It is reported that in 2011 nearly 60% (30.1 million) of the adult population used the internet on a daily basis (see Figure 4.1).[218] In 2006 the figure was only 16.5 million.

---

[217] Office for National Statistics, 'Internet Access', http://www.statistics.gov.uk/cci/nugget.asp?id=8, accessed 18 January 2011.
[218] Office for National Statistics, Internet Access.

Table 4.1 Sales and purchases over ICTs as a proportion of total sales and purchases, 2005 to 2009 (per cent)

	2005	2006	2007†	SIC 2003 2008	SIC 2007 2008	2009
Sales over the internet	5.4	6.3	7.4	9.6	9.3	–
Sales over ICTs other than the internet	10.9	11.3	11.6	5.1	5.1	–
Sales over a website	–	–	–	4.3	4.1	4.7
Sales over ICTs other than a website	–	–	–	10.4	10.3	12.0
Purchases over the internet	5.6	6.9	9.4	–	–	–
Purchases over ICTs other than the internet	18.6	20.7	19.4	–	–	–
Purchases over ICTs	–	–	–	22.4	22.0	26.5

Notes:
Coverage: UK non-financial sector businesses with 10 or more employees.
– not available
† estimates since 2007 have been revised. Since 2008 estimates for sales over ICTs other than the internet, and purchases over ICTs, exclude transactions over manually typed email.

Source: E-commerce and ICT Activity, 2009 e-commerce Survey of Business datasets, http://www.statistics.gov.uk/downloads/theme_economy/ecommerce-2009/dataset-links2009.pdf, accessed 18 January 2011.

Table 4.2 Businesses with a website, by size of business, 2005 to 2009 (per cent)

Employment size			10–49	50–249	250–999	1000+	All size-bands
Website, own or		2005	65.0	86.6	94.7	97.6	69.2
third party		2006	65.5	89.0	96.0	97.9	69.9
		2007†	66.1	89.3	95.7	98.0	70.3
	SIC 2003	2008	69.6	89.7	94.6	98.2	73.3
	SIC 2007	2008	71.3	91.3	94.3	97.9	75.1
	SIC 2007	2009	72.3	91.8	97.3	98.5	76.0

Notes:
Base: UK businesses with 10 or more employees.
† estimates since 2007 have been revised.

Source: E-commerce and ICT Activity, 2009 e-commerce Survey of Business datasets, http://www.statistics.gov.uk/downloads/theme_economy/ecommerce-2009/dataset-links2009.pdf, accessed 18 January 2011.

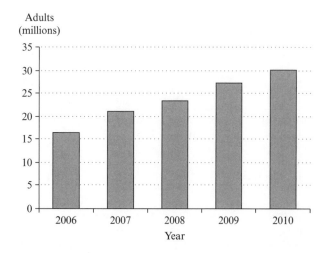

Note: Adults using the internet everyday.

Source: Office for National Statistics, internet Access.

Figure 4.2   Internet access 2006–2010

The Office for National Statistics reported that in the UK 9.2% of adults surveyed in 2010 had never used the internet, falling from 10.2% in 2009. Internet use is also connected to demographic and social indicators such as age, location, marital status and education.[219] For example, the majority of those aged 65 and over (60%) had never accessed the internet, compared with just 1% of those aged 16 to 24. While 97% of adults educated to degree level had accessed the Internet, 45% without any formal qualifications had done so.[220]

One interesting trend has been the use of social media as a form of networking, socialising and interacting. Although e-commerce has allowed us to shop and purchase goods, in a different manner use of the internet has reconnected people via social media such as Facebook and Twitter. In 2010 43 million adults used social media routinely in their daily lives, compared with 6.4 million in 2006. The number of households with internet connections has also grown to around 73% of households.[221]

Apart from shopping and social media, the Office for National Statistics

---

[219] Ibid.
[220] Office for National Statistics, Internet access.
[221] Ibid.

Table 4.3   Adults using internet banking: EU Comparison (per cent)

Country	2006	2007	2008	2009
Estonia	79	83	84	87
Finland	81	84	87	87
Netherlands	73	77	79	82
Sweden	66	71	73	79
Denmark	69	70	73	77
Latvia	44	50	64	66
Belgium	46	52	57	62
Luxembourg	58	58	60	62
France	39	51	59	60
Lithuania	35	43	51	56
Malta	42	48	52	56
United Kingdom	42	45	49	55
Germany	46	49	51	53
Austria	44	44	47	48
Ireland	40	42	–	46
Spain	32	31	35	39
Slovenia	32	36	38	39
Poland	23	29	35	38
Slovakia	25	27	37	38
Portugal	27	29	32	37
Italy	25	31	32	34
Cyprus	18	31	30	32
Czech Republic	22	24	25	31
Hungary	18	23	23	27
Greece	9	12	13	13
Romania	3	7	7	7
Bulgaria	6	5	4	4
EU Average	40	44	47	50

Note: Individuals aged 16–74 who had used the internet in the last three months for an activity.

Source: Office for National Statistics, Social Trends pt 81, http://www.statistics.gov.uk/ articles/social_trends/e-society-2010.pdf, accessed 18 January 2011.

has stated that 54% of people interviewed used internet banking, making it the UK's fourth most well used Internet activity.[222] Additionally, research has also indicated that with the increase in the use of internet banking,

[222]   BBC News, 'UK Net Use Grows Despite Digital Inequalities', 11 November 2010, http://www.bbc.co.uk/news/technology-11734910, accessed 18 January 2011.

there has been a dramatic rise in internet banking crime, with over £59.7mn lost through crime in 2009.[223]

In a National Fraud Authority (NFA) Report out in January 2011, it was reported that online banking fraud increased from £53mn in 2008 to £60mn in 2009, an increase of 14%.[224] The NFA stated that they believed this increase was because criminals were using more sophisticated methods of fraud online. The rise in economic online crime was also linked to the growth in use of online banking.

We can therefore conclude that in terms of technology and evolution of banking, commerce and finance, society's perceptions and acceptance are changing. Along with the change in the dynamics of how people operate through the use of the internet, we can see that criminals are also changing the way in which they commit crimes, and are now using the internet as a means of accessing victims. The internet is an almost universally accepted form of technology and it will not be long before it becomes an essential part of everyday life for the majority of society. Along with this growth and acceptance, crime will continue to evolve and grow. Use of the internet as a method of banking and commerce, which might once have been considered unusual, is now normal.

SUMMARY

The aim of this chapter was to consider the proposition that throughout history money has been a continuously changing phenomenon and that today we are entering a dramatic new phase of monetary exchange which will lead to different regulatory and legal issues arising. The rise of banks and the use of money has been charted and discussed, and the present financial crisis and incumbent regulatory structure have also been explored. This examination has provided evidence that money is evolving and that the next step towards a virtual economy and virtual currencies is not too far away. As iterated throughout this book, what was once unreal will soon become real, and the legal system must be ahead of the criminals who are all too quick to exploit any weakness in the system. It is this idea which will be considered in detail in Chapters 5 and 6, providing an argument for robust legal regulation to be put in place in the virtual world.

---

[223] Office for National Statistics, *Social Trends*, http://www.statistics.gov.uk/articles/social_trends/e-society-2010.pdf, accessed 18 January 2011.

[224] National Fraud Authority, 'Annual Fraud Indicators', January 2011.

5.   A real crime in a virtual world

> But they that will be rich fall into temptation and a snare, and into many
> foolish and hurtful lusts, which drown men in destruction and perdi-
> tion. For the love of money is the root of all evil: which while some coveted
> after, they have erred from the faith, and pierced themselves through
> with many sorrows. But thou, O man of God, flee these things; and follow
> after righteousness, godliness, faith, love, patience, meekness. (1 Timothy 6:
> 4–11)

INTRODUCTION

So far in this book the nature and development of virtual worlds has
been discussed with particular reference to legal jurisdiction and also
virtual crimes, namely the financial crime of money laundering. Within
this chapter, virtual money laundering will be discussed. In order to do
this the chapter will set out what virtual money laundering is and how
it occurs within virtual worlds. The chapter also acknowledges that not
all academics are of the belief that virtual money laundering occurs,
thereby discussing the arguments for and against the presence of virtual
money laundering. This bifurcation of beliefs about virtual money
laundering stems from the lack of prosecutable evidence owing to the
lack of legal structure and jurisprudence in the virtual worlds. This
book expresses the opinion that virtual money laundering does indeed
occur and therefore, having presented both academic viewpoints, it will
further continue to discuss virtual money laundering within this chapter.
In doing so the statistics and case studies of virtual money laundering
instances will be explored, along with presenting interviews with the law
enforcement agencies which work towards combating virtual financial
crime, namely Interpol and the state police in the USA. The chapter
will conclude that although relatively little is known about the true
amounts being laundered in virtual worlds, there is a true and tangible
threat present and only a joined-up international legal structure will be
able to combat virtual money laundering. This flows from the thinking that, as iterated in the book previously, virtual crime is merely a
continuum of the real world crime of money laundering, which is taken

seriously, especially after the terrorist attacks of 9/11 (USA) and 7/7 (London).[1]

WHAT IS VIRTUAL MONEY LAUNDERING AND HOW DOES IT OCCUR?

Definitions

Before defining what virtual money laundering is, it is prudent to determine what cyber crime is. Cyber crime 'is one of the fastest growing areas of crime, as more and more criminals exploit the speech, convenience and anonymity that modern technologies offer in order to commit a diverse range of crimes'.[2]

One of the earliest detected virtual crimes was that of virtual rape,[3] which took place in the LambdaMOO MUD.[4] The rapist, known as Mr Bungle, described the rape of another MUD user graphically. His actions were insufficient for a successful prosecution. There is an academic bifurcation as to whether Mr Bungle's actions amounted to an actual rape capable of prosecution or whether it was insufficient because it lacked real world consequences. Susan Brenner referred to the rape as a 'true virtual crime',[5] whereas Julian Dibbell commented that he 'was fascinated by the concept of a virtual rape, but I was even more so by the notion that anyone could take it altogether seriously'.[6] Brenner explored what would make a virtual crime successful at prosecution and she determined that the virtual crime would need to have real world elements, and thus were not new criminal activity but a continuum of the real world crimes carried out in a new way.[7] Professor Lessig opined that there could be a valuable link between actual rape and the LambdaMOO rape in cyberspace,[8] but this opinion was criticised by Professor Kerr who stated that the link 'is tenuous at best. It is a link between a brutal rape and a

---

[1] For a good discussion on the history of combating financial crime, see: Levi (2010), 650.

[2] Interpol. 'Cybercrime fact sheet', 2008. COM/FS/2008-07/FHT-02.

[3] Dibbell (1993).

[4] MUDs are text based virtual worlds. For a discussion on this see Bartle (2004); Dibbell (1998), at pp. 51–65; Lastowka and Hunter (2004), at pp. 14–21.

[5] Brenner S. (2001).

[6] Dibbell (1998), p. 21.

[7] Brenner S. (2001).

[8] Lessig L. (1999).

fictional story of a brutal rape. Surely the difference is more striking than any similarity'.[9]

Although this argument may be considered credible, the author is of the opinion that if there are real world effects stemming from in-world action/crime, then such a crime is a real world crime and should be met with the same real world consequences. Comparing virtual rape and virtual financial crime is like comparing apples and bananas, but it is a useful point from which to consider the notion of virtual financial crime. In this sense virtual financial crime is a crime which takes place in-world but which has a true and real effect on the real world. Therefore this book is of the standpoint that virtual crimes, in the sense of financial crime, are true crimes. We shall now consider virtual financial crime in more detail.

As just mentioned one element of cyber crime which is pertinent in this book is that of financial crime. Interpol, acting to combat virtual financial crime, states that, 'the global nature of the Internet allows criminals to commit almost any illegal activity anywhere in the world, which makes it essential for all countries to adopt their domestic offline controls to cover crimes committed in cyberspace'.[10] Therefore Interpol, the international law enforcement agency, is stating that to combat this new wave of criminal activity, domestic governments should tailor their domestic real world laws to fit the crimes that are being carried out in cyberspace. This has two important implications; first, they acknowledge that there is a real threat of financial crime being committed over the internet and secondly, because the virtual is a continuum of the real, domestic laws should be applied to the virtual worlds. However, this causes problems of its own. With the internet crossing a multitude of boundaries and therefore laws, it is unclear which domestic law should apply in each instance of a crime being committed. There are no international standards which have to be met. More discussion will be made concerning the international regulations later in the book.

Given that cyber crime is a real threat to society, we must explore the inherent aspects of money laundering and financial crime. To be able to commit virtual financial crime, the overreaching term we use for all financial crimes here, then real money must pass into the virtual ether and then be able to be extracted. Real money is therefore turned into virtual money. 'Virtual money is defined as money value represented by a claim on the issuers which is stored on an electronic device and accepted as

---

[9]   Kerr (2002–3), at pp. 372–3, n. 66.
[10]   Ibid.

a means of payment by persons other than the issuer'.[11] Virtual money is therefore the digital currency which can then be used by the criminal to either launder or commit fraud. Virtual money can be said to be real money. It is an encrypted code representing money, which is accepted as money. This is very similar to the discussion in Chapter 3 whereby grain was slowly considered to be money and then this property was transferred to metal, then to paper. It is this same gradual acceptance by society which ascribes to the encrypted code the property of having monetary value.

There are two types of virtual money: identified virtual money and anonymous virtual money. Identified virtual money can be identified as belonging to someone and as having been withdrawn from a banking institution. In other words it is traceable. Anonymous virtual money – or what is known as virtual cash – is untraceable. Once it is withdrawn, it leaves no discernible trace. There are plenty of criminal activities which can then take place with this money. For example, Interpol states that the main areas are:

- Unauthorised creation, transfer or redemption of virtual money;
- Criminal access to computer systems being used to change illicitly the attribution of funds within the system;
- Criminal attacks on virtual money systems leading to a loss of virtual money value or loss of function on the virtual money system;
- Criminal misuse of virtual money systems for financial crimes or as a tool to subvert or misuse other financial systems; and
- Criminals may use virtual money to reduce the likelihood of capture – for example, the cases of blackmail, kidnapping or extortion, where in the past, collection of money has been problematic for perpetrators. This is particularly significant for anonymous virtual money.[12]

So why is there virtual money in the first place? Virtual money was created along with the advancement of technology to create faster and more convenient ways of transferring money through commerce. In other words, it is a development in the process of doing business in the industrial world. The internet has now become a major part of global commerce and where there is a means of conducting a criminal act, the criminal will exploit it. The internet is no exception.

---

[11] Interpol, 'Virtual Money', 27 May 2010, http://interpol.int/Public/ TechnologyCrime/CrimePrev/VirtualMoney.asp, accessed 27 May 2010.
[12] Ibid.

The British Fraud Advisory Panel describes virtual money laundering as where 'A fraudster converts the proceeds of illegal activities into online currency, which is then used to purchase goods and/or services from you before being exchanged into real world currency'.[13]

In the real world there are three stages in laundering money from illegal gains. These three stages are placing, layering and integration. The first stage, placing, consists of putting the money (which is normally cash) in a place such as a bank. In the case of virtual money laundering, this could also be a PayPal account. The second stage, layering, aims to ensure that the money does not look suspicious. The criminal carries out many complicated and intricate transactions with the money so that any traces are hard to follow. The final stage, integration, is where the criminal combines so-called dirty money with legitimate money, giving the money the appearance of being clean. From this very brief description you can already see how the virtual world, the virtual economy and virtual money transfers can be manipulated by the criminal mind in laundering money. The dirty money can enter the virtual world through a pre-paid card, such as PayPal, where little identification is required. The money can be used to buy in-world goods, passing through numerous accounts, and then the criminal can sell these goods in-world. The money from investments in-world can then be withdrawn from the world via an ATM or money account and the money appears to be from a legitimate source. It has therefore been laundered.[14]

The Financial Action Task Force highlighted concerns about the new method of electronic monetary transfers in 2006, taking the view to that this was a new method of financial crime for criminals.[15] However, during the last four years little has been put in place to provide deterrence, nor have any regulations been brought in to ensure successful prosecutions. It is important to understand the ideology behind electronic or digital money and this chapter will now move on to discuss this.

Although this book is looking at money laundering in virtual worlds, it is important to note that the issues discussed within these pages can be translated to other economic virtual crimes such as online fraud. Fraud, whether virtual or real, can lead to other criminal activities such as drug

---

[13] Fraud Advisory Panel, 'Cyber Crime: Social Networking and Virtual Worlds', Issue 4, October 2009, http://www.fraudadvisorypanel.org/new/pdf_show.php?id=119, accessed 15 July 2010.

[14] Ryder (2008).

[15] Financial Action Task Force, 'Report on New Payment Methods', October 2006, http://www.fatf-gafi.org/dataoecd/30/47/37627240.pdf, accessed 16 July 2010.

trafficking, people trafficking and terrorist financing. Other cyber crimes that are of interest are e-banking fraud and identity theft. The law in all these areas is falling behind the advancements in technology and there are few legislative provisions to combat these crimes. Furthermore without clear legislative provisions it is nearly impossible to quantify how frequent these crimes are.[16]

Digital currencies and money laundering

To be able to launder money through the internet, there needs to be a method by which to do this. Money is therefore converted into digital money, used within a virtual game, which has now converted real money into a virtual in-world currency and the means by which a criminal can launder criminal money is in place. 'All virtual games use some sort of electronic monetary system. Electronic money is used as an "electronic replacement for cash"'.[17] There are various methods of using electronic money to facilitate money laundering: through an electronic purse, mobile payments, and internet payment services and through digital precious metals. An electronic purse is a pre-paid card, which looks like a credit or debit card. There is an electronic chip within the card which stores data as to how much money has been loaded onto the card. Money can be put on these cards at various tellers and shop stores. The cards can then be used to pay for goods and services, where accepted, the destination being another electronic purse, but they leave no transaction record. Recently the major credit card companies have also been providing these new payment methods.[18]

The second method of payment is through mobile and wireless telecommunications. These mobile payments mostly require financial institutions as part of the transaction; however, this can be avoided should the mobile payment go through a broker account. Broker accounts are normally prepaid with cash and operate in the same way as an electronic purse. This will then lend itself to money laundering because of the lack of verification of identification and lack of traceability.

The third method is through internet payment. 'Internet payment services either rely on an associated bank account and use the internet as a means of moving funds to and from the associated bank account or they operate entirely on the Internet and are indirectly associated with a bank

---

[16]   House of Lords Science and Technology Committee (2007), p. 10.
[17]   Desguin (2008), p. 15.
[18]   For more information on electronic purses, please see: Open University Computer Laboratories (2000).

account'.[19] When the payments are not associated with a bank account, there is again a lack of identification and traceability required for the process to occur. Furthermore, most providers will accept cash and may not want to participate in money laundering regulations because of the red tape that would be required before the completion of a transaction.

The final method is through digital precious metal methods, whereby digital precious metal brokers allow customers to purchase digital precious metal on the world commodity market at market prices. By using a broker, there is again another level of anonymity and lack of traceability for the transaction. 'The basis for using digital precious metals is to make online transactions possible without regard for underlying currencies or access to foreign exchange'.[20]

So why is digital money an effective way of laundering criminal gains? This reason is because 'digital currencies provide an ideal money laundering instrument because they facilitate international payments without the transmittal services of traditional financial institutions'.[21] Many 'digital currencies are privately owned online payment systems that allow international payments'.[22] Furthermore, an additional feature of virtual world money is that digital currency is sometimes used to buy real world metals, which can then be traded. The people that buy the metals with digital cash are allegedly linked to the real commodities stock market. These digital currencies are as bespoke as any real world currency. As the US Department of Justice National Drug Intelligence Center states: 'Each digital currency functions as a transnational currency; however none are recognised as currencies by the US government'.[23]

Global Digital Currency Association (GDCA)[24] digital transactions account for billions of dollars each year – digital gold currency transactions alone increased from $3bn in 2004 to $10bn (approx) in 2006.[25] The benefit of digital currencies is that they are always available and thus 'digital currencies are more convenient than other methods of funds transfer which may be limited by normal business hours and international timezones'.[26] Therefore it is more appealing to the criminal to choose this

---

[19] Desguin (2008).

[20] Ibid., p. 18.

[21] US Department of Justice National Drug Intelligence Center (NDIC). (2008), p. 1.

[22] Ibid.

[23] Ibid.

[24] http://www.gdcaonline.com/, accessed 26 May 2010.

[25] NDIC (2008), p. 2.

[26] Ibid.

method of laundering because of the availability and convenience of the transactions.

Digital currency transactions are also available through mobile payment systems via web-enabled phones. This allows the criminal even more anonymity if the phone is a pre-paid phone with no traceability. The transactions are therefore instantaneous and irreversible,[27] not to mention anonymous.

Many of these digital currencies are not thought to fall inside federal or state laws within the US.[28] There is a belief that because these are digital currencies and digital transactions, the normal law of the land does not apply. However, because of the interaction with the real world economy there is an argument that the normal laws should be applicable to them.

Another problem of digital currencies is their anonymity. 'Anonymity is a heavily marketed characteristic of the digital currency industry'.[29] This allows the cyber criminal an extra layer of protection when laundering money though digital methods. Some issuers of digital currency do require some form of identification but because this is done via the internet the documents can be scanned or emailed or faxed, allowing for easy doctoring of the documents. There are several means of converting real money into digital money and each offers the criminal an easy method of laundering money. For example, one can pay in cash to the issuer's exchange bank account; thus the money is not traceable. Secondly, exchanges also accept wire transfers or postal money orders, adding another layer of difficulty in determining the source of the original money. Thirdly, money can be transferred via electronic money orders, cheques, and online banking transfers etc., all of which make it hard to determine the true source of the money. Fourthly, money can be transferred into the exchanges via pre-paid cards[30] and money can be taken out via ATMs (automated telling machines).

The use of advanced technology allows the cyber criminal further anonymity and networking ability.[31] The use of IP (Internet Protocol) addresses link the user with their computer and therefore their actions allow identification of cyber criminals. However, there are various ways round this identification, such as using mobile devices, i.e. mobile phones that are internet enabled; hijacking wireless networks, encrypted chat

---

[27] Ibid.
[28] Ibid., p. 3.
[29] Ibid.
[30] NDIC (2006).
[31] NDIC (2008), p. 4.

rooms and using public internet access, all of which allows anonymity for the criminal.

It is reported that 'because digital currency is increasingly misused to purchase drugs and other illicit materials that are sold online, the proceeds of that activity are essentially pre-laundered'.[32] Additionally, some digital exchanges allow for transactions to be unlimited in value, thus allowing drug trafficking to occur in ready abundance.[33] The criminals can launder larger amounts, with total anonymity, using fewer transactions.[34]

The US government acknowledges that there are regulatory loopholes which must be closed in relation to digital currencies and money laundering.[35] However, regulatory action by one nation will not be enough to combat multinational, even global, cyber crime. There must be a joined-up multinational regulatory position that is devised to prevent further cyber financial crimes and money laundering.

There are several major problems associated with virtual money laundering (hereafter VML), these being: the issues of anonymity of transactions and digital and real world account details through online transactions; the lack of jurisdiction surrounding these transactions and how they interact with the real world; that there is a trading feature associated with the real world, namely that of digital cash, which also interacts with the real world; and finally, the issues around payment methods from the real world to the virtual world are the same as if for a transaction within the real world. These four issues link the virtual to the real and vice versa allowing the continuum of the real into the virtual and will be discussed in detail now.

How does real money get into the virtual world?

As briefly mentioned above, real money can be transferred into the virtual world through various means such as cash, pre-paid cards, and credit cards and through the relatively new electronic payment method PayPal. Of course there are other electronic payment methods, but PayPal, a wholly owned subsidiary of eBay, is the most famous. However, although these electronic payment methods are making internet commerce more readily accessible for the majority of the population, it does 'open the doors to alternative forms of money laundering'.[36] PayPal used to be solely used for settling transactions in traditional forms of money, such as dollars, pounds, yen, etc., but with the new forms of virtual money being

---

[32]   Ibid.
[33]   Ibid., p. 6.
[34]   Ibid.
[35]   Ibid.
[36]   Virtual World News (2008).

banded around in the virtual worlds, PayPal has also entered into these new financial transactions. The problem with this is that virtual money, because of its anonymity, is opens to the possibility of financial crime. As Virtual World News states:

> Given the vast sums of money being transferred among parties around the world, it should not be surprising of course that criminals would want to take advantage of this money flow. With little if any regulation, virtual world economies are ripe for exploitation by organised crime, terrorists and others who wish to launder large sums of money.[37]

WHY IS THERE DISCOURSE AS TO WHETHER VIRTUAL MONEY LAUNDERING EXISTS OR NOT?

Within this next part of the chapter the academic bifurcation of whether virtual money laundering exists or not will be discussed. The view put forward in this book is clearly that virtual money laundering exists, but that it is part of the real world problem of money laundering, financial crime and terrorist financing and therefore should be considered to be a real and present threat to society. However, it would be foolish not to consider both sides of the academic discussion as to whether virtual money laundering exists. This is where the discussion gets pretty hypothetical. Let's set out some of the positions on whether virtual money laundering is an urban or virtual myth.

For some academics, the virtual world is completely separate from the real, and therefore no laws exist since the virtual world is lawless and unregulated. For others, the virtual and the real merge and are a continuum of each other and therefore real world laws should apply to the virtual world. The problem here lies in the appropriate jurisdiction in which to prosecute, govern and from which to control. Moreover, other academics just do not believe that virtual worlds can and do provide a platform for financial crime and money laundering. This is because there is little factually based evidence, although law enforcement agencies around the world are targeting this as a future area of crime. The other reason for disbelief in virtual money laundering is that there is a lack of prosecutions. As mentioned above, this could be because of the lack of legal jurisdiction clarification and not because there is a lack of money laundering occurring in virtual worlds. Finally, virtual money laundering is hard to detect. Virtual money laundering and financial crime are being carried out by very

---

[37]   Ibid.

sophisticated criminals who use advanced and complicated technology and computer code to launder the money through virtual worlds.

Having discussed why some believe that virtual money laundering does not exist, it is only right to discuss the view that virtual money laundering does exist and is a present and real threat to society.

The overwhelming argument for virtual money laundering and virtual financial crime is international governments' and international law enforcement's response to the threat. Interpol, the US State police and the London Metropolitan police force are all targeting virtual financial crime as a major problem in the fight against terrorism. In addition to this, there are new reports, which detail the ongoing problem of fraud and financial crime occurring within the virtual worlds. In the economic chapter of this book, we saw that the economy of virtual worlds is similar to those in the real world, barring the legitimate control over the supply and demand of goods. By acknowledging this as a fact about virtual worlds, we can then proceed to the assumption that if an abstract phenomenon of replicating economies in virtual worlds occurs, then we can logically extrapolate from it that criminals will find a way of using the virtual worlds as a means of committing crimes. If we also appreciate that the virtual world is a continuum of the real, then it should come as no surprise that criminals are using the internet and virtual worlds as a means of laundering money. Where there is a loophole, criminals will find a way to exploit it. This is what is occurring in the virtual worlds currently. Because there is a lack of clear legal structure and parameters, the criminals are using this black hole in the law as an opportunity to launder money for their criminal activities. Just because little is widely known about virtual money laundering does not mean that we cannot target it as a crime.

The British Fraud Advisory Panel (FAP) has said 'there is nothing virtual about online crime, it is all too real. It is time the government took this seriously'.[38] The FAP has further opined that 'money laundering is the obvious risk. There will be a migration of fraudsters into these sites when they see all of the opportunities'. They describe the virtual world as 'a parallel universe with almost no external rule of law, no enforced banking regulations or compliance, no policing and no government oversight'.[39]

One of the major problems is that little work is being conducted into this problem. Since the economic decline in 2007 to the present day, the government (past and present) has been preoccupied with keeping the UK's and the USA's economies solvent. Although some work is being

---

[38] Fraud Advisory Panel (2009).
[39] Ibid.

done, the latest Fraud Advisory research was conducted in 2007 and although it does start to promote awareness of the latest crime, much more needs to be done currently.

How Big is the Problem of Virtual Money Laundering?

To combat virtual financial crime there needs to be action taken internationally by government. Interpol states that there are four main aspects to consider in the future in combating virtual financial crime, namely:

- Law enforcement agencies need to know where servers are based in instances of financial crime. These may be located in different countries which may pose a problem when it comes to locating the legal form which is to be taken.
- Law enforcement agencies need to influence legislatures in the future to take into account virtual financial crime when drafting new pieces of legislation. Consideration needs to be given not only to prosecution but also the recovery of assets and information from each virtual crime committed.
- Barriers between law enforcement agencies and the industry must be broken down to ensure accountability of data crossing networks.
- Law enforcement agencies need to learn how to investigate virtual crimes.[40]

There has been an increase in internet malicious activity globally. A report detailing this increase in 2010 shows the top ten countries which have recorded internet malicious activity (see Table 5.1).

The two most significant movers in 2009 were Brazil and India. Due to the increase in activity in Brazil and the increase in malicious activity via the internet, a Cyber Crime Bill has been proposed.[41] Malicious activity appears to increase in countries that are rapidly expanding their broadband infrastructure and connectivity, such as India and other Asian countries.[42]

---

[40] Interpol, 'Virtual Money', 27 May 2010, http://interpol.int/Public/TechnologyCrime/CrimePrev/VirtualMoney.asp, accessed 27 May 2010.

[41] Please see for more detail: Electronic Frontier Foundation, 'President Lula and the Cyber Crime Bill', 17 July 2009, http://www.eff.org/deeplinks/2009/07/lula-and-cybercrime, accessed 15 July 2010.

[42] Point Topic, http://point-topic.com/dslanalysis.phpaccessed, 15 July 2010 and/or India Broadband Forum, http://www.indiabroadband.net/india-

Table 5.1   Table demonstrating global internet malicious activity

Overall Rank 2009	Overall Rank 2008	Country	Percentage 2009	Percentage 2008
1	1	United States	19	23
2	2	China	8	9
3	5	Brazil	6	4
4	3	Germany	5	6
5	11	India	4	3
6	4	United Kingdom	3	5
7	12	Russia	3	2
8	10	Poland	3	3
9	7	Italy	3	3
10	6	Spain	3	4

Source: Symantec Internet Security Threat Report, Trends for 2009, Vol. XV (2010), http://eval.symantec.com/mktginfo/enterprise/white_papers/b-whitepaper_internet_security_threat_xv_04-2010.en.us.pdf, accessed 10 February 2012.

HOW DOES VIRTUAL MONEY LAUNDERING WORK?

As Kevin Sullivan states in his anti-money laundering training materials, 'the virtual world with little regulation or observation by law enforcement is fertile ground and ripe with opportunity for the criminal element'.[43] He continues to bemoan the lack of adequate regulation in virtual worlds. 'In the virtual world there is negligible means of monitoring financial activity, sparse due diligence, paltry customer identification rules, nor any mandatory forms or reports to complete'.[44] So how does it work? How do criminals use virtual worlds to launder money? We have seen above that money comes into the virtual world through electronic means. In terms of preventing money laundering electronic payment methods are relatively unregulated. The UK and US are aware of this problem and have started to work in conjunction with the virtual world providers to counter this.

PayPal is an example of an electronic payment system. Its system of

broadband-telecom-news/11682-india-register-500-growth-broadband-services-within-5-years.html, accessed 15 July 2010.
[43]   Sullivan (2008).
[44]   Ibid.

regulation and jurisdiction has altered in the last four years. Previously PayPal was registered in the United Kingdom. It was registered as an electronic payment issuer and was regulated by the Financial Services Authority (FSA) from 2004. However, in 2007 PayPal moved its registered office to Luxemburg and became a bank. Subsequently PayPal become regulated by the Commission de Surveillance du Secteur Financier (CSSF). UK customers can no longer seek redress from PayPal under the UK legal system. The situation is different again in the US where it is seen not as a bank, in the narrow sense of a money service business, but as a payment intermediary. Federal law does not apply to PayPal but it could be subject to State regulations. However, each State differs in its application of laws. The law most applicable to PayPal in the US is the one which regulated person-to-person (P2P) payments using credit cards known as the Truth in Lending Act 15 U.S.C. §§ 1601–67f implemented by Regulation Z, 12 C.F.R. pt. 226. Furthermore, the Electronic Funds Transfer Act 15 U.S.C. §§ 1693–1693r, as implemented by Regulation E, 12 C.F.R. pr. 205, could be seen to define the relationship between debit card holder and issuer bank. This Act's primary aim is to protect the consumer and as PayPal is seen as a payment intermediary and not a bank, this legislation too poses jurisdictional problems.

In the UK the Electronic Money Directive came into force on 1 May 2011. The issuance of electronic money has been regulated under the FSA since 2002. However, the new rules alter the regulations. The main changes are:

- Electronic money issuers (EMI) are no longer allowed to set a time limit on the e-money holder's right to redeem (although a proportionate fee can be charged for redemption in certain circumstances). They are also not allowed to refuse to redeem e-money if it is worth less than €10.
- Electronic money issuers are not allowed to grant interest or other benefits related to the length of time e-money is held.
- EMIs can provide payment services that are unrelated to the issuing of e-money without additional authorisation/registration and engage in other business activities, subject to relevant EU and UK law.
- Businesses with average outstanding e-money not exceeding €5 million can apply to be registered as small EMIs. They will not be able to passport into other EEA states.
- The initial and minimum ongoing capital requirement for authorised EMIs has been reduced. There are initial and minimum ongoing capital requirements for some small EMIs.

- All EMIs must safeguard funds received from customers for e-money so that, if it becomes insolvent, the e-money issued will be protected from other creditors' claims and can be repaid to customers.[45]

As can be seen throughout this book, the law is complex and diverse, with very little correlation between countries. This allows criminals to take advantage of this regulatory loophole and avoid prosecution or even detection. For a criminal to launder money, very little needs to be done. A resident or a user will open numerous fictitious accounts to be able to access the online world. Little verification of true identity is required which means this is the first gap in the virtual world regulation. Money can then be transferred into the virtual world through PayPal or credit card. This is where most forms of verification and tracking ability take place. However, the procedure is far from foolproof and many criminals can get around it by creating a fictitious PayPal account. Once money is transferred into the virtual world, the resident/user can purchase whatever he or she wants within that virtual world. There is no way to trace where the money has come from, few security checks and no regulation. Once the resident/user wants to cash out his laundered money from the virtual world, all they need to do is to use the virtual exchange in-world to reap the rewards of laundering their money. The resident/user can then withdraw his cash through the normal real world means, i.e. cash point, ATM, banks etc. It is here that it is nearly impossible to trace these funds. To all intents and purposes this money now looks like the proceeds from a virtual world game and not the proceeds of crime. The money is therefore clean and can be used undetected to fund other criminal activities.

These virtual worlds 'have no police force, no courts, no taxes. The fast growing economy is lightly controlled, and banks and the stock exchange'[46] have been lightly regulated if at all in some situation. It is unsurprising therefore that criminals have sought out this virtual world as a place for laundering their illegal money.

THE TECHNOLOGY

Virtual money laundering could not even be in existent were it not for the advancement of technology. Various types of technology can facilitate

---

[45] FSA, 'Electronic Money Regulations', 1 May 2011, http://www.fsa.gov.uk/Pages/About/What/International/emoney/index.shtml, accessed 1 June 2011.
[46] Leapman (2007).

money laundering or financial crime. Within the next section of the chapter different forms of money laundering-assisted technology will be discussed. These types of technology are by no means designed to facilitate criminal activity, but, as indicated above, criminals will find any means of carrying out illegal activities, and technology in virtual worlds is just one of these new methods. One thing that unites all these methods of virtual world payments methods is their lack of traceability, affording the criminal anonymity and secrecy.

PayPal

Within this chapter PayPal has been mentioned as a method of getting money in and out of virtual worlds. In a sense PayPal has revolutionised the electronic payment system. PayPal is an e-commerce business formed through the merger of x.com and Confinity. It allows for electronic transfer of money from accounts to other accounts. The PayPal account can be funded using a credit or debit card issued by a normal bank account. In 2005 PayPal become a fully owned subsidiary of eBay, an online auction site. Fully aware of their responsibilities towards anti-money laundering, PayPal insists: 'As a global financial institution, PayPal is committed to full compliance with all applicable laws and regulations regarding Anti-Money Laundering ('AML'). PayPal's policy is to prevent people engaged in money laundering, fraud, and other financial crimes, including terrorist financing, from using PayPal's services'.[47] Yet PayPal is still considered in the main to be antagonistic to the control of virtual payments. In 2009 PayPal was found to be in breach of Australia's anti-money laundering laws.[48] Having said that though, each year PayPal takes steps to try and stay ahead of the virtual financial criminals, yet staying ahead of criminals, especially in the virtual world, is not an easy task.[49] Caution must be taken when entering into a contract with any virtual financial provider because of the inherent risk of criminal activity taking place on your account. Criminals can hack into your own account and proceed to carry

---

[47]   PayPal, 'PayPal Anti-money Laundering and Counter terrorist-financing Statement', 11 May 2009, https://cms.paypal.com/us/cgi-bin/?&cmd=_render-content&content_ID=ua/AML_full, accessed 21 July 2010.

[48]   Finextra, 'PayPal Found in Breach of Australia's Anti-money Laundering Laws', 23 November 2009, http://www.finextra.com/news/fullstory.aspx?newsitemid=20781, accessed 21 July 2010.

[49]   Computer Weekly, 'PayPal Launches Multipronged Attack on E-crime', 17 March 2008, http://www.computerweekly.com/Articles/2008/03/17/229884/paypal-launches-multi-pronged-attack-on-e-crime.htm, accessed 21 July 2010.

out criminal activities through your account. It is the lack of identification which causes most of the problems with any of these virtual payment methods as we shall discover with each method below.

The Virtual Wallet

The virtual wallet is a term which encompasses all the different types of virtual monetary transaction. For example, the virtual wallet can be imagined as a real world wallet. It allows you to make payments from it and also allows payments to be made to it. In the future, it is expected that the virtual wallet will be the only thing you carry around with you. This has already been discussed as a possible option for many universities, schools and festivals where it is easy to lose cash, cards and other forms of payment. The virtual wallet will be your one stop to your money. There are two methods of using the virtual wallet at present. One method is to allow your mobile phone to link to your m-accounts, allowing transfers to go ahead and the other is to allow mobile phone companies to act as a bank to allow transactions to be carried out. Although this is not a universal method of monetary transactions, it is being used in the United Kingdom, Japan, Korea and also developing countries such as in Africa. One such company is Moneybookers which operates all over Europe and in over 40 countries, dealing with customers in 12 languages.[50] Another company is MoPay, which opened its offices in the United States for the first time in 2010.

Virtual ATM

The virtual ATM is already in existence in many supermarkets around the world. Here you can purchase goods in store and then ask for cash back for a small fee. This is a relatively easy way to obtain cash and as long as you know the pin number of the card you are using you can withdraw up to £50 per transaction. This level of anonymity further explains the rise in money laundering through virtual methods.

Person-to-Person Transfer

A person-to-person transfer is exactly as it sounds. One person with an m-account can transfer money to another person with an m-account via

---

[50] For more information please see: www.moneybookers.com, accessed 21 July 2010.

their mobile phone. This level of monetary transfer lays itself open to abuse by criminals. Relatively small amounts of money can be transferred to others without trace or identification. This is a perfect disguise for many money laundering transactions and financing.

Wire Transfer via Mobile Phone

Wire transfer via mobile phone is similar to person-to-person transfer, but this time the money is transferred from an m-account to a bank account. It is used in America predominantly by Mexicans sending money home to relatives still living in Mexico.

Virtual Traveller's Cheque

This is one of the newest forms of mobile financing technology. Before a traveller leaves home they can load up their mobile phone with money. The phone then acts as a traveller's cheque.

Pre-paid Mobile Phones and M-payments

Pre-paid mobile phones are an excellent means of communicating without an identification or authorisation. These pre-paid mobile phones can also be used as a mobile virtual wallet and as such monetary transactions can take place without trace or identification. Small amounts can be moved easily around the criminal community.

Smurfing

In the above descriptions, mention has been made of the relatively small amounts of money changing hands and which could be used by criminals for illegal activities. Criminals generally try to keep their financial transactions below $1000. Therefore to ensure that the money they require is being transferred without implicating themselves, they use multiple 'smurfs' who traffic the money on the lead/head criminal's behalf. Small amounts will generally go unnoticed, but collectively huge sums of money are being transferred daily through the above payment methods.

Although the above methods have not been designed for criminal activities, criminals have used these methods to launder money and commit financial crimes. Most of these methods are relatively unregulated and certainly where money is crossing borders via mobile payments, it is incredibly hard to detect criminal activity. Lack of identification and criminal anonymity are among the major causes of lack of prosecution in these areas. Lack of awareness within crime enforcement agencies and lack of international cooperation are also further issues to be dealt with.

However, one advocate of digital cash as a means of promoting monetary freedom and free-market cash, Jon Matonis, welcomes this new age of e-commerce but also recognises the importance of trying to eradicate financial crime within these new systems of payment.[51] Matonis points to ten elements which are required in an e-commerce monetary system to ensure it is secure and free from criminal activity. These are: for it to be secure, portable, two way, offline capabilities, divisible, infinite duration, wide acceptability, user-friendly and unit or value freedom. However, Matonis states that 'he had not found a system which meets all ten criteria yet'.[52] Matonis further alludes to the thoughts of Hayek that 'money does not have to be created legal tender by governments like law, language and morals; it can emerge spontaneously. Such private money has often been preferred to government money, but the government has soon suppressed that'.[53] Hayek's thoughts on the development of money in a capitalist and free society are not too dissimilar to those of the developers of virtual money. However idealistic this notion is, if virtual money can assist the real economy, especially in times of economic decline, more should be done by regulators to ensure that the system is free from criminal activity.

CASE STUDIES FOR VIRTUAL MONEY LAUNDERING

As seen above, amongst academics and practitioners virtual money laundering is sometimes considered nebulous. This part of the chapter examines the reported instances of money laundering and/or financial crime taking place within virtual online games. In some situations, little is known about the case. This is sometimes because businesses or game owners do not want to release information for fear of opening the floodgates to other potential launderers and criminals. However, just because information is limited does not mean that virtual financial crime does not exist. In fact, it is even more important to outline these cases here to make society aware of the instances of virtual money laundering.

---

[51] Matonis (1995).
[52] Ibid.
[53] Hayek (1978).

Gold Farming[54]

Financial crime is not just limited to money laundering. Gold farming has become an increasing problem, especially in Asian countries, and governments have gone to certain extremes to try and control and govern this area of virtual currency. Gold farming is where in in-world games, players repeatedly purchase online goods which are then sold for virtual currency or real world currency. A gold farmer could sit at a computer all day, every day, each week of each month and purchase goods repeatedly, selling them for virtual or real money. They have no interest in the virtual world, game or the social interaction designed for these worlds; the gold farmer's concern is with the money which they are making from this farming. You may ask who would want to buy such goods from the gold farmers when they can often be won or purchased cheaply once they play the game or transverse the world? Yet it is those players that enter the world and want to progress quickly that are eager to part with real money for the virtual goods. This is big business and gold farmers can earn a good wage from carrying out this activity. Gold farming is particularly prolific in Asian countries. World of Warcraft (www.worldofwarcraft.com) is the most popular venue for gold farming among virtual worlds.

In 2008 it was estimated by the Chinese Government that 1 billion yen or $146m was spent on virtual world currency transactions.[55] It is also estimated that the marketplace is growing by 20% each year,[56] in spite of the global economic crisis which occurred from 2007 to date. China has taken an unusual step by banning gold farming and it has limited the use of virtual currencies in the first official rules issued by the Chinese government on the trade of virtual goods and services. It issued the rules because of the real and possible future impact the virtual financial system could have on the real financial system. The new rules prevent virtual money being traded for real money. The reason for this is to stop competition with real world currencies. Edward Castronova, stated that: 'These virtual currencies, as they grow, are going to become competitors to real-world currencies – and apparently that's what happening in China. These QQ coins are becoming things you can use at the corner store to top off your bill'.[57]

---

[54]   See Chapter 3 for a more in-depth discussion.
[55]   DGC Magazine, 'China Bans Gold Farming & Limits Virtual Currency', 21 November 2009, http://www.dgcmagazine.com/dp/content/china-bans-gold-farming-limits-virtual-currency.htm, accessed 27 May 2010.
[56]   Ibid.
[57]   Sutter, J. D., 'China Restricts Virtual Economies', 1 July 2009, CNN

Virtual Money Inc

In 2008 the owner of Virtual Money Inc was indicted on drug trafficking and money laundering charges. Robert Hodgins is the owner and CEO of the virtual pre-paid cards[58] which have come under scrutiny in the USA over the lack of regulation surrounding the fledgling industry. Hodgins is currently on the run from the police[59] and the case remains open. However, he is said to have laundered drug money through Virtual Money Inc on pre-paid cards from Colombia. In 2010 Federal Prosecutors announced five convictions of drug related money laundering in relation to the Virtual Money Inc case, known as VM. VM is said to have been part of the AdSurfDaily and other auto surf companies. One of those convicted, Juan Merlano Salazar, 35, of Medellin, Colombia, pleaded guilty in the US District Court in Connecticut to 11 counts of money laundering and one count of conspiracy to commit money laundering. He is facing a 240 year prison sentence and a $6 million maximum fine.[60]

In 2011 the US Treasury Department are still struggling to write pre-paid credit card rules so as to not to stifle growth. The Credit Card Accountability Responsibility and Disclosure Act of 2009 ensured that the Treasury would incorporate money laundering regulations within any new policy surrounding the movement of money. This job fell to the Financial Crime Enforcement Network but this has now been reformed and in the process the incorporation of such a rule has been overlooked. Senators Dianne Feinstein, Chuck Grassley and Sheldon Whitehouse believe that urgent action needs to be taken.

E-Gold Case

E-gold was a digital gold currency which traded gold and allowed the instant transfer of gold between users until 2009. E-gold was owned by Gold & Silver Reserve Inc and traded under e-gold inc. In 2009 trading was

---

News, http://edition.cnn.com/2009/TECH/07/01/china.virtual.currency/index. html, accessed 27 May 2010.

[58] For a good discussion on pre-paid cards, see Linn (2008), p. 146.

[59] Interpol. 'Robert Hodgins', http://www.interpol.int/public/Data/Wanted/ Notices/Data/2010/56/2010_7456.asp, accessed 1 June 2011.

[60] PatrickPretty.com, '5 Convicted to Date in Money Laundering Case Involving Colombian Drug Operation that Used the Same Debit Card as AdSurfDaily Autosurf', 17 April 2010, http://www.patrickpretty.com/2010/ 04/17/update-5-convictions-to-date-in-money-laundering-cases-involving-colombi an-drug-operation-that-used-same-debit-card-as-adsurfdaily/, accessed 1 June 2011.

suspended because of illegal trading activity and its owners were indicted under money laundering legislation. E-gold was known to the authorities as being a safe haven for money laundering, online con schemes and fraud. E-gold also had strong links with the ShadowCrew Ring which was a 4000 strong international crime syndicate that specialised in identity theft and fraud. Omar Dhanani of Fountain Valley, California, connected with the ShadowCrew Ring, held an e-gold account and is said to have pushed through thousands of dollars of proceeds of crime money through his e-gold account. In July 2008 e-gold and its three directors pleaded guilty to conspiracy to engage in money laundering and conspiracy to operate an unlicensed money-transmitting business. Later in 2008 Gold & Silver Reserve CEO Douglas Jackson was sentenced to 300 hours of community service, a $200 fine, and three years of supervision, including six months of electronically monitored home detention. It is said that the judge was lenient to him because he was not aware of the illegal activity and because he was deeply in debt at the time.

The ShadowCrew Ring

The ShadowCrew Ring as iterated above was a 4000 strong international crime syndicate which operated from 2002–04 through an online message board, shadowcrew.com. This message board assisted criminals with illegal activities and to provide a meeting place where illegal goods and services could be traded. The United States Secret Service disbanded the organisation in 2004 after a year-long undercover operation. The online site was a haven for criminals to sell and purchase stolen online accounts, email addresses, eBay accounts, stolen identities, to name but a few. In June 2006 Andrew Mantovani, one of the leaders of ShadowCrew, was sentenced to 32 months in prison, a $5000 fine and three years probation.

Western Express International Currency Exchange Company

Western Express International Currency Exchange was a currency exchange company that acted for known criminals in laundering proceeds of crime between 2002–05. Customers used various forms of cyber crime such as phishing, spoofing and spamming to obtain money, which was then used to purchase e-gold which was then laundered through Western Express. In 2006 the owners of Western Express were indicted for illegal cheque cashing and illegal money transmittance.

Korea

In 2008/9 it was discovered that a group of Chinese and Korean game players were able to defraud other virtual players and launder the proceeds back into mainland China through a number of business front companies. The process of defrauding was through gold farming from Korea back to mainland China. It is estimated that $38m was wired from Korea to Hong Kong over an 18-month period. The company in Hong Kong bought virtual money in mainland China with the gold farmed money, charging a commission of 3–5%.[61]

Furthermore a study by Jang has indicated the current situation of cyber crime and cyber terror in Korea.[62] In his study, Jang indicates the dramatic increase of take-up by Koreans over the last decade, but along with this increase there has been an increase in cyber crime within the country. Although Jang does not specifically touch upon the cyber crime of money laundering or financial crime, it is understood that these crimes are among the cyber crimes that are being explored by the Republic of Korea.

In one such step toward further regulation and control of virtual money within Korea, the Supreme Court made a historic judgment in 2010, allowing virtual money used in virtual games to be exchanged for real money.[63] This is likely to have far reaching consequences as China found out when it banned virtual money converting since it was affecting its own economy.[64]

Sony Online Entertainment

It is not just large games that have encountered money laundering; organisations that have an online presence have also been affected. In 2006 Sony Online Entertainment realised that money was being laundered through their internet-based role-playing games. A player was transferring large amounts of money through Sony's online site and when located in Europe, he said that he used the site because it was cheaper than laundering the money through a normal bank.[65]

Attorney turned Launderer

Ken Rijock is an attorney turned launderer and works for financial crime consultant World-Check. Ken describes virtual money laundering as 'the

---

[61] Virtual World News (2008).
[62] Jang J. (2008).
[63] Si-Soo (2010).
[64] *The Wall Street Journal* (2009).
[65] Monroe (2007).

perfect crime'.[66] He says that 'there is no way law enforcement can even enforce the laws, because they don't apply', and Ken should know being an ex-Attorney. One of the main reasons he believes that virtual money laundering is a crime of the future is because of the ease with which money can be laundered without detection or repercussions. He gives an example of how virtual money laundering works.

> A drug dealer using fake IDs opens numerous virtual bank accounts through online games. He deposits money into those virtual accounts through ATMs. The criminal's online persona buys, say, virtual real estate from a co-conspirator – or even from one of his other accounts – and transfers payment to the seller's virtual account. The seller can then convert the virtual currency into real money through a virtual money exchange and withdraw it from an ATM or a bank.[67]

Ken further states that it is impossible to police and counter the criminal act because there is a total lack of clarity over the legal position of virtual worlds. Greg Short, director of Web presence for San Diego, California-based Sony Online Entertainment, agrees and states: 'The legal system doesn't extend here, there really aren't any laws that govern what happens [in-world]'.[68] So whether a crime can ever be perfect is not a question for this book, but from the criminal's perspective, the method is as near as perfect as you can get.

2010 Eve Online Virtual Credit Crunch and Bank Run

In June 2009 space trading game, Eve Online encountered a massive theft in one of its largest financial institutions. The theft was an inside job, one of the bank's controllers stole about 200bn kredits, the online currency used in Eve Online and exchanged this stolen money for real world currency. This amounted to the sum of £3,115. This theft however, was not just a crime on the bank, it started a run on the bank caused by worried customers withdrawing their funds for fear that their money would be lost.[69]

Virtual Banking Licences

Mobile banking is now a commonly accepted function of our high street banks. However, virtual electronic banking is a new twist to online

---

[66]   Ibid.
[67]   Ibid.
[68]   Ibid.
[69]   BBC News, 'Billions Stolen in Online Robbery', BBC News, 3 July 2009, http://newsvote.bbc.co.uk/mpapps/pagetools/print/news.bbc.co.uk/1/hi/technolo gy/81325, 29 January 2010.

banking. In 2007 Entropia Universe, another virtual world, sold five virtual electronic banking licences for a total of $400,000 in real money. Each licence is a two-year agreement, allowing the holder to integrate real world banking into the virtual world. Virtual banks can offer real interest payments legitimately through these licences but they are not beholden to real world banking regulations. To safeguard users' money the holder of the licence must initially put forward $100,000 of real money. Entropia's currency is called PED and it is fixed against the US dollar. Furthermore, users of Entropia can also be offered a debit card from these virtual banks, allowing the residents of Entropia to transfer their in-world money onto the card and use it in the real world. The card, known as the Entropia Universe Cash Card, is not associated with any real world bank, and is reloadable.[70]

Future Areas for Concern

Sullivan is also concerned that the criminal will find other ways of exploiting these virtual worlds for their own illegal use. For example, Sullivan points out his concern over whether virtual currencies could be counterfeited in the future, allowing even more criminal financial activity to occur. Secondly, Sullivan is concerned that due to the lack of regulation, verification and identification requirements in-world and in the real world regarding virtual worlds, can there be any trail to follow in order to catch these criminals? Thirdly, Sullivan asks how law enforcement agencies investigate possible money laundering through virtual worlds.

LEGISLATION OF ANTI-ML IN THE REAL WORLD AND HOW THIS CAN BE TRANSPOSED INTO THE VIRTUAL WORLD, UK, USA, AND ASIA – CHINA AND KOREA

Within the next section of this chapter we shall be examining the laws of those countries which are seen as the major participants in thwarting cyber crime and virtual money laundering. First, the laws of real world money laundering are set out in detail, and categorised as to whether they are likely to be used to capture cyber criminals. Then the chapter will move

---

[70] For more detail, please see Mark, 'World's First Virtual Currency Banking Licences issued at Entropia Universe', *Money World*, ed. Doug Hanna, 8 May 2007, b5 Media, 17 July 2007, http://www.digitalmoneyworld.com/worlds-first-virtual-currency-banking-licenses-issued-at-entropia-universe, accessed 21 July 2010.

Table 5.2   United Kingdom

	The law explained	Applicable to electronic ML?
Money Laundering Regulations		
Money Laundering Regulations 1993	These Regulations give effect to articles 3, 4, 10 and 11 of the Council Directive No. 91/308/ EEC on prevention of the use of the financial system for the purpose of money laundering (OJ No. L166, 28.6.91, p. 77). In so far as other new legislative provisions were needed to implement the other provisions of the Directive, this provision is contained in the Criminal Justice Act 1993 (c. 36). The Regulations came into force on 1 April 1994.	Probable
Financial Services and Markets Act 2000 (Regulations relating to Money Laundering) Regulations 2001	These Regulations prescribe the Money Laundering Regulations 1993 (SI 1993/1933), ('the 1993 Regulations'), as amended, for the purposes of s168(4)(b) of the Financial Services and Markets Act 2000 ('the Act'). The effect of this is that the Financial Services Authority may, under s168(5) of the Act, appoint a competent person to conduct an investigation on its behalf where it appears to it that a person may be guilty of an offence under the 1993 Regulations. The 1993 Regulations are also prescribed for the purposes of s402(1)(b) of the Act. This will enable the Financial Services Authority (except in Scotland) to institute proceedings for any offence under the 1993 Regulations.	Probable
Money Laundering Regulations 2001	These Regulations give effect to articles 12 and 15 of the Council Directive No. 91/308/ EEC on prevention of the use of the financial system for the purpose of money laundering. They supplement the provisions of the Money Laundering Regulations 1993 ('the 1993 Regulations').	
Proceeds of Crime Act 2002	Amongst other things, the 2002 Act made it easier to convict criminal suspects because prior to it being enacted prosecutors had to rely on the Drug Trafficking Act 1994 for offences of drug trafficking, and the Criminal Justice Act 1988 as amended by the Criminal Justice Act 1993 regarding the proceeds of other crimes. In essence, prior to 2002 a prosecuting	Probable

Legislation	Description	Status
	lawyer had to prove that the monies or assets were the proceeds of crime and also what 'type' of crime the proceeds came from. The 2002 Act makes convictions more likely by removing the need to make a distinction between the types of crime the money from which was made.	
Proceeds of Crime Act 2002 (Failure to Disclose Money Laundering: Specified Training) Order 2003	This Order specifies training for the purposes of s330 of the Proceeds of Crime Act 2002. If a person has not been provided by his employer with the specified training, he may have a defence to the offence in s330 of failure to disclose money laundering by a person in the regulated sector. The defence only applies where the employee does not actually know or suspect that another person is engaged in money laundering, but would still commit the offence by virtue of having reasonable grounds for knowing or suspecting that another person is engaged in money laundering.	Probable
Serious Organised Crime and Police Act (SOCA) 2005	Created the Serious Organised Crime Agency.	Probable
Proceeds of Crime Act 2002 (Money Laundering: Exceptions to Overseas Conduct Defence) Order 2006	This Order sets out exceptions to the defences in sections 327(2A), 328(3) and 329(2A) of the Proceeds of Crime Act 2002 ('the 2002 Act'), as inserted by s102 of the Serious Organised Crime and Police Act 2005. Sections 327(1), 328(1) and 329(1) of that Act create offences relating to 'criminal property'. That expression is defined by s340(3) by reference to benefit from 'criminal conduct'. The definition of 'criminal conduct' includes conduct that would constitute an offence in any part of the United Kingdom if it occurred there (see s340(2)). Sections 327(2A), 328(3) and 329(2A) create defences in respect of the offences in ss327(1), 328(1) and 329(1) (respectively) if the person who would otherwise commit such an offence knows, or believes on reasonable grounds, that the 'relevant criminal conduct' occurred in a particular country or territory outside the United Kingdom and was not, at the time it occurred, unlawful under the criminal law then applying in that country or territory. 'Relevant criminal conduct' is defined in ss327(2B), 328(4) and 329(2B)	Probable

Table 5.2 (continued)

Money Laundering Regulations	The law explained	Applicable to electronic ML?
	(respectively) as the criminal conduct by reference to which the property concerned is criminal property. By virtue of ss327(2A)(b)(ii), 328(3)(b)(ii) and 329(2A)(b)(ii), this defence does not apply in respect of relevant criminal conduct of a description prescribed in an order. Article 2(2) of this Order prescries conduct which would be an offence punishable by imprisonment for a maximum term in excess of 12 months in any part of the United Kingdom (subject to the exceptions set out in article 2(2)).	
Proceeds of Crime Act 2002 and Money Laundering Regulations 2003 (Amendment Order 2005)	Section 330 of the Proceeds of Crime Act 2002 requires a person to make a disclosure in accordance with s330(4) (as substituted by s104(3) of the Serious Organised Crime and Police Act 2005) where he knows or suspects, or has reasonable grounds for knowing or suspecting, that another person is engaged in money laundering and the information or other matter came to him in the course of a business in the regulated sector. Schedule 9 to that Act (as amended by the Proceeds of Crime Act 2002 (Business in the Regulated Sector and Supervisory Authorities) Order 2003 (SI 2003/3074)) has effect for determining what is a business in the regulated sector. Failure to make such a disclosure is an offence under s330(1). Section 330(6)(b) (as substituted by s104(3) of the 2005 Act) provides a defence to this offence where the person is a professional legal adviser and the information or other matter came to him in the circumstances set out in s330(10). In order to give full effect to Directive 2001/97/EC, article 2(2) of this Order amends s330(6)(b), (9A)(a) and (10) to extend the persons to whom the defence applies to a 'relevant professional adviser', as defined by s330(14), which is inserted by article 2(5). The amendments made by article 2(3) and (4) provide a defence for a person who is employed by (or in partnership with) the professional legal adviser or other relevant professional adviser to provide assistance or support.	Probable

| Proceeds of Crime Act 2002 and Money Laundering Regulations 2003 (Amendment Order 2006) | | Probable |

The Money Laundering Regulations 2003 also give effect to that Directive. Article 3 of this Order makes the same amendments to regulation 7 of those Regulations as the amendments made by article 2 to section 330. Regulation 7 provides for the internal reporting procedures with which a person must comply in the course of relevant business (regulation 3(1) of those Regulations). 'Relevant business' is defined by regulation 2(2) of those Regulations.

Section 330 of the Proceeds of Crime Act 2002 requires a person to make a disclosure in accordance with s330(4) (as substituted by s104(3) of the Serious Organised Crime and Police Act 2005) where he knows or suspects, or has reasonable grounds for knowing or suspecting, that another person is engaged in money laundering and the information or other matter came to him in the course of a business in the regulated sector. Schedule 9 to that Act (as amended by the Proceeds of Crime Act 2002 (Business in the Regulated Sector and Supervisory Authorities) Order 2003 (SI 2003/3074)) has effect for determining what is a business in the regulated sector. Failure to make such a disclosure is an offence under s330(1). Section 330(6)(b) (as substituted by s104(3) of the 2005 Act) provides a defence to this offence where the person is a professional legal adviser and the information or other matter came to him in the circumstances set out in s330(10). In order to give full effect to Directive 2001/97/EC, article 2(2) of this Order amends s330(6)(b), (9A)(a) and (10) to extend the persons to whom the defence applies to a 'relevant professional adviser', as defined by s330(14), which is inserted by article 2(5). The amendments made by article 2(3) and (4) provide a defence for a person who is employed by (or in partnership with) the professional legal adviser or other relevant professional adviser to provide assistance or support. The Money Laundering Regulations 2003 also give effect to that Directive. Article 3 of this Order makes the same amendments to regulation 7 of those Regulations as the amendments made by article 2 to s330. Regulation 7 provides for the internal reporting procedures with which a person must comply in the course of relevant business (regulation 3(1) of those Regulations). 'Relevant business' is defined by regulation 2(2) of those Regulations.

131

Table 5.2 (continued)

Money Laundering Regulations	The law explained	Applicable to electronic ML?
SI 2003/3075 The Money Laundering Regulations 2003	Requirements for persons carrying out registered activities.	Probable
Money Laundering Regulations 2003	These Regulations replace the Money Laundering Regulations 1993 and 2001 with updated provisions which reflect Directive 2001/97/EC of the European Parliament and of the Council amending Council Directive 91/308/EEC on prevention of the use of the financial system for the purpose of money laundering.	Probable
Money Laundering Regulations 2007	The Treasury are a government department designated (1) for the purposes of s2(2) of the European Communities Act 1972(2) in relation to measures relating to preventing the use of the financial system for the purpose of money laundering; The Treasury, in exercise of the powers conferred on them by s2(2) of the European Communities Act 1972 and by ss168(4) (b), 402(1)(b), 417(1)(3) and 428(3) of the Financial Services and Markets Act 2000(4), make the following Regulations:	Probable

SI 2007/3299 The Money Laundering Regulations 2007	These Regulations, which come into force on 15 December 2007, amend the Money Laundering Regulations 2007 (SI 2007/2157) ('the 2007 Regulations'). The 2007 Regulations implement in part Directive 2005/60/EC (OJ No. L309, 25.11.2005, p.15) of the European Parliament and of the Council on the prevention of the use of the financial system for the purpose of money laundering and terrorist financing. Regulation 2(b) specifies that 'communications' in relation to the grounds of confidentiality of communications in Scotland means communications between a lawyer and his client or in contemplation or in connection with legal proceedings. Regulation 2(f) provides for the treatment of determinations by the Commissioners for Revenue and Customs to refer matters to the Scottish prosecuting authorities as assigned matters within the meaning of s1(1) of the Customs and Excise Management Act 1979 (c. 2). Regulation 2(g) adds the International Association of Book-keepers as a supervisory authority who may supervise persons regulated by it for compliance with the 2007 Regulations. Regulations 2(a), (c), (d) and (e) make minor amendments to the 2007 Regulations.	Probable
Money Laundering (Amendment) Regulations 2007	These Regulations replace the Money Laundering Regulations 2003 (SI 2003/3075) with updated provisions which implement in part Directive 2005/60/EC (OJ No. L309, 25.11.2005, p.15) of the European Parliament and of the Council on the prevention of the use of the financial system for the purpose of money laundering and terrorist financing.	Probable

Table 5.3   United States

Money Laundering Regulations	The law explained	Applicable to electronic ML?
Bank Secrecy Act (BSA) 1970	Established requirements for recordkeeping and reporting by private individuals, banks and other financial institutions; designed to help identify the source, volume, and movement of currency and other monetary instruments transported or transmitted into or out of the United States or deposited in financial institutions; required banks to (1) report cash transactions over $10,000 using the Currency Transaction Report; (2) properly identify persons conducting transactions; and (3) maintain a paper trail by keeping appropriate records of financial transactions.	Probable
Money Laundering Control Act of 1986	Established money laundering as a federal crime; prohibited structuring transactions to evade CTR filings; introduced civil and criminal forfeiture for BSA violations. Directed banks to establish and maintain procedures to ensure and monitor compliance with the reporting and recordkeeping requirements of the BSA.	Probable
Anti-Drug Abuse Act of 1988	Expanded the definition of financial institution to include businesses such as car dealers and real estate closing personnel and required them to file reports on large currency transactions; required the verification of identity of purchasers of monetary instruments over $3000.	Probable
Annunzio-Wylie Anti-Money Laundering Act (1992)	Strengthened the sanctions for BSA violations; required Suspicious Activity Reports and eliminated previously used Criminal Referral Forms; required verification and recordkeeping for wire transfers; established the Bank Secrecy Act Advisory Group (BSAAG).	Probable
Money Laundering Suppression Act (1994)	Required banking agencies to review and enhance training, and develop anti-money laundering examination procedures; required banking agencies to review and enhance procedures for referring cases to appropriate law enforcement agencies. Streamlined CTR exemption process; required each Money Services Business (MSB) to be registered by an owner or controlling person of the MSB; required every MSB to maintain a	Probable

list of businesses authorized to act as agents in connection with the financial services offered by the MSB; made operating an unregistered MSB a federal crime; recommended that states adopt uniform laws applicable to MSBs.

Money Laundering and Financial Crimes Strategy Act (1998)	Required banking agencies to develop anti-money laundering training for examiners. Required the Department of the Treasury and other agencies to develop a National Money Laundering Strategy; created the High Intensity Money Laundering and Related Financial Crime Area (HIFCA) Task Forces to concentrate law enforcement efforts at the federal, state and local levels in zones where money laundering is prevalent. HIFCAs may be defined geographically or they can also be created to address money laundering in an industry sector, a financial institution, or group of financial institutions.	Probable
The US Patriot Act 2002 Laundering Abatement and Financial Anti-Terrorism Act of 2001	Criminalized the financing of terrorism and augmented the existing BSA framework by strengthening customer identification procedures; prohibited financial institutions from engaging in business with foreign shell banks; required financial institutions to have due diligence procedures (and enhanced due diligence procedures for foreign correspondent and private banking accounts); improved information sharing between financial institutions and the US government by requiring government–institution information sharing and voluntary information sharing among financial institutions; expanded the anti-money laundering program requirements to all financial institutions; increased civil and criminal penalties for money laundering; provided the Secretary of the Treasury with the authority to impose 'special measures' on jurisdictions, institutions, or transactions that are of 'primary money laundering concern'; facilitated records access and required banks to respond to regulatory requests for information within 120 hours; required federal banking agencies to consider a bank's AML record when reviewing bank mergers, acquisitions, and other applications for business combinations.	Probable
Intelligence Reform & Terrorism Prevention Act of 2004	Amended the BSA to require the Secretary of the Treasury to prescribe regulations requiring certain financial institutions to report cross-border electronic transmittals of funds, if the Secretary determines that such reporting is 'reasonably necessary' to aid in the fight against money laundering and terrorist financing.	

Table 5.4 Korea

Money Laundering Regulations	The law explained	Applicable to electronic ML?
Financial Provision Reports Act 2001	It is the purpose of this Act to prevent criminal activities and furthermore, to contribute to the establishment of a sound and transparent financial system, by stipulating provisions necessary to regulate money laundering activities through the financial transactions including foreign transactions, with respect to the reporting and using specific financial transaction information.	Probable
Proceeds of Crime Act 2001	It is the purpose of this Act to contribute to the maintenance of sound social order by eliminating, from the root, economic factors that induce predicate offences, through stipulating provisions that conceal criminal proceeds with the purpose of disguising the obtainment of criminal proceeds relating to predicate offences or inducing predicate offences, disguising illegally obtained properties as legal ones; and by stipulating provisions about forfeiture and confiscation of criminal proceeds relating to predicate offences.	Probable
International Conventions for the Suppressing of the Terrorist Financing 2004	It requires Member States to take measures to protect their financial systems from being misused by persons planning or engaged in terrorist activities.	Probable

Prohibition of Financing for Offences of Public Intimidation Act 2007	The purpose of this Prohibition of Financing for Offences of Public Intimidation Act (the '*Act*' hereinafter) is to implement the 'International Convention for the Suppression of the Financing of Terrorism(1999)' by setting forth matters necessary to prohibit financing for offences of public intimidation.	Probable
The Suppression of Terrorist Financing Act 2008	Provides a legal outline for the prevention of terrorist financing.	
Financial Transaction Report Act 2008	The purpose of the Financial Transaction Reports Act (hereinafter the '*Act*') is to set forth matters related to the filing and the use of financial transaction reports required to regulate money laundering activities and financing for offences of public intimidation using financial transactions including foreign currency transactions, thereby preventing crimes and contributing to establishment of a sound and transparent financial system.	Probable
Act on Real Name Financial Transactions and Secrecy Guarantee Act 2008	The purpose of this Act is to realise economic justice and to facilitate the sound development of national economy by implementing real name financial transactions and protecting secrets through normalised financial transactions.	Probable

Table 5.5 China

Money Laundering Regulations	The law explained	Applicable to electronic ML?
Anti Money Laundering Laws 2007	Establishes for the first time AML laws in the People's Republic of China.	Probable
Criminal Law of PRC (1997)	Adopted by the Second Session of the Fifth National People's Congress on 1 July 1979 and amended by the Fifth Session of the Eighth National People's Congress on 14 March 1997. Article 319: Whoever defrauds people, in the name of labour export and economic and trade exchanges or for other reasons, of their exit documents such as passports and visas through fraud and deception for use in organizing people in the secret crossing of the national boundary (border) shall be sentenced to not more than three years of fixed-term imprisonment, and may in addition be sentenced to a fine; and when the circumstances are serious, not less than three years and not more than ten years of fixed-term imprisonment, and may in addition be sentenced to a fine.	Probable
Anti-Money Laundering Law of China (2010)	The definition of money laundering has been expanded to include corruption and bribe taking, violating financial management regulations and financial fraud. Came into force 1 January 2007. The People's Bank of China, or central bank, is the nerve centre of the anti-money money laundering campaign. Its provincial branch offices are authorised to investigate suspect fund transfers by financial institutions.	Probable

Table 5.6 European Union

Money Laundering Regulations	The law explained	Applicable to electronic ML?
Basel II Accord	Basel II is the second of the famous Basel Accords, issued by the Basel Committee on Banking Supervision. Basel II replaced the 1998 Basel I Accord, and serves as a regulatory framework for strengthening the stability of the international banking system. It also includes explicit measurement criteria for operational risk, and essentially serves to foster a stronger risk mitigation and AML compliance culture within the financial services sphere.	Probable
EU Second Money Laundering Directive (2MLD)	Constituted a significant expansion of cross-border anti-money laundering legislation. The Directive increased the regulatory scope in terms of the types of financial and serious crimes being combated to include all serious crimes, but also placed AML obligations on a far wider range of industries. Newly regulated industries included estate agencies, casinos and the purveyors of high-value goods, as well as the legal and accounting sectors. 2MLD outlined procedures for reporting suspicious transactional activities, and had the task of ensuring that a uniform enforcement framework was adhered to in six Member States, namely the UK, Greece, Italy, Spain, Lithuania and Poland. Although the Directive expressly named money laundering and fraud, Member States were also given permission to define any other offences for the purposes of the Directive.	Probable
EU Third Money Laundering Directive (3MLD)	Incorporates the objectives of the EU Second Money Laundering Directive and is intended to further curb abuses of the European financial and banking systems. Its stated primary aim is to include anti-terrorist financing within anti-money Laundering provisions, and it has served to expand and consolidate the provisions of 2MLD.	Probable

Table 5.7   UN

Money Laundering Regulations	The law explained	Applicable to electronic ML?
United Nations Convention against the Illicit Traffic in Narcotic Drugs and Psychotropic Substances 1988	First international legal instrument to embody the money laundering aspect of this new strategy; is also the first international convention which criminalises money laundering.	Probable
UN Convention against Transnational Organized Crime 2003	Widens the scope of the money laundering offence by stating that it should not only apply to the proceeds of illicit drug trafficking, but should also cover the proceeds of all serious crimes. Urges States to create a comprehensive domestic supervisory and regulatory regime for banks and non-bank financial institutions, including natural and legal persons, as well as any entities particularly susceptible to being involved in a money laundering scheme. The Conventions also call for the establishment of Financial Intelligence Units (FIUs).	Probable
UN Convention against Corruption 2005	The Convention introduces a comprehensive set of standards, measures and rules that all countries can apply in order to strengthen their legal and regulatory regimes to fight corruption. It calls for preventive measures and the criminalization of the most prevalent forms of corruption in both public and private sectors. And it makes a major breakthrough by requiring Member States to return assets obtained through corruption to the country from which they were stolen.	Probable

	These provisions – the first of their kind – introduce a new fundamental principle, as well as a framework for stronger cooperation between States to prevent and detect corruption and to return the proceeds. Corrupt officials will in future find fewer ways to hide their illicit gains.	Probable
International Convention for the Suppression of the Financing of Terrorism 2002	It requires Member States to take measures to protect their financial systems from being misused by persons planning or engaged in terrorist activities.	Probable
Resolution 1373	Imposes certain obligations on Member States, such as the prevention and the suppression of the financing of terrorist acts, the criminalisation of terrorism-related activities and of the provision of assistance to carry out those acts, the denial of funding and safe haven to terrorists and the exchange of information to prevent the commission of terrorist acts. In the same resolution, the Council also established the Counter-Terrorism Committee (CTC) to monitor the implementation of the resolution.	Probable

on to outline the cyber crime laws which could capture virtual economic crime.

The tables above demonstrate that although there are adequate provisions for the prevention of money laundering and terrorist financing in countries, these are not specific to virtual crime. However, it is the opinion of the author that it is probable that these laws could be used by the judiciary to fit cyber crimes.

The next section examines the laws which are applicable directly to cyber crimes. A marriage between the money laundering and financial crime laws stated above and the laws set out below is essential to forge a new joined-up piece of legislation. At the end of the section, the Cyber Crime Initiative will be examined in light of the Commonwealth's plan to create model laws for the inception of a legislation combating cyber crime. This is a start, but countries have a long way to go before effectively tackling not only cyber crime but also virtual economic crime.

UNITED KINGDOM CYBER CRIME LAWS

The Police and Justice Act 2006 Chapter 48
This amends the Computer Misuse Act.

See Part 5, ss 35–38. The new amendments came into force on 1 October 2008, and read as follows:

35 Unauthorised access to computer material

   (1)   In the Computer Misuse Act 1990 (c. 18) ('the 1990 Act'), section 1 (offence of unauthorised access to computer material) is amended as follows.

   (2)   In subsection (1)–

      (a)   in paragraph (a), after 'any computer' there is inserted, 'or to enable any such access to be secured';

      (b)   in paragraph (b), after 'secure' there is inserted, 'or to enable to be secured,'.

   (3)   For subsection (3) there is substituted–

'(3   A person guilty of an offence under this section shall be liable–

      (a)   on summary conviction in England and Wales, to imprisonment for a term not exceeding 12 months or to a fine not exceeding the statutory maximum or to both;

      (b)   on summary conviction in Scotland, to imprisonment for a term not exceeding six months or to a fine not exceeding the statutory maximum or to both;

      (c)   on conviction on indictment, to imprisonment for a term not exceeding two years or to a fine or to both.'

36 Unauthorised acts with intent to impair operation of computer, etc.

For section 3 of the 1990 Act (unauthorised modification of computer material) there is substituted–

'3 Unauthorised acts with intent to impair, or with recklessness as to impairing, operation of computer, etc.
(1) A person is guilty of an offence if
  (a) he does any unauthorised act in relation to a computer;
  (b) at the time when he does the act he knows that it is unauthorised; and
  (c) either subsection (2) or subsection (3) below applies.
(2) This subsection applies if the person intends by doing the act–
  (a) to impair the operation of any computer;
  (b) to prevent or hinder access to any program or data held in any computer;
  (c) to impair the operation of any such program or the reliability of any such data; or
  (d) to enable any of the things mentioned in paragraphs (a) to (c) above to be done.
(3) This subsection applies if the person is reckless as to whether the act will do any of the things mentioned in paragraphs (a) to (d) of subsection (2) above.
(4) The intention referred to in subsection (2) above, or the recklessness referred to in subsection (3) above, need not relate to–
  (a) any particular computer;
  (b) any particular program or data; or
  (c) a program or data of any particular kind.
(5) In this section–
  (a) a reference to doing an act includes a reference to causing an act to be done;
  (b) "act" includes a series of acts;
  (c) a reference to impairing, preventing or hindering something includes a reference to doing so temporarily.
(6) A person guilty of an offence under this section shall be liable–
  (a) on summary conviction in England and Wales, to imprisonment for a term not exceeding 12 months or to a fine not exceeding the statutory maximum or to both;
  (b) on summary conviction in Scotland, to imprisonment for a term not exceeding six months or to a fine not exceeding the statutory maximum or to both;
  (c) on conviction on indictment, to imprisonment for a term not exceeding ten years or to a fine or to both.'

37 Making, supplying or obtaining articles for use in computer misuse offences

After section 3 of the 1990 Act there is inserted–

'3A Making, supplying or obtaining articles for use in offence under section 1 or 3

(1) A person is guilty of an offence if he makes, adapts, supplies or offers to supply any article intending it to be used to commit, or to assist in the commission of, an offence under section 1 or 3.

(2) A person is guilty of an offence if he supplies or offers to supply any article believing that it is likely to be used to commit, or to assist in the commission of, an offence under section 1 or 3.

(3) A person is guilty of an offence if he obtains any article with a view to its being supplied for use to commit, or to assist in the commission of, an offence under section 1 or 3.

(4) In this section "article" includes any program or data held in electronic form.

(5) A person guilty of an offence under this section shall be liable–

    (a) on summary conviction in England and Wales, to imprisonment for a term not exceeding 12 months or to a fine not exceeding the statutory maximum or to both;

    (b) on summary conviction in Scotland, to imprisonment for a term not exceeding six months or to a fine not exceeding the statutory maximum or to both;

    (c) on conviction on indictment, to imprisonment for a term not exceeding two years or to a fine or to both.'

38 Transitional and saving provision

(1) The amendments made by–

    (a) subsection (2) of section 35, and

    (b) paragraphs 19(2), 25(2) and 29(2) of Schedule 14,

apply only where every act or other event proof of which is required for conviction of an offence under section 1 of the 1990 Act takes place after that subsection comes into force.

(2) The amendments made by–

    (a) subsection (3) of section 35, and

    (b) paragraphs 23, 24, 25(4) and (5), 26, 27(2) and (7) and 28 of Schedule 14,

do not apply in relation to an offence committed before that subsection comes into force.

(3) An offence is not committed under the new section 3 unless every act or other event proof of which is required for conviction of the offence takes place after section 36 above comes into force.

(4) In relation to a case where, by reason of subsection (3), an offence is not committed under the new section 3–

    (a) section 3 of the 1990 Act has effect in the form in which it was enacted;

    (b) paragraphs 19(3), 25(3) to (5), 27(4) and (5) and 29(3) and (4) of Schedule 14 do not apply.

(5) An offence is not committed under the new section 3A unless every act or other event proof of which is required for conviction of the offence takes place after section 37 above comes into force.

(6) In the case of an offence committed before section 154(1) of the Criminal Justice Act 2003 (c. 44) comes into force, the following provisions have effect as if for '12 months' there were substituted 'six months'–
   (a) paragraph (a) of the new section 1(3);
   (b) paragraph (a) of the new section 2(5);
   (c) subsection (6)(a) of the new section 3;
   (d) subsection (5)(a) of the new section 3A.
(7) In this section–
   (a) 'the new section 1(3)' means the subsection (3) substituted in section 1 of the 1990 Act by section 35 above;
   (b) 'the new section 2(5)' means the subsection (5) substituted in section 2 of the 1990 Act by paragraph 17 of Schedule 14 to this Act;
   (c) 'the new section 3' means the section 3 substituted in the 1990 Act by section 36 above;
   (d) 'the new section 3A' means the section 3A inserted in the 1990 Act by section 37 above.

Computer Misuse Act 1990 Chapter 18

1 Unauthorised access to computer material.
(1) A person is guilty of an offence if–
   (a) he causes a computer to perform any function with the intent to secure access to any program or data held in any computer, or to enable any such access to be secured,
   (b) the access he intends to secure, or to enable to be secured, is unauthorised, and
   (c) he knows at the time when he causes the computer to perform the function that that is the case.
(2) The intent a person has to have to commit an offence under this section need not to be directed at:
   (a) any particular program or data,
   (b) a program or data of any particular kind, or
   (c) a program or data held in any particular computer.
(3) A person guilty of an offence under this section shall be liable–
   (a) on summary conviction in England and Wales, to imprisonment for a term not exceeding 12 months or to a fine not exceeding the statutory maximum or to both;
   (b) on summary conviction in Scotland, to imprisonment for a term not exceeding six months or to a fine not exceeding the statutory maximum or to both;
   (c) on conviction on indictment, to imprisonment for a term not exceeding two years or to a fine or to both.

2 Unauthorised access with intent to commit or facilitate commission for further offences.
(1) A person is guilty of an offence under this section if he commits an offence under section 1 above ('the unauthorised access offence') with intent

       (a) to commit an offence to which this section applies; or

       (b) to facilitate the commission of such an offence (whether by himself or by any other person); and the offence he intends to commit or facilitate is referred to below in this section as the further offence.

(2) This section applies to offences

       (a) for which the sentence is fixed by law; or

       (b) for which a person of twenty-one years of age or over (not previously convicted) may be sentenced to imprisonment for a term of five years (or, in England and Wales, might be so sentenced but for the restrictions imposed by section 33 of the Magistrates Courts Act 1980).

(3) It is immaterial for the purposes of this section whether the further offence is to be committed on the same occasion as the unauthorised access offence or on any future occasion.

(4) A person may be guilty of an offence under this section even though the facts are such that the commission of the further offence is impossible.

(5) A person guilty of an offence under this section shall be liable

       (a) on summary conviction, to imprisonment for a term not exceeding the statutory maximum or to both; and

       (b) on conviction on indictment, to imprisonment for a term not exceeding five years or to a fine or to both.

3 Unauthorised acts with intent to impair, or with recklessness as to impairing, operation of computer, etc.

(1) A person is guilty of an offence if–

       (a) he does any unauthorised act in relation to a computer;

       (b) at the time when he does the act he knows that it is unauthorised; and

       (c) either subsection (2) or subsection (3) below applies.

(2) This subsection applies if the person intends by doing the act–

       (a) to impair the operation of any computer;

       (b) to prevent or hinder access to any program or data held in any computer;

       (c) to impair the operation of any such program or the reliability of any such data; or

       (d) to enable any of the things mentioned in paragraphs (a) to (c) above to be done.

(3) This subsection applies if the person is reckless as to whether the act will do any of the things mentioned in paragraphs (a) to (d) of subsection (2) above.

(4) The intention referred to in subsection (2) above, or the recklessness referred to in subsection (3) above, need not relate to–

       (a) any particular computer;

       (b) any particular program or data; or

       (c) a program or data of any particular kind.

(5) In this section–

       (a) a reference to doing an act includes a reference to causing an act to be done;

       (b) 'act' includes a series of acts;

(c)　a reference to impairing, preventing or hindering something includes a reference to doing so temporarily.

(6)　A person guilty of an offence under this section shall be liable–

    (a)　on summary conviction in England and Wales, to imprisonment for a term not exceeding 12 months or to a fine not exceeding the statutory maximum or to both;

    (b)　on summary conviction in Scotland, to imprisonment for a term not exceeding six months or to a fine not exceeding the statutory maximum or to both;

    (c)　on conviction on indictment, to imprisonment for a term not exceeding ten years or to a fine or to both.

3A　Making, supplying or obtaining articles for use in offence under section 1 or 3.

(1)　A person is guilty of an offence if he makes, adapts, supplies or offers to supply any article intending it to be used to commit, or to assist in the commission of, an offence under section 1 or 3.

(2)　A person is guilty of an offence if he supplies or offers to supply any article believing that it is likely to be used to commit, or to assist in the commission of, an offence under section 1 or 3.

(3)　A person is guilty of an offence if he obtains any article with a view to its being supplied for use to commit, or to assist in the commission of, an offence under section 1 or 3.

(4)　In this section 'article' includes any program or data held in electronic form.

(5)　A person guilty of an offence under this section shall be liable–

    (a)　on summary conviction in England and Wales, to imprisonment for a term not exceeding 12 months or to a fine not exceeding the statutory maximum or to both;

    (b)　on summary conviction in Scotland, to imprisonment for a term not exceeding six months or to a fine not exceeding the statutory maximum or to both;

    (c)　on conviction on indictment, to imprisonment for a term not exceeding two years or to a fine or to both.

UNITED STATES CYBER CRIME LAWS

Substantive cyber crime laws (e.g. laws prohibiting online identity theft, hacking, intrusion into computer systems, child pornography, intellectual property, online gambling):

18 U.S.C. § 1028 – Fraud and related activity in connection with identification documents, authentication features, and information

18 U.S.C. § 1028A – Aggravated identity theft

18 U.S.C. § 1029 – Fraud and related activity in connection with access devices

18 U.S.C. § 1030 – Fraud and related activity in connection with computers
18 U.S.C. § 1037 – Fraud and related activity in connection with electronic mail
18 U.S.C. § 1343 – Fraud by wire, radio, or television
18 U.S.C. § 1362 – [Malicious mischief related to] Communications lines, stations, or systems
18 U.S.C. § 1462 – Importation or transportation of obscene matters
18 U.S.C. § 1465 – Transportation of obscene matters for sale or distribution
18 U.S.C. § 1466A – Obscene visual representation of the sexual abuse of children
18 U.S.C. § 2251 – Sexual exploitation of children
18 U.S.C. § 2252 – Certain activities relating to material involving the sexual exploitation of minors
18 U.S.C. § 2252A – Certain activities relating to material constituting or containing child pornography
18 U.S.C. § 2252B – Misleading domain names on the Internet [to deceive minors]
18 U.S.C. § 2252C – Misleading words or digital images on the Internet
18 U.S.C. § 2425 – Use of interstate facilities to transmit information about a minor
18 U.S.C. § 2319 – Criminal infringement of a copyright
17 U.S.C. § 506 – Criminal offenses [related to copyright]
47 U.S.C. 605 – Unauthorized publication or use of communications
The Unlawful Internet Gambling Enforcement Act of 2006
Procedural cyber crime laws (e.g. authority to preserve and obtain electronic data from third parties, including internet service providers; authority to intercept electronic communications; authority to search and seize electronic evidence):
18 U.S.C. §§ 2510-2522 – Interception of wire, oral, or electronic communication
18 U.S.C. §§ 2701-2712 – Preservation and disclosure of stored wire and electronic communication
18 U.S.C. §§ 3121-3127 – Pen registers and trap and trace devices[71]

---

[71] Cyber Crime Laws of the United States, http://www.oas.org/juridico/spanish/us_cyb_laws.pdf.

TITLE 18. CRIMES AND CRIMINAL PROCEDURE
PART I – CRIMES

Chapter 47 – Fraud and False Statements

Section 1030. Fraud and related activity in connection with computers

(a) Whoever–

(1) having knowingly accessed a computer without authorization or exceeding authorized access, and by means of such conduct having obtained information that has been determined by the United States Government pursuant to an Executive order or statute to require protection against unauthorized disclosure for reasons of national defense or foreign relations, or any restricted data, as defined in paragraph y of section 11 of the Atomic Energy Act of 1954, with reason to believe that such information so obtained could be used to the injury of the United States, or to the advantage of any foreign nation willfully communicates, delivers, transmits, or causes to be communicated, delivered, or transmitted, or attempts to communicate, deliver, transmit or cause to be communicated, delivered, or transmitted the same to any person not entitled to receive it, or willfully retains the same and fails to deliver it to the officer or employee of the United States entitled to receive it;

(2) intentionally accesses a computer without authorization or exceeds authorized access, and thereby obtains–

(A) information contained in a financial record of a financial institution, or of a card issuer as defined in section 1602 (n) of title 15, or contained in a file of a consumer reporting agency on a consumer, as such terms are defined in the Fair Credit Reporting Act (15 U.S.C. 1681 et seq.);

(B) information from any department or agency of the United States; or

(C) information from any protected computer if the conduct involved an interstate or foreign communication;

(3) intentionally, without authorization to access any nonpublic computer of a department or agency of the United States, accesses such a computer of that department or agency that is exclusively for the use of the Government of the United States or, in the case of a computer not exclusively for such use, is used by or for the Government of the United States and such conduct affects that use by or for the Government of the United States;

(4) knowingly and with the intent to defraud, accesses a protected computer without authorization, or exceeds authorized access, and by means of such conduct furthers the intended fraud and obtains anything of value, unless the object of the fraud and the thing obtained consists only of the use of the computer and the value of such use is not more than $5,000 in any one year period;

(5)

(i) knowingly causes the transmission of a program, information, code, or command, and as a result of such conduct, intentionally causes damage without authorization, to a protected computer;

(ii) intentionally accesses a protected computer without authorization, and as a result of such conduct recklessly causes damage; or

(iii)   intentionally accesses a protected computer without authorization, and as a result of such conduct, causes damage; and

(B)   by conduct described in clause (i), (ii), or (iii) of subparagraph (A), caused (or, in the case of an attempted offence, would, if completed, have caused)–

    (i)   loss to 1 or more persons during any 1-year period (and, for purposes of an investigation, prosecution, or other proceeding brought by the United States only, loss resulting from a related course of conduct affecting 1 or more other protected computers) aggregating at least $5000 in value;

    (ii)   the modification or impairment, or potential modification or impairment, of the medical examination, diagnosis, treatment, or care of 1 or more individuals;

    (iii)   physical injury to any person;

    (iv)   a threat to public health or safety; or

    (v)   damage affecting a computer system used by or for a government entity in furtherance of the administration of justice, national defence, or national security;

(6)   knowingly and with intent to defraud traffics (as defined in section 1029) in any password or similar information through which a computer may be accessed without authorization, if

(A)   such trafficking affects interstate or foreign commerce; or

(B)   such computer is used by or for the Government of the United States;

(7)   with intent to extort from any person any money or other thing of value, transmits in interstate or foreign commerce any communication containing any

(a)   threat to cause damage to a protected computer . . . shall be punished as provided in subsection (c) of this section.

(b)   Whoever attempts to commit an offense under subsection (a) of this section shall be punished as provided in subsection (c) of this section.

(c)   The punishment for an offense under subsection (a) or (b) of this section is–[72]

    . . . .

(f)   This section does not prohibit any lawfully authorized investigative, protective, or intelligence activity of a law enforcement agency of the United States, a State, or a political subdivision of a State or of an intelligence agency of the United States.[73]

---

[72]   See http://www.usdoj.gov/criminal/cybercrime/1030NEW.htm.

[73]   For a legislative analysis, see: http://www.usdoj.gov/criminal/cyber-crime/1030_anal.html.

CHINA CYBER CRIME LAWS

Criminal Law of the People's Republic of China

(14 March 1997)

ARTICLE 285   Whoever violates state regulations and intrudes into computer systems with information concerning state affairs, construction of defence facilities, and sophisticated science and technology is be sentenced to not more than three years of fixed-term imprisonment or criminal detention.

ARTICLE   286 Whoever violates state regulations and deletes, alters, adds, and interferes in computer information systems, causing abnormal operations of the systems and grave consequences, is to be sentenced to not more than five years of fixed-term imprisonment or criminal detention; when the consequences are particularly serious, the sentence is to be not less than five years of fixed-term imprisonment.

Whoever   violates state regulations and deletes, alters, or adds the data or application programs installed in or processed and transmitted by the computer systems, and causes grave consequences, is to be punished according to the preceding paragraph.

Whoever   deliberately creates and propagates computer virus and other programs which sabotage the normal operation of the computer system and cause grave consequences is to be punished according to the first paragraph.

ARTICLE 287   Whoever uses a computer for financial fraud, theft, corruption, misappropriation of public funds, stealing state secrets, or other crimes is to be convicted and punished according to relevant regulations of this law.

Hong Kong Telecommunications Ordinance

Section 27A: unauthorized access to computer by telecommunication
(1)   Any person who, by telecommunication, knowingly causes a computer to perform any function to obtain unauthorized access to any program or data held in a computer commits an offence and is liable on conviction to a fine of $20 000.
(2)   For the purposes of subsection (1)–
    (a)   the intent of the person need not be directed at–
        (i)   any particular program or data;
        (ii)   a program or data of a particular kind, or
        (iii)   a program or data held in a particular computer;
    (b)   access of any kind by a person to any program or data held in a computer is unauthorized if he is not entitled to control access of the kind in question to the program or data held in the computer and–

       (i)   he has not been authorized to obtain access of the kind in question to the program or data held in the computer by any person who is entitled;

       (ii)   he does not believe that he has been so authorized; and

       (iii) he does not believe that he would have been so authorized if he had applied for the appropriate authority.

(3) Subsection (1) has effect without prejudice to any law relating to powers of inspection, search or seizure.

(4) Notwithstanding section 26 of the Magistrates Ordinance (Cap 227), proceedings for an offence under this section may be brought at any time within 3 years of the commission of the offence or within 6 months of the discovery of the offence by the prosecutor, whichever period expires first.

Section 161: Access to computer with criminal or dishonest intent

(1) Any person who obtains access to a computer–
    (a)   with intent to commit an offence;
    (b)   with a dishonest intent to deceive;
    (c)   with a view to dishonest gain for himself or another; or
    (d)   with a dishonest intent to cause loss to another,

whether on the same occasion as he obtains such access or on any future occasion, commits an offence and is liable on conviction upon indictment to imprisonment for 5 years.

(2) For the purposes of subsection (1) 'gain' and 'loss' are to be construed as extending not only to gain or loss in money or other property, but as extending to any such gain or loss whether temporary or permanent; and–
    (a)   'gain' includes a gain by keeping what one has, as well as gain by getting what one has not; and
    (b)   'loss' includes a loss by not getting what one might get, as well as a loss by parting with what one has.

KOREA CYBER CRIME LAWS

Article 141 (invalidity of public documents, etc. and destruction of public goods)

(1) A person who damages or conceals documents or other goods, or special media records, such as electromagnetic records, etc., used by public offices, or spoils its utility by other methods, shall be punished by imprisonment with prison labour for not more than 7 years or by a fine not exceeding 10 million won.

Amended by Act No. 5057, Dec. 29, 1995

Article 227-2 (false preparation or alteration of public electromagnetic records)

A person with the intention of disrupting business falsely or alters electromagnetic documents of public official or public office shall be punished by imprisonment with prison labor not more than 10 years.
This Article Wholly Amended by Act No. 5057. Dec. 29, 1995

Article 232-2 (falsification or alteration of private electromagnetic records)

A person who falsifies or alters, with the intention of making any error in the management of affairs, any special media records, such as another person's electromagnetic records concerning any years, shall be punished by imprisonment with prison labor for not more than 5 years, or a fine not exceeding 10 million won.
This Article Wholly Amended by Act No. 5057. Dec. 29, 1995

Article 316 (violation of secrecy)

(1)   A person who opens a sealed or other secretly composed letter, document, or drawing shall be punished by imprisonment with or without labor for not more than 3 years or by a fine not exceeding 5 million won.

Amended by Act No. 5057. Dec. 29,1995
(2)   Any person who detects the contents of another person's sealed or secretly designed letter, document, drawing, picture, or special media records, such as electromagnetic records, using any technical means, shall be subject to the same punishment referred to in paragraph (1).
Newly Inserted by Act No. 5057. Dec. 29, 1995

Article 347-2 (fraud by the use of computer, etc.)

Any person who acquires any benefits to property or has a third person acquire them, by making any data processed after inputting a false information or improper order, or inputting or altering the data without any authority into the data processor, such as computer, etc., shall be punished by imprisonment with prison labor for not more than 10 years, or a fine not exceeding 20 million won.
This Article Wholly Amended by Act No. 5057. Dec. 29, 1995

Article 366 (destruction and damage, etc. of property)

A person who, by destroying, damaging, or concealing another's property document or special media records, such as electromagnetic records, etc., or by any other means, reduces their utility, shall be punished by imprisonment with prison labor for not more than 3 years or a fine not exceeding 7 million won.
Amended by Act No. 5057. Dec. 29, 1995

2. ACT ON PROMOTION OF INFORMATION AND COMMUNICATIONS NETWORK UTILIZATION AND INFORMATION PROTECTION, ETC.

Chapter VI Stability of the Information and Communications Network

Article 48 (prohibition on act of infiltrating into information and communications networks, etc.)

(1) Any person shall be prohibited from infiltrating into information and communications networks without any justifiable access right or beyond his/her permitted access right.

(2) Any person shall be prohibited from transmitting or distributing any program (hereinafter referred to as a 'malicious program') that may damage, disrupt, and destroy the information and communications system, alter and forge the data or programs, etc., or hinder the operation thereof without any justifiable reasons.

(3) Any person shall be prohibited from sending a large volume of signals or data for the purpose of hindering the stable operation of information and communications networks or from causing troubles in information and communications networks using the method of getting unfair instructions processed.

Article 49 (protection of secrets, etc.)

Any person shall be prohibited from damaging the information of other persons or from infringing, stealing or leaking the secrets of other persons, which are processed, stored or transmitted by information and communications networks.

Chapter IX Penal Provisions

Article 61 (penal provisions)

(1) Any person who has defamed any other person by alleging openly facts through information and communications network with the purpose of slandering him/her shall be punished by imprisonment with or without prison labor for not more than 3 years or by a fine not exceeding 20 million won.

(2) Any person who has defamed any other person by alleging openly false facts through information and communications network with the purpose of slandering him/her shall be punished by imprisonment with prison labour for not more than 7 years or the suspension of disqualification for not more than 10 years, or by a fine not exceeding 50 million won.

Article 62 (penal provision)

Any person falling under any of the following subparagraphs shall be punished by imprisonment with prison labour for not more than 5 years or by a fine not exceeding 50 million won.

(1) A person who has utilized the personal information or provided it to any third person beyond the scope of the notification or the limit specified in a standardized contract under Article 22(2) in contravention of Article 24 (1) (including a case where the provisions are applied mutatis mutandis in Article 58);

(2) A person who has utilized the personal information of users for other purpose than the purpose for which such personal information has been provided or provided such personal information to any other person in contravention of Article 24(2) (including a case where the provisions are applied mutatis mutandis in Article 58);

(3) A person who has damaged, infringed or leaked the personal information of users in contravention of Article 24(4) (including a case where the provisions are applied mutatis mutandis in Article 58);

(4) A person who has transmitted or distributed malicious programs in contravention of Article 48(2);

(5) A person who has caused troubles in information and communications networks in contravention of Article 48(3); and

(6) A person who has damaged the information of any other person, or infringed, stolen or leaked the secrets of any other person in contravention of Article 49.

Article 63 (penal provisions)

Any person falling under any of the following subparagraphs shall be punished by imprisonment with the prison labour for not more than 3 years or by a fine not exceeding 30 million won;

(1) A person who has infiltrated information and communications networks in contravention of Article 48(1); and

(2) A person who has leaked the secrets to any other person, which he/she has learned while performing his duties, or utilized such secrets for other purpose than the purpose of his/her duties in contravention of Article 57.

Article 65 (penal provisions)

(1) Any person falling under any of the following subparagraphs shall be punished by imprisonment with prison labour for not more than 1 year or by a fine not exceeding 10 million won;

(2) A person who has put any label or similar one on goods or sold such goods bearing such label or displayed such goods for the purpose of selling them in contravention of Article 8(4);

(3) A person who has distributed, sold, rented, or openly displayed lascivious codes, letters, sounds, visuals, or films through information and communications networks; and

(4) A person who has repeatedly sent words, sounds, letters, visuals, or films inciting fears and uneasiness to any other person through information and communications networks.

3.   INFORMATION INFRASTRUCTURE PROTECTION ACT

Article 28

Any person who disrupts, paralyzes, or destroys a Critical Information Infrastructure shall be punished by imprisonment with prison labour for not more than 10 year or by a fine not exceeding 100 million won.

Justification

The above countries were chosen for the purposes of this book because of the prevalence within them of virtual economic crime or because of work towards a joined-up cyber legislation.

The Commonwealth are beginning to take cyber crime seriously and have drafted the Cyber Crime Initiative which will be worked on over the next couple of years. It is hoped that a draft model law will be created which will pave the way for Commonwealth countries to enact harmonised legislation to create a platform to prevent cyber crime. Virtual economic crime may also fall under this model law but for now it is too soon to tell.

Summary

Throughout this chapter a discussion has taken place as to the mechanics and intricacies of virtual money laundering. Virtual money laundering is a real and viable criminal activity and is now globally recognised. Some work is now being done by law enforcement agencies and international groups (which will be discussed in Chapter 7). However, as we have discussed above, there is very little domestic regulation which effectively combats, detects and prosecutes virtual economic criminals. There are even fewer effective international regulations in place to counter this ever growing criminal activity. The EU Convention on Cyber Crime is considered in Chapter 7 because it is used as a model for creating an international convention on virtual financial crime. In the following chapters of the book, the legal structure and the complexities of creating a cyber law for countering virtual money laundering will be discussed.

6. Law and the virtual world

INTRODUCTION

The British Fraud Advisory Panel (FAP) has said 'there is nothing virtual about online crime, it is all too real. It is time the government took this seriously'.[1] The FAP has further opined that 'money laundering is the obvious risk. There will be a migration of fraudsters into these sites when they see all of the opportunities'.[2] They describe the virtual world as 'a parallel universe with almost no external rule of law, no enforced banking regulations or compliance, no policing and no government oversight'.[3] Similarly, Field Fisher Waterhouse Solicitors iterated that 'the law doesn't stop just because this is a virtual world, but with its borderless nature, it may be challenging to determine whose laws apply. And there's a culture of anonymity, so it is often difficult to known whom you are dealing with'.[4] So the question is: are there laws relating to the virtual worlds? If so, what are these laws and if there are none, how can we create laws that still comply with the rule of law? It is true 'that the law often lags behind technology and this is certainly the case in virtual worlds and social networking sites'.[5]

Throughout the book thus far we have discussed virtual worlds, their economic nature and progress through time, and their impact on the real world, all of which has culminated in the proposition that virtual worlds are a continuum of the real world and thus should have the necessary legal culpability of any other state within the real world. Within the present chapter this discussion will continue in more depth. There is academic debate as to whether there should be virtual world self-regulation, as opposed to a separatist point of view that virtual world laws should be distinct from real world laws or the inclusionist view that real world laws should be applicable in the virtual world too, given the real world effect

---

[1] Fraud Advisory Panel (2009).
[2] Ibid.
[3] Ibid.
[4] Ibid.
[5] Bond (2009).

and consequences these virtual worlds have. Caution must be exercised with regard to the wealth of academic literature available on IT and cyber law and jurisdiction. In this book we are not primarily concerned with the implications of IT laws and cyber jurisdiction, but rather with the laws contained within the virtual worlds which are impacting on real world society. From this point of view, there is relatively little literature available, so parallels must be drawn with the nearest legal element, namely IT and cyber law. In this sense, IT and cyber law do play an important part in the theoretical underpinnings of the book, but it cannot be an exact match.

The chapter will therefore be divided into six main areas. First, the chapter will discuss the laws of constraint within the natural and the virtual worlds. Secondly, it will examine Private and Public International law and whether comparisons can be drawn to outline a determinate virtual world legal system. Thirdly, the chapter will move on to analyse International Economic Law so as to marry public and private international law with the concepts of international economic law for the purposes of transposition into the virtual world. Penultimately, the academic debate between the separatists, inclusionist and legal pluralists will be analysed in relation to virtual world jurisdictions. The chapter will conclude by considering the rule of law and its impact on both cyber jurisdictions and also virtual world jurisdictions.

However, to begin this chapter it is important to examine the statement made by John Perry Barlow in 1996 on behalf of cyberspace (see Box 6.1).[6] In this, Barlow provides an explosive piece of work, demonstrating the attitudes towards the US Communications Decency Act, the first piece of legislation in the US which prohibited pornography on the internet. This Act engendered outrage that freedom of speech and communication were being curtailed by a government which, in the opinion of a few, to be examined later in the chapter, did not have jurisdiction over cyberspace. It is this separatist view, that there should be a separate law for the internet, that will be examined and compared to the inclusionist viewpoint, which believes that cyber law should be an extension of real world laws. Barlow's declaration demonstrates the many points of tension between the two sides.

It is important to examine the statement fully, to provide clarification as to how difficult it is to regulate such a nebulous matter when there is lack of democracy and governmental control. This book is written with the philosophical stance that the internet should be ruled by the laws of the

---

6   Barlow (1996).

BOX 6.1 BARLOW'S DECLARATION OF CYBERSPACE INDEPENDENCE

Governments of the Industrial World, you weary giants of flesh and steel, I come from Cyberspace, the new home of Mind. On behalf of the future, I ask you of the past to leave us alone. You are not we come among us. You have no sovereignty where we gather.

We have no elected government, nor are we likely to have one, so I address you with no greater authority than that with which liberty itself always speaks. I declare the global social space we are building to be naturally independent of the tyrannies you seek to impose on us. You have no moral right to rule us nor do you possess any methods of enforcement we have true reason to fear.

Governments derive their just powers from the consent of the governed. You have neither solicited nor received ours. We did not invite you. You do not know us, nor do you know our world. Cyberspace does not lie within your borders. Do not think that you can build it, as though it were a public construction project. You cannot. It is an act of nature and it grows itself through our collective actions.

You have not engaged in our great and gathering conversation, nor did you create the wealth of our marketplaces. You do not know our culture, our ethics, or the unwritten codes that already provide our society with more order than could be obtained by any of your impositions.

You claim there are problems among us that you need to solve. You use this claim as an excuse to invade our precincts. Many of these problems don't exist. Where there are real conflicts, where there are wrongs, we will identify them and address them by our means. We are forming our own Social Contract. This governance will arise according to the conditions of our world, not yours.

Our world is different.

Cyberspace consists of transactions, relationships, and thought itself, arrayed like a standing wave in the web of our communications. Ours is a world that is both everywhere and nowhere, but it is not where bodies live.

We are creating a world that all may enter without privilege or prejudice accorded by race, economic power, military force, or station of birth.

We are creating a world where anyone, anywhere may express his or her beliefs, no matter how singular, without fear of being coerced into silence or conformity.

Your legal concepts of property, expression, identity, movement, and context do not apply to us. They are all based on matter, and there is no matter here.

Our identities have no bodies, so, unlike you, we cannot obtain order by physical coercion. We believe that from ethics, enlightened self-interest, and the commonweal, our governance will emerge. Our identities may be distributed across many of your jurisdictions. The only law that all our constituent cultures would generally recognize is the Golden Rule. We hope we will be able to build our particular solutions on that basis. But we cannot accept the solutions you are attempting to impose.

In the United States, you have today created a law, the Telecommunications Reform Act, which repudiates your own Constitution and insults the dreams of Jefferson, Washington, Mill, Madison, DeToqueville, and Brandeis. These dreams must now be born anew in us.

You are terrified of your own children, since they are natives in a world where you will always be immigrants. Because you fear them, you entrust your bureaucracies with the parental responsibilities you are too cowardly to confront yourselves. In our world, all the sentiments and expressions of humanity, from the debasing to the angelic, are parts of a seamless whole, the global conversation of bits. We cannot separate the air that chokes from the air upon which wings beat.

In China, Germany, France, Russia, Singapore, Italy and the United States, you are trying to ward off the virus of liberty by erecting guard posts at the frontiers of Cyberspace. These may keep out the contagion for a small time, but they will not work in a world that will soon be blanketed in bit-bearing media.

Your increasingly obsolete information industries would perpetuate themselves by proposing laws, in America and elsewhere, that claim to own speech itself throughout the world. These laws would declare ideas to be another industrial product, no more noble than pig iron. In our world, whatever the human mind may create can be reproduced and distributed infinitely at no cost. The global conveyance of thought no longer requires your factories to accomplish.

These increasingly hostile and colonial measures place us in the same position as those previous lovers of freedom and self-determination who had to reject the authorities of distant, uninformed powers. We must declare our virtual selves immune to your sovereignty, even as we continue to consent to your rule over our bodies. We will spread ourselves across the Planet so that no one can arrest our thoughts.

We will create **a** civilization of the Mind in Cyberspace. May it be more humane and fair than the world your governments have made before.

Davos, Switzerland, February 8, 1996

real world, since the internet is run and used by humans and when things go wrong on the internet, there are real human consequences. Therefore although the separatist point of view is considered and examined, it is from the viewpoint of an inclusionist.

Barlow does not accept this view. In his opening paragraph, he addresses the 'weary giants of flesh and steel', whereas he states that he comes from 'the new home of Mind'. Human beings will always be the controllers of the internet. However indirectly, it is the human will which directs robots to use the internet,[7] and it is the human mind which has created the internet. The internet can never be separated from this innate link to humans. To argue that the internet is the new Mind is treacherous to the very being and uniqueness of the human evolution.

Barlow moves on to rightly point out that cyberspace has no elected government, thereby identifying the very essence of the problem of governance and control. If there is no democracy, then who runs the internet and who makes the rules? There is no elected government because there is no body within the internet. To have an elected government to control the internet, there needs to be human intervention. Barlow's declaration was written 14 years ago and the debate as to who has jurisdiction and governance is still proceeding. The opinion expressed in the declaration is that humans 'are not welcome' and that humans 'have no sovereignty'. These statements are harmful to the movement towards protecting the individual who uses the internet for business and social interactions. To have a wealth of information laid out for the use of humans without

---

7   BBC News, 'Robots to Get their Own Internet', 9 February 2011, http://www.bbc.co.uk/news/technology-12400647, accessed 9 February 2011.

control or governance will prove to be harmful to the well-being of human life and the morals by which we abide. Indeed the statement has been thwarted through legislation that controls pornographic sites as well as providing legal remedies for intellectual property disputes and contractual issues. Whether Barlow et al. like it or not, real world laws do have an impact. Why is this? The reason is because inherently humans have a need to protect others and to create a society which is fair and safe. We question later in the chapter whether this need for protection goes too far in instances where states limit their people's use of the internet and therefore their freedom of information, speech and communication. A modicum of control should be exercised. Barlow goes on to say that humans 'have no right to rule over us and no moral right to rule us'. The right to rule is contained in the right of humans who created the internet, the right of users and the right to protect the vulnerable. It is irresponsible to say that we humans have no right to govern when there are real world consequences.

Moving through Barlow's speech, in his third paragraph Barlow makes the claim that humans do not know the users of the internet or cyberspace and that it does not lie within our borders. Again, it can be contended that this is wrong: the users of the internet are human, as are those who understand the remit of the internet. It is implausible to state such an assumption and does not make theoretical sense. The internet, although cross-jurisdictional in places, lies within the earth's realm and as such within our (human) borders. Barlow's assumption that we (humans) do not know the culture, ethics or unwritten codes of the internet is nonsense, since it is ours – we have created it. Humans cannot be seen as discrete entities from the internet. Yet Barlow continues to opine that the people of cyberspace are creating their own social contract. If this were true, then 14 years later, we should be able to see it and use it. The further assumption that their world is different from ours can be refuted through the laws of physics. We created the internet; it cannot be anything but a human creation with human physical restraints. As we shall see later, Lessig[8] is of the opinion that both the real and the virtual worlds can be set upon the foundation of four issues, the difference between them being the architecture of the worlds. The real world architecture operates through nature's laws; on the internet it is mediated through human creation and imagination.

Barlow states that they are 'creating a world where anyone, anywhere may express his or her beliefs, no matter how singular, without fear of being coerced into silence or conformity'. This is a dangerous assumption and set of beliefs. It is not a matter of inhibiting civil liberties to have a

---

[8]   Lessig (1995–6).

method of controlling the internet; rather it is a means of creating a safe environment where children and the vulnerable will not be preyed upon by the prejudices and beliefs which we as humans hold to be harmful and against our moral codes. A place where 'anything' goes can only hold harmful consequences for human beings.

Going beyond this, Barlow proclaims that 'your legal concepts of property, expression, identity, movement and context do not apply to us'. Legally, over the past 14 years the courts have succinctly disagreed with Barlow. Barlow further opines that 'the only law that all our constituent cultures would generally recognize is the Golden Rule', this being 'Remember the Human'. In other words, users of cyberspace, in whatever capacity they are using it, must remember that there are humans out there. This one singular rule encompasses, if we really think about it, all the inherent moral codes and beliefs that we as humans live by. This therefore recognises the importance of the human and the human interaction with cyberspace. In fact, it acknowledges that without humans there would be no internet. Why then, is it so important to have a distinct set of laws when users must abide by the Golden Rule which encompasses all human moral codes and norms? Why should it be seen as them and us, for the Golden Rule is inclusive in its very nature? An answer to this could be the argument that the internet embodies freedom of information, freedom of communication and freedom of knowledge. Barlow typifies this argument by naming several countries that restrict the use of cyberspace within their territories. Barlow insists the internet should span borders and frontiers and argues that by interfering with the cyberspace realm, governments are restricting the very essence of the internet: freedom of information across borders.

Although it is the opinion of this author that information in countries should not be restricted in such a way as to breech human right laws, the internet should not have separate laws for the real world since the virtual world has real world consequences. No matter how idyllic use of the Golden Rule is, human beings, in the real world, breach these rules and just stating 'remember there are humans out there' will not prevent wrongdoing and crimes being committed. As we can see, 14 years after this declaration was written, more and more crime is being committed online. The Golden Rule has since been used as the catalyst for developing what is known as Netiquette, the rules which govern the internet. These will be discussed later in the chapter. What this chapter will now discuss is the development of the argument between separatists and inclusionists and how democracy and governance can be built in cyberspace. Furthermore, the chapter will also argue that although the laws for the internet in general can be discussed in this fashion, thought must also be given to the virtual worlds. In essence, the virtual worlds are a world within the internet and when economic crime is committed within them, how do we, as regulators, manage to control and govern them?

The questions to be considered in this chapter are the following:

- Who can govern the internet?
- How is the internet different from the virtual world?
- Who holds the democratic authority to decide what is right and wrong within the virtual worlds?
- Can you implement laws within the internet and thus virtual worlds?
- Can virtual world laws be part of the real world legal system, and if so, of what legal system, or are they separate from the real world?
- How can you impose laws on a virtual world which crosses borders and jurisdictions?
- Where can people who have committed a wrong in a virtual world be held accountable?

During the following discussion we shall consider these questions and although there may not be a satisfactory answer or conclusion to many of them, it is important to discuss them. We can be sure that economic crime and money laundering is occurring within virtual worlds. We can be sure that it is having an effect on the real world and real human beings. We know that it is real humans who have committed these acts of wrongdoing. What are we are unclear about is if there is any law present to prevent this from occurring.

LAWS OF CONSTRAINT

One of the first things that must be considered is the notion of what is the internet and where is it located. As we have discussed previously, the internet was designed as a method of communication for the military. The growth of the internet has been enormous, surpassing anyone's expectations. The internet is a global system of interconnected computer networks that use the standard Internet Protocol Suite (TCP/IP) to serve billions of users worldwide. It is a *network of networks* that consists of millions of private, public, academic, business, and government networks, of local to global scope, that are linked by a broad array of electronic, wireless and optical networking technologies. Therefore there is not just one network to govern but many. Within these networks and on the internet, there are many virtual worlds. To gain access to these networks and thus virtual worlds a person has to register with an Internet Service Provider

(ISP). These IPSs are private companies that offer their customers access to the internet through their network. You can already see that even within one country there are many networks with many ISPs. This poses problems when tracking users down. Adding an additional layer of complexity is the use of networks which are not registered to a person but to a company, such as a business, a university or an internet café, where access to the internet is provided by the person contracting with the IPS, not the person using the internet. Therefore accountability can be lost. Just as this is the case for one country, so it is also the case for another country, and when a person uses the internet and accesses data from another country, they may cross thousands of networks and hundreds of jurisdictions. This is why economic crime and money laundering are so difficult to monitor and control within the internet, but the difficulties are compounded when the crime takes place within a virtual world.

Bond[9] outlines that there is also potential liability for a game developer as well as for ISP providers. For instance, liability could rest with the game developer in the design of the platform, access to the platform and/ or control of the platform. The E-commerce Directive 2000 has already had a host of cases which have set standards for content and host or access providers. However, as Bond notes, virtual worlds have not come under such scrutiny and as such there is no legal precedent as to what is acceptable and where liability rests. The E-commerce Directive, which is intended to provide guidelines for Member States in regulating the liability of information providers, determines that, under Article 15 para 1, there is no general obligation on a provider to monitor the information which they transmit. The E-commerce Directive is not directly applicable since Member States need only interpret the Directive in a manner which fits best with their individual policies on regulation.

In other words, virtual worlds add another layer of Internet 'bubble' around the crime. As we have discussed, a virtual world is a world within the internet that provides space for people to create their own world in which to live. Many are worlds without laws or rules but that do have an effect on the real world. Academic debate has occurred as to whether the internet should be real world law free, as Barlow declares above, overlooking his indiscretion in using the Golden Rule, thus negating his whole argument. Others believe that a legal system should be in place to provide protection to end users. After all, it is humans who are using the Internet and participating in virtual worlds. Moreover, there is another point of contention in that there is a belief that the internet is not global but rooted

---

[9] Bond (2009).

in state control, in other words *Lex Electronica*. In other words, the internet and control of the internet are governed by each country's own laws.

As Schultz states, 'the Internet and its regulation cannot be seen a single phenomenon',[10] therefore for regulation to work effectively, we need to 'challenge the conventional wisdom that the Internet is inexorably global'.[11] Zekos propounds that sovereignty of any one state is founded on the notion of territories and in the case of the internet, there are no boundaries which signify territories. Schultz argues that the answers may be found in the 'reconsideration of private international law standards in the light of public international law standards of jurisdiction'.[12] He argues in 'favour of double standards of jurisdiction for the regulation of internet content; one based on the principle of targeting, used to sanction behaviour, the other an incarnation of the effects doctrine, used to prevent actions and fulfil the cathartic function of law'.[13] Furthermore, Shultz believes that regulation of the internet is entirely possible and indeed integral to its importance in society. The idea that the internet is a borderless world[14] has dominated jurisprudential thinking about internet law for many years. Today we can move on and see that in fact the internet does have borders and can be regulated.

The problem with the internet is that it has no central authority through which all communications can flow.[15] This is known as cloud computing and demonstrates the unpredictability of the route communication through the internet will take. Zittrain[16] represents this as shown in Figure 6.1.

The intention of the internet creators was to create a world connected through networks, where computers spoke one common language (internet protocol language) and thus created a global network. However, through day-to-day use of the internet, aspects of undesirable behaviour occurred and the internet community has moved away from a desire to have the internet recognised as a single entity towards having many entities under the umbrella of the name internet. The internet community has largely, according to Engle and Keller, decided that they want each country to decide on the regulation of the internet according to their own values and moral

---

[10]   Schultz (2008), p. 801.
[11]   Ibid.
[12]   Ibid., p. 800.
[13]   Ibid.
[14]   For examples of this thinking see Goldsmith and Wu (2006), 181–3 and Benkler (2006).
[15]   For more information see Zittrain (2003), at p. 13.
[16]   Zittrain (2003b), at p. 656.

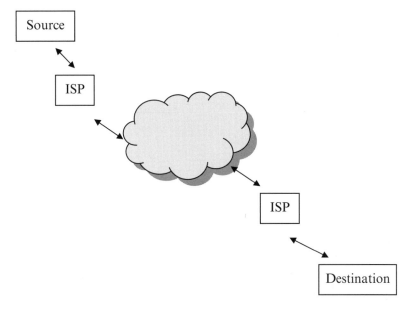

Figure 6.1   Zittrain's representation of the unpredictability of the route of communication

code.[17] Therefore the notion that the internet is borderless is false. Each country's own law and moral codes depict what is and what is not acceptable to be published on the internet. Schultz argues that 'safeguarding local values is one of the foundational roles of the state'.[18] Therefore this social contract must be upheld in relation to the Internet. It is this notion which leads us into the realms of sovereignty and jurisdiction. If each country has an overwhelming need and right to protect their own country, and each country's set of laws differs in relation to the protection right, then the internet, which does cross boundaries, could be in breach of those laws in another country. The idea of where jurisdiction lies is often debated[19] and will be considered later in the chapter, but for now we shall consider the application of constraints in both the virtual and the real world.

Lessig[20] is one of the main commentators advocating a continuation of laws for cyberspace which mirror those in the real world. Lessig does

---

17   Engle and Keller (2002), at pp. 46ff.
18   Schultz (2008), p. 806.
19   Wang (2008).
20   Lessig (1998), p. 2.

not see the internet or cyberspace as being an entity distinct from the real world. His work has drawn upon inferences of real world application in cyberspace.[21] Lessig sees that any type of behaviour, whether conducted in the real world or the virtual, is constrained by four factors. These are:

1. Law
2. Social norms
3. Market and price
4. Nature and architecture.[22]

Law is but one of four restraints on people's behaviour and it is how the government or people in control monitor and regulate these that can affect the outcome of the application of the law. Laws regulate by issuing sanctions, so that anyone who does not comply will be punished through a sanction imposed by the rule maker. The second constraint, social norms, refers to those socially accepted trends which depict how one will behave in society. For example, if you drink a cup of tea, you drink it from the cup rather than the saucer. The third constraint Lessig identifies is that of the marketplace, which sets the price of goods and what one is willing or can afford to pay for them. Lessig notes that, through the device of price, the market sets many opportunities and the range of opportunities available is regulated. Finally, Lessig opines that nature or architecture constrains behaviour. Lessig states that this constraint is 'the constraint of the world as I find it, even if this world as I find it is a world that others have made'. For example, if no one has made a ramp to the library then you cannot go up the ramp.[23] If in the real world gravity and bone structure means you cannot fly, you cannot fly. However, in the realms of cyberspace worlds, this architecture can be changed via the coding of the program, thus allowing a ramp to be present or a human avatar to fly.

The one major variance between real world constraints and virtual world or cyberspace constraints is that of anonymity, which is built into the architecture of cyberspace through code. In cyberspace, 'hiding who you are, or more precisely features about who you are is the simplest thing in the world. The default in cyberspace is anonymity'.[24] Lessig believes this is the key to 'regulability – the ability of governments to regulate

---

[21] Ibid.; Lessig (1995–6); Lessig, et al. (2002); Lessig (1999, 2001a, 2001b, 2003).

[22] Lessig (1998), p. 2.

[23] Ibid., p. 2.

[24] Ibid., p. 6.

behaviour there'.[25] A consequence of this use of code or architecture, Lessig has previously argued, is that 'it renders [cyberspace] essentially unregulable'.[26] Lessig believes that cyberspace 'has the potential to be the antithesis of a space of freedom'[27] contrary to the mainstream view that 'cyberspace is unregulable. [Where] [n]o national can live without it, yet no nation will be able to control it'.[28] This now rather out-of-date view was anticipated by Lessig in 1998. Throughout his writing on the subject, Lessig has criticised this notion of cyberspace as unregulated; arguing rather that the manner in which cyberspace is regulated must recognise the four constraints, as outlined above. He believes that the laws, norms, marketplace and architecture in cyberspace do regulate the internet. It is not the actions of the individuals within the space but locating the people who commit acts of wrongdoing. Lessig calls this the 'regulability of Cyberspace'.[29] In other words, regulability is the government's ability to regulate behaviour in cyberspace. 'Cyberspace is a less regulable space than real space. There is less that governments can do'.[30] However, Lessig believes that to get round an unregulable cyberspace governments need to govern within state boundaries of jurisdiction. It is when the internet crosses state or country boundaries that the internet, due to its anonymity, becomes unregulable. Lessig also notes that within cyberspace there are many different architectures which are controlled and monitored by many different governments. Each of these different architectures reflects the political will of the government. Therefore the architecture for the internet is akin to it having its own constitution. Lessig's argument is as follows:

> It sets the terms upon which people get access; it sets the rules, it control their behaviour. In this sense it is its own sovereignty. An alternative sovereignty, competing with real space sovereigns, in the regulation of behaviour by real space citizens.[31]

Although we can draw comparisons with the real world, it must not be forgotten that cyberspace constraints and sovereignty are not the same as in the real world. In cyberspace, architecture can be changed; therefore the rules, remit and the law can be changed through a change of code. Lessig

25 Ibid.
26 Ibid.
27 Ibid.
28 Ibid.
29 Ibid.
30 Ibid.
31 Ibid., p.9.

believes that this is where the judiciary and theorists keep causing confusion in regulation issues concerning the internet. Governments cannot regulate the behaviour of people on the internet because of the inherent freedom that the internet bestows. However, what the government can do to directly influence behaviour is to regulate the architecture. In other words, the government can regulate to change the very regulability of the space so that behaviour in cyberspace becomes more 'regulable'.[32] Lessig argues that, as in the real world, we could have passports in cyberspace too, enabling governments to track our movements so that if there is a crime committed, then the problem of anonymity is negated. However, this does pose issues of freedom of speech and movement and liberty and control within cyberspace and will be covered later in the chapter. For now if we take this idea, we can see that it does allow governments to control and regulate and monitor the behaviour of internet users through the control and regulation of the architecture of the net. What should be taken into account, according to Lessig, is 'to find a way to translate what is salient and important about present day liberties and constitutional democracy into this architecture of the net'.[33] Furthermore, we as citizens of the real and the virtual worlds must also be as critical of the emerging governance of the net as we would be of any laws affecting our lives. Doing so would produce a democratic authority which could control behaviour on the net. Lessig therefore sees that the internet is regulated by laws of constraint and that these mirror those of the real world with some differences. The process of regulability over people's behaviour on the net is an organic process which requires us all to participate in monitoring and criticising its development. 'Code is an efficient means of regulation'.[34] What does become problematic though is when the real world government is overtly controlling freedom of information and as such does not allow its citizens this right of information. There will certainly be tension between local, national and international sovereignty over rule application and code alterations. This tension will create voids in compliance and agreement and allow criminal activity to flourish. What is important is that Lessig sees regulation being controlled by governments over their jurisdictions. Whether there can be a single set of rules for the internet to govern all people who use it regardless of their physical location is yet to be decided.

---

[32]   Ibid., p. 11.
[33]   Ibid., p. 15.
[34]   Lessig (1995–6), p. 1408.

NETIQUETTE

In this chapter we have discussed two opposing views. The first is one offered by Barlow, who believes the internet is an entity separate from the real world, where laws and governance are bespoke to cyberspace. The other view, is offered by Lessig, who believes that laws are present in cyberspace but that behaviour can be controlled and monitored by governments through the fragmentation of regulation of the architecture. We move on to dispel the reasoning offered by Barlow in his 'Declaration of Independence of Cyberspace'. In Barlow's pronouncement, he states: 'The only law that all our constituent cultures would generally recognize is the Golden Rule'.[35] This Golden Rule comes from Netiquette. *Netiquette*, a book written by Virginia Shea in 1994, was updated online in 1997.[36] It articulates the do's and don'ts of online interaction. The intentions of the core rules proposed by Shea are for 'net newbies' who may forget that when online their actions may have real world consequences. These being:

- *Rule 1:* Remember the human
- *Rule 2:* Adhere to the same standards of behaviour online that you follow in real life
- *Rule 3:* Know where you are in cyberspace
- *Rule 4:* Respect other people's time and bandwidth
- *Rule 5:* Make yourself look good online
- *Rule 6:* Share expert knowledge
- *Rule 1:7* Help keep flame wars under control
- *Rule 1:* 8 Respect other people's privacy
- *Rule 1:* 9 Don't abuse your power
- *Rule 1:* 10 Be forgiving of other people's mistakes

Rule number 1 is the Golden Rule, as referenced and used by Barlow. The Golden Rule or rule number 1, remember the human, dispels Barlow's argument that the users of cyberspace are separate from the real world. By remembering the human, Barlow is acknowledging that every act or behaviour undertaken on the internet has a real world effect and that users must be aware of this. It acknowledges the constraints on both worlds as outlined by Lessig above. The Golden Rule therefore accepts the presence of law in the virtual world and makes the statement offered by Barlow obsolete.

---

35 Barlow (1996).
36 Shea (1994).

Rule 2 is also important as it enforces the same standards of law and ethics within cyberspace. Shea asserts that sometimes in cyberspace people are tempted to commit crimes they normally would not, because they think the chances of getting caught are slim.[37] Shea notes that 'this is a book on manners, not a legal manual. However, Netiquette mandates that you do your best to act within the laws of society and cyberspace'.[38] Therefore the set of rules which Barlow bases all his cyberspace governance on comes, in fact, from a book about manners assimilated from the behavioural norms and laws of the real world. Rule 8 also outlines the importance of privacy and copyright and enforces the need to abide by the laws of the country the user is in. Thus, it asserts the basic foundation that although the Internet can be considered as a separate entity, it is based on the rules and governance of the real world.Within this book we are concerned with the regulation of economic crime within virtual worlds. From Lessig we can assert that there are rules present on the internet and within each country's jurisdiction such that users' behaviour can be controlled through the use of architecture and code alteration. From Barlow, despite his argument in the declaration of independence, there is a notion that despite the division of the worlds, the users of cyberspace must 'remember the human', and therefore not act outside the remit of real world constraints. The question is, therefore, how is law from the real world translated into the virtual worlds through the middle layer of internet and cyberspace? For example, if we see the real world as the inner layer of a circle, with the internet being the middle layer and the virtual worlds being the outer circle, it is hard to transpose real world laws into the many virtual worlds through the many internet service providers (see Figure 6.2). Regulation of the internet has and is being discussed, but regulation of the virtual world is one step removed from this discussion as the regulations or change in code has to transverse yet another layer of anonymity and jurisdictional lines.

Figure 6.2 shows the inherent difficulties in regulating not only the internet but the virtual worlds. From many jurisdictions, real world laws pass through many ISPs to many virtual worlds. It is almost impossible to monitor, control and regulate the origins and the end of one law passing through these complex coding systems. The question posed above, 'how is the internet different from the virtual worlds?' amounts to this: a complex web of interconnected networks, each providing access to different virtual worlds. Thus virtual worlds add another layer of complexity

---

[37]   Ibid.
[38]   Ibid.

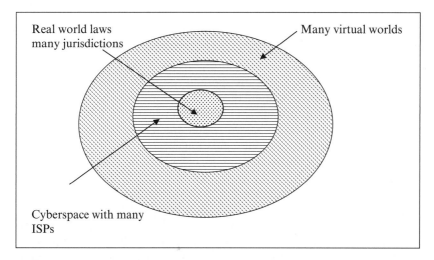

Figure 6.2   Layers of cyberspace

to the jurisdictional issues of cyberspace. To regulate and monitor virtual worlds is even harder for state authorities because of the lack of accountability and the anonymity of not only the end user but the ISP and the country's jurisdiction. The starting point therefore has to be to gauge what is achieved in terms of legality in cyberspace and to try to find a solution capable of transferring these complex webs of the net and virtual worlds. What is clear is that there needs to be international cooperation to maintain a level playing field across all jurisdictions over what is condoned as acceptable behaviour on the net. However, this would be very hard to achieve given the dramatic differences in countries' laws and applications of even basic human rights and civil liberties. Public policy and generally accepted norms would have to be considered, and again this poses issues, given societal differences globally. Whether a unified agreed set of rules can ever be agreed upon is nebulous at best. An additional issue is that that even if rules are agreed upon and the above issues are resolved, the organic evolution of the virtual worlds will ensure that the laws are out of date before they become applicable. The time sensitivity of laws within the virtual world means that real world laws will struggle to maintain pace with the technology. Reidenberg articulates that 'the current internet technology creates ambiguity or sovereign territory because network boundaries intersect and transcend national borders'.[39]

---

[39]   Reidenberg (2005).

LEGAL INTERACTION

To say that the internet or cyberspace is free from law is untrue. To say that virtual worlds are without laws is also untrue. However, the laws are not joined up; in other words, they are sporadic, piecemeal and do not provide the protection required. Why is this? Jurisdictions globally are struggling with the notion of cyberspace and how all the many networks, IPSs and virtual worlds can be encompassed within one set of rules of regulations. Within this section the laws and regulations which have been enacted will be discussed, along with some landmark cases in terms of jurisdiction over behaviour on the net. However, we cannot discuss all the laws applicable to the internet; rather we shall examine those that create the most important discussion points for us in terms of the questions outlined above.

Courts have had problems applying national and international decision in cases involving the internet. According to Reidenberg, the courts are 'ill-equipped' to deal with internet cases. Two cases which are essential to discuss are the Yahoo and Zippo cases.

Zippo[40]

In this case Zippo Manufacturing Company, based in Pennsylvania, is a company which makes the well-known Zippo lighters. Zippo DotCom is a company based in California which is internet based and offers access to USENET newsgroups. DotCom registered the name zippo.com and zippo.net. DotCom did not have a physical presence in Pennsylvania and had access to Pennsylvania only through the internet as with everywhere else. DotCom had entered into a contract with seven ISPs based in Pennsylvania to allow subscribers access to the USENET newsgroups. Manufacturing claimed that DotCom had infringed copyright and were guilty of false designation. DotCom claimed that they did not have personal jurisdiction to be held accountable. In other words, they were not physically present in Pennsylvania for the courts to have jurisdiction over their company. The courts dismissed this and said that personal jurisdiction for internet companies must be decided on a sliding scale using a three stage test. The court must take into account that 'the likelihood that personal jurisdiction can be constitutionally exercised is directly proportionate to the nature and quality of the commercial activity that an entity conducts over the internet'.[41] This case is seen as a seminal case,

---

[40] *Zippo Mfr. Co. v. Zippo Dot Com, Inc.*, 952 F. Supp. 1119 (W.D. Pa. 1997).
[41] Ibid.

determining the minimum standard of contact that can be used to establish jurisdiction.[42] Though *Zippo* is not without its critics, it has been used in five federal appellate court cases. The judges within the case did not decide on what would amount to 'interactivity' of a website, as might have been expected, so as to avoid a floodgate of litigation. Furthermore, the notion of interactivity is less relevant now due to the increasing interactivity contained on the majority of all websites.

The US further developed an alternative to establishing jurisdiction over the internet in *Calder v. Jones*.[43] In this case, Calder brought a suit against Florida residents who published libellous materials about her in the newspapers. The courts decided that it was the 'effect' of the matter which constituted her jurisdiction in the case. In other words, the emotional suffering and distress, as well as harm to her reputation, was deeply felt in California where she lived and not just on the internet. The court acknowledged that this 'effect' test established by the case does not apply with the same force to corporations as it does to individuals.[44]

Yahoo[45]

The *Yahoo* case is a landmark case which demonstrates how courts are willing to apply their nation or state's moral or legal code on a multinational platform such as the internet. In this case, the plaintiffs filed suit against Yahoo because a French auction site containing anti-Semitic and Nazi-related paraphernalia was accessible via French Yahoo on Yahoo.com. In the first case, the French court held that French users of the auction site were contravening French law. The court ordered Yahoo to inform all users of the potential risk of using the site and also to make it impossible for Yahoo.com users to find the auction site. Yahoo argued that the French court had no jurisdiction over this issue as its defendants were in the US. The court responded by rejecting Yahoo's claim and appointed consultants to help Yahoo to comply with the findings.[46] The Director of Yahoo.fr, Philippe Guillanton, said in response to the case: 'The point is whether we want the internet to be closed the same way that

---

[42] Wang (2011), p 68

[43] *Calder v. Jones*, 465, US 783 (1984).

[44] *Calder v. Jones*, 465, US 783 (1984); *Cybersell, Inc. v Cybershell, Inc.*, 130, F. 3d 414, 420 (9th Circuit 1997).

[45] *Ligue contre le racisme et l'antisémitisme et Union des étudiants juifs de France c. Yahoo! Inc. et Société Yahoo! France* (*LICRA v. Yahoo!*) 2000.

[46] Akdenzi (2001).

the media have traditionally been closed by frontiers'.[47] Several years since the court's decision, this statement can be looked at again and although freedom of information is still integral to the internet, when it affects the real world and has real world consequences, its remit must surely be curtailed.

The *Yahoo* case demonstrated that the first wave of cases sought to deny jurisdiction, choice of law and enforcement to states where users and victims are located, constituting a type of 'denial or service attack against the legal system'.[48] The view that the technology does not exist to establish sufficient contact for jurisdiction is expounded by internet separatists. This standpoint means that separatists view the state as being unable to protect their citizens from online matters. Reidenberg, however, argues the opposite to this opinion and believes that because technology keeps advancing, technology itself will be able to uphold law and the rule of law.[49] Reidenberg comments on this irony by stating; 'just as the internet attack uses technological infrastructure to challenge jurisdiction technological innovation also empowers sovereign states to assert their rules on internet activity'.[50]

CYBER JURISDICTION

Within this section an overview will be provided of the international regulation of the internet. The internet has three levels of regulation, these being direct regulation of the internet infrastructure itself; regulation of activities that can be conducted only over the internet; and regulation of activities which can be, but need not be, conducted over the internet.[51] According to Froomkin, the first sphere of direct regulation of the internet infrastructure itself includes: (a) standards of communication, (b) the equipment used to provide and access internet communication, (c) intermediaries engaged in the provision of internet communications, e.g. ISPs.

The second sphere relates to the regulation of activities that can be

---

[47] BBC News, 'France Bans Internet Nazi Auctions.' 23 May 2000, http:// news.bbc.co.uk/1/hi/world/europe/760782.stm, accessed 23 February 2011.

[48] Reidenberg (2005), p. 1953.

[49] Ibid.

[50] Ibid., p. 1960.

[51] Froomkin, A. M. 'International and National Regulation of the Internet', University of Miami School of Law, froomkin@law.miami.edu, submitted 8 December 2003, http://law.tm/docs/International-regulation.pdf, accessed 28 February 2011.

conducted only over the internet and which have no significant offline analogues. The third sphere is where there is regulation of activities which may or may not be conducted over the internet, e.g. e-commerce in both tangible and intangible goods. This can be divided into categories too, for example some internet versions of an activity may be regulated in a different way from an online version or where special regulations are devised because use of the internet makes existing rules impossible to implement, such as e-cash or e-banking.[52] It is therefore very difficult to come to a consensus nationally or internationally on what should or should not be implemented to regulate Internet activities. The regulations which are in place to regulate contractual activity on the internet are as follows. Contractual activities are important here as this is where most of the legislation is found due to the expansion of business and commerce via the net. We can draw inferences from international cooperation in e-commerce situations and transpose these to virtual economies.

In the EU, the UNCITRAL (United Nations Commission on International Trade Law) model law on Electronic Commerce and the UN Convention on the Use of Electronic Communications in International Contracts do not contain any jurisdiction provisions.[53] Furthermore, the EC Directive on Electronic Commerce[54] does not provide further clarification on private international law or court jurisdiction. The Brussels I Regulation, based on the old Brussels Convention, provides some remit of jurisdiction guidance in the absence of legislation in the EU. Article 2 of the Brussels I Regulation provides the general jurisdiction rule which states that any defendant who is domiciled in any one of the contracting states shall be sued at their place of domicile. Therefore whether the person is an individual or a corporation, Brussels I regulation provides general jurisdiction based on domicile regardless of nationality.[55] Article 5 provides the claimant with the opportunity to derogate from the general provision just mentioned and allows the defendant to be sued despite their domicile being outside the Member States. However, these are general considerations of jurisdiction under the banner of contract law and not criminal economic law. Within the US there are two types of jurisdiction, general and specific, and as can be seen above, jurisdiction is interpreted liberally by the courts. The use of establishing a criminal jurisdiction falls under the guise of personal jurisdiction.

---

52 Ibid.
53 Wang (2008).
54 Recital 23 and Article 1(4) of Directive 2000/21/EC.
55 Article 60 Brussels I Regulation.

The Organisation for Economic Co-operation and Development (OECD) is an 'intergovernmental organisation whose purpose is to provide its 29 Member countries with a forum in which governments can compare their experiences, discuss the problems they share and seek solutions which can then be applied within their own national contexts'.[56]

Chik believes that 'the speed at which information technology has developed requires a faster, more reactive and automatic response for the law and that is not currently met by the existing law-making framework'.[57] Chik therefore propounds a new method of law which is separate from private and public international law: customary internet-ional law, a term coined by using custom and practice as a means of agreeing on an international standard of internet regulation. Chik's proposed new methods of law will be examined later in the chapter when we discuss different theorists' approaches to internet law regulation.

SEPARATISTS, INCLUSIONISTS AND LEGAL PLURALISM – NOT TO MENTION SELF-REGULATION, NATIONAL REGULATION AND INTERNATIONAL REGULATION

It is not surprising that the regulation of the internet and especially the regulation of virtual worlds have no agreed legislative structure. Even a quick glance at the existing literature in the area is confusing at best and contradictory at worse. Within this section, the chapter will break the literature down into manageable and sensible chunks in order to achieve a more sensible overview of the area of regulation of the internet. However, what cannot be achieved in this book is a consensus of thought by academics and practitioners as to what is the best method of regulating the internet and this can be seen as one of the major pitfalls and stumbling blocks in the growth of Internet regulation.

There are many groups into which theorists and academics can be categorised when discussing the regulation of the internet: separatists, inclusionists, legal pluralists, realists and liberalists. In addition to these three groups of theorists there are those who determine how regulation should be and these can also be seen as three separate groups: (1) self-regulation; (2) national regulation of the internet and (3) international cooperation. It

---

[56]   OECD, http://www.oecd.org/dsti/sti/it/index.htm, accessed 28 February 2011.
[57]   Chik (2010), p. 3.

is therefore important to clarify the situation according to how the authors view internet theory and regulation. It is by no means an inclusive list and the author does accept variations of beliefs and crossovers in beliefs, terminology and norms. However, if the author may beg indulgence and proffer the following summation for ease.

Before we turn to the issue of theorists we must tackle the regulation of the internet. The question constantly being asked is what is the regulation of the internet, who governs it and how can we use it to protect the ordinary citizen? Regulation of the internet can be seen in three ways as outlined above: (1) self-regulation; (2) national regulation of the internet and (3) international cooperation.

If we consider these in terms of economic virtual crime and not just regulation of the internet as a whole, self-regulation of the internet is where internet users themselves regulate and monitor behaviour on the internet. However, this poses several problems. Would normal users of the internet know about economic crime? Would they be able to spot economic crime occurring? Would they have the necessary tools to locate economic crime? Would they be able to do anything to prevent economic crime from occurring? Do they have the power to prevent economic crime? These questions would have to be answered in the negative for the majority of people using the internet.

The second method of regulating the internet is through national laws. This too poses problems such as cross-border jurisdictional issues and deciding upon who has the legitimate right to adjudicate on such matters. Similarly, if there are cross-border issues, which jurisdiction has precedence and should there be a difference in legislation on the same matter? Although, as we shall see shortly in the chapter, countries can use technological barriers to prevent users going outside a nation's borders in their use of the internet, which allows control by the government, this is rarely done in democratic societies and only in cases where there is an immediate threat present. Should jurisdictional issues arise in cross-border cases, the place and location of the server of the implicated IPS is often where jurisdiction is located. Furthermore, domicile of the implicated user has also been identified as a reasonable source of jurisdiction location. However, there is no standard or codified practice on this and certainly not for economic crime in virtual economies. Lessons from the jurisprudence of contractual law could be sought for best practice, but whether they can be assimilated into economic crime is nebulous. Contract law and criminal law have different standards of test which determine liability and therefore although the lessons could be pertinent, caution must be exercised in assimilating them in totality. Finally, regulation can be seen as international cooperation. As we have seen above, several law agencies have tried to implement legal standards that apply to all jurisdictions on the use and standards of the internet. This would be the most useful approach to apply in virtual economic crime. However, as with the other two forms of regulation, it poses problems. For example, to create an international law to control virtual economic crime, there would have to be an agreement from all countries as to who controlled the internet, who governed the internet laws, who would enforce the laws. There would also have to be an agreed set of rules by which countries would have to abide. This would be extremely difficult to achieve since a consensus would be nearly impossible to achieve at the present moment due to the complexity of economic crime and the acknowledgement that it poses a serious threat to public life.

Therefore it is hard to see what would be the best form of regulation for controlling virtual economic crime. In theory, an international agreement to prevent virtual economic crime would be best, since it would create a level playing field for all users of the internet. However, in practice obtaining agreement from all countries would be nearly impossible. Therefore the second-best option would be to have each individual country create rules and procedures under which virtual economic crime could be monitored and controlled. From this would flow an expectation that an international agreement would one day be reached. An international group could be created to advise governments on regulating virtual economic crime in their countries and this would hopefully permeate other countries' legislative frameworks.

A possible solution that could be offered to countries draws upon real world laws. In most real world legal systems, economic crime and money laundering are against the law. Criminals are using the internet to create new ways of committing crime and because of the network of ISPs and many virtual worlds, jurisdiction is hard to establish. Theoretically, though, if we take the inclusionist point of view, we can use real world laws to establish a legal system within virtual worlds. To enter a virtual world, everyone needs to go through an IPS in order to log onto the Internet and sign into the virtual world. Each IPS is registered and controlled in a real world jurisdiction. Each of these ISPs could ensure that all their users are required to sign a contract which overtly acknowledges that they shall not commit economic crime or launder money and that if they do so, they shall (a) be reported to the relevant authority and (b) have their ISP rights revoked and be banned from access to the internet for a period of time. This would allow each jurisdiction to deal with the person under their own legal system but also would prevent virtual worlds harbouring criminals. In many ways, this resembles the technological blocking which many countries use to prevent access to the internet. In the UK a Digital Economy Bill has been proposed to prevent illegal downloading of copyright sensitive materials from the internet. Many parallels can be drawn from this Bill. However, many questions still remain: e.g. how do you locate the criminal activity? International cooperation would be required. Who holds the power of jurisdiction over the internet? Should an international agreement be developed which would allow a standard of real world laws to be applicable to the virtual worlds? If so, would it follow the rule of law? Who holds the democratic authority to decide what is right and wrong within virtual worlds? To answer all these questions fully is outside the remit of this book, but as iterated above, would form part of a larger study into the jurisdiction of virtual worlds. Technological blocking will be covered later in the chapter.

If we move from the legal stance of regulation to the theoretical and philosophical stance of regulation, we can see even more divergence and nebulousness created among protagonists. At the beginning of this chapter, we discussed Barlow. Barlow is a separatist. He views the internet as a separate being from real world laws and as such, considers no real world laws should be placed in the realm of the internet. As we can see from the Declaration of the Independence of Cyberspace, the Internet, according to Barlow, should be free from human interference as this interference will only curtail the pure freedom of the internet. However, Barlow disproves his own theory when he states that the only rule that should be remembered is the 'Golden Rule': to remember the human. If any act done within the confines of the internet has an effect on the human being, then it should have real world laws applicable to it. Barlow is not alone, however, in his beliefs that the internet should have its own separate laws. Johnson and Post[58] also proclaim this view and argue against Lawrence Lessig, the main supporter for real world laws to be used within the virtual world. Johnson and Post see that because internet communication cuts across jurisdictions, this undermines the legitimacy of applying real world laws to new human activities.[59] Johnson and Post further argue that cyberspace 'needs and can create new law and legal institutions of its own'.[60] However, they ignore throughout their argument the real world effects that virtual world actions can have. The starting point of their assumption is that the physical location of the internet and the online act means that real world laws simply cannot apply to the internet. Therefore such laws should not be followed. They believe that the internet has no territorial boundaries. We can already see that this is not the case through the use

---

[58] Johnson and Post (1996); Johnson (2007).
[59] Johnson and Post (1996).
[60] Ibid.

of case law and existing legislation, legislating activities on the internet. Johnson and Post proclaim:

> The laws of any given place must take into account the special characteristics of the space it regulates and the types of persons, places and things found there. Just as a country's jurisprudence reflects its unique historical experience and culture, the law of cyberspace will reflect its special character, which differs markedly from anything found in the physical worlds.[61]

There are many contentious aspects of this statement. First, it can be conceded that each country does reflect its own individual characteristics, but this reflects the human life occupying that space. For the internet to have anything other than human characteristics when cyberspace has such an influence on the real world would be unthinkable. Secondly, cyberspace is not so different from the real world. Virtual worlds, although differing in architectural terms, do reflect the human world in many ways. To regulate it in any other way would be impossible, since it is human beings who will still monitor and regulate. Although cyberspace does pose interesting legal questions, it is still an earthly phenomenon and should be treated as such.

Another term for separatists is legal pluralism. Griffiths defines legal pluralism as the presence in a social field of more than one legal order.[62] Van den Bergh suggests that pluralism should be viewed not as a situation but as a process that develops in time, a complex pattern of continuous interactions.[63] Pluralism within the internet would suggest that it is possible to have more than one legal order, not in order to have several rules applicable to one situation, but to provide mechanisms that allow conflicting rules to co-exist, thereby enabling and encouraging their interaction. This would rightly describe the existence of cyber law created by those who use the internet as iterated by Barlow and Johnson and Post. However, there are many issues with this. First, although two systems may exist in one social field, legal pluralism does not suggest that it ignores the basic human laws already in existence. In fact, legal pluralism could be applied to the creation and existence of a universally applied law which regulated the internet in various fields which are of interest to all states. Johnson and Post require a system of rules quite distinct from the laws that regulate physical, geographically defined territories. Cyberspace challenges the law's traditional reliance on territorial borders; it is a 'space' bounded by

---

[61] Ibid.
[62] Griffiths (1986).
[63] Van den Bergh (1992).

screens and passwords rather than physical markers.[64] Professors Johnson and Post illustrate how 'taking Cyberspace seriously' as a unique place can lead to the development of both clear rules for online transactions and effective legal institutions.[65] Although the author agrees with Johnson and Post on the point that cyberspace must be taken seriously, Johnson and Post's work moves too far from the realms of reality to assist in the creation of a serious legal system.

Another school of thought regarding the regulation of the internet is that associated with Lawrence Lessig. Lessig[66] opposes the view of Johnson and Post and compares his view with that of Faber.[67] Faber proffers a three-tiered approach to legislative jurisdiction: the localist, the globalist and the evolutionary.[68] Lessig sees that there is a correlation between his work and the first two tiers of Faber's theory. Lessig notes, 'a localist looks for strong links with stuff that happens in local space before she claims an authority to regulate beyond her borders. A globalist is far less picky. Everything affects everything, the globalist insists, and our regulation should reach anything that affects this'.[69] Therefore if we take this analogy, we can see that Lessig, Faber and the author are globalists, for, to us, if something, i.e. economic crime, affects humans, then our regulation should be used to control and regulate it. Therefore an inclusionist theory is where the internet is seen as an international regime which must be governed by real world laws and beliefs.

Lessig's work has been discussed at length above in this chapter and therefore his views will not be repeated here, but will be used to critique those posed by the separatists. Lessig criticises Johnson and Post's theory[70] of cyberspace regulation for mixing up the first two of Faber's theories, in other words they see the internet as being both local and global at the same time. Johnson and Post state that the Internet is global and therefore everywhere, but at the same time it is nowhere as it cannot be pinned down.[71] Therefore its global-ness creates its

---

[64]   Jones, R., 'The Internet, Legal Regulation and Legal Pluralism', British and Irish Legal Education and Technology Conference, 27 and 28 March 1998, Dublin, http://www.bileta.ac.uk/Document%20Library/1/The%20Internet,%20 Legal%20Regulation%20and%20Legal%20Pluralism.pdf, accessed 1 March 2011.
[65]   Ibid.
[66]   Lessig (1995–6), pp. 1403–4.
[67]   Faber (1996).
[68]   Ibid.
[69]   Lessig (1995–6), p. 1404.
[70]   Johnson and Post (1996).
[71]   Ibid.

separateness.[72] They also state that it is local in so far as they insist that cyberspace does not affect the real world and therefore is self-contained. It cannot be everywhere and nowhere in one breath and local and self-contained in the next. This is not possible even for the virtual world. Lessig expounds that, 'There will be a law of cyberspace, it will be regulated by real space regulation to the extent that it affects real space life'.[73] This persuasive argument demonstrates the ability cyberspace has to create a new philosophical divide among academics and theorists. Lessig further claims that cyber law will evolve as a separate form of law driven by the needs of the real world and will arise because of the necessity to negate cross-border irregularities.[74] Lessig believes that a form of cyber common law will be developed and used by judiciaries around the globe to form a body of cyber common law which will allow cyber law as a distinct entity to be created. However, this law will reflect the needs and demands of the real world.

Johnson and Post's insistence that there will be a democracy in cyberspace,[75] where its citizens will regulate and control their actions within the space, is, as Lessig describes it, 'a romantic'[76] notion. 'The separation that they argue for comes then from the respect that we owe this autonomy'.[77] In other words, the separateness and utopian democracy that they believe is created by cyberspace stems from global rules and regulations which have taken millennia to evolve.

Lessig also points to the effectiveness of code alteration as a means of regulation and control. As discussed earlier in the chapter, we can see that if code is changed or altered in cyberspace, the architecture of the space is changed or regulated. According to Lessig, this form of regulation is not the same as abiding by a legal code where we as sentient human beings can choose whether to abide by it or not. Within cyberspace there is no way around a code change; you have no choice but to abide by it. This is a different form of jurisdiction and governance.[78] This is the perfect state where there is no law breaking but human nature's freedom of choice is curtailed. Lessig believes that cyberspace is changing and growing continually; for an effective legal system to evolve, it may be prudent to create zones for internet regulation. Zoning would allow larger groups of countries to develop a legal system or cyber common law which would later in cyberspace's

---

72   Lessig (1995–6), p. 1404.
73   Ibid., p. 1406.
74   Ibid., p. 1407.
75   Johnson and Post (1996).
76   Lessig (1995–6), p. 1407.
77   Ibid.
78   Ibid., p. 1408.

evolution be joined by other zones to create a utopian legal system. However, we are not there yet and due to the acts of crime being committed in cyberspace, action must be taken to prevent further acts of criminality from occurring. Finally, Lessig states that we cannot predict what the legal system of cyberspace will be like; rather it will evolve organically and through common law precedents, changing the path of cyber law.

As iterated above, Chik[79] believes that a new form of law will evolve for the internet and this will be based on custom and practice. This is very similar to Lessig's view of the cyber common law. Chik draws on the real world and states that, as in real space, law often follows 'change', therefore cyber law will be directly affected by occurrences in cyberspace. In this way, Chik argues for of a set of rules to be created which are based on customs and norms specially created to suit cyberspace stakeholders, relationships, transactions and environment with its idiosyncrasies.[80] Chick has termed this 'customary internet-ional law'. Furthermore, Chik believes that this is the default law-making device and will act to fill the gaps left by other laws of the real world, allowing the customary internet-ional law to develop organically.

The third theoretical position that will be covered within the chapter is that of internet liberalism. Liberalism is defined as a belief that politics should not be constrained by legally constituted boundaries. Classical liberalism is a philosophy which is rooted in the ideals of freedom of speech, communication, movement, economics and markets. It typifies a belief in progress and embraces the utilarian views offered by Jeremy Bentham (5 February 1748–6 June 1832) and John Stuart Mills (20 May 1806–8 May 1873).

Wu's[81] argument that Johnson and Post's descriptive assumptions that the 'territorial' powers of the world will, or already do, respect an emergent cyberspace sovereignty, and that state regulation of the internet will be impossible or futile, is incorrect, according to Jones.[82] Wu feels that 'Internet regulation, although difficult, is possible and stands to become increasingly so regardless of its desirability on normative grounds'.[83] Wu further opines the difficulty of internet regulation on an international platform by using liberal theory as a means of explanation. Several academics such as Wu and Netanel[84] have used Liberal theory or liberal democratic

---

[79]   Chik (2010).
[80]   Ibid.
[81]   Wu (1997).
[82]   Jones, 'The Internet, Legal Regulation and Legal Pluralism'.
[83]   Ibid.
[84]   Netanel (2000).

theory as a means of explaining internet regulation. Wu begins his argument by stating how liberal theory could be used as a form of regulation. He states the similarities between liberal theory and international regulation. The leap from there to cyberspace is synonymous with the thought that there are many different jurisdictions and principles within cyberspace. Wu states that there are three assumptions that liberal theory makes about international regulation. First, the primary actors are those individuals who constitute domestic societies or groups.[85] Secondly, governments represent some segment of domestic society[86] and thirdly, state behaviour will be determined by the configuration and the nature of state preferences.[87] Liberal theory, as Wu proclaims it, sees sovereignty as a much more flexible meeting of minds between states.[88] If we transpose this and the three assumptions above into cyberspace jurisdiction, we can see that each zone of cyberspace will be monitored and regulated in a different way as regulation will grow from the demands of the individual and the individual state. Therefore, in the example of economic crime, where states see this as a problem occurring frequently, regulation would be in place; in countries where it is less prevalent, regulation would be more flexible and soft. The idea is to control the problems that are occurring rather than to inhibit freedom on the internet. As such, politics or society should not be constrained by the constitution. Issues with cross-border jurisdictions would pose a problem under this arrangement, since questions would arise over where a perpetrator would be held accountable if his/her country of domicile had a soft approach to economic crime, but the crime occurred in a virtual world which was supplied and run by an ISP in another country which had a hard line on economic crime. An international agreement would have to be in place. Netanel bemoans the fact that 'the most egregious illiberal practices and norms of the virtual world demand the cautious, by resolute intervention of international institutions and the territorial liberal state'.[89]

Within this section we have heard from many different academics as to what is the best and most logical manner of regulating cyberspace and the internet, and thus also the virtual worlds. We have seen that on the one hand, internet regulation should be separate from real world laws since it

---

[85]   See: Moravcsik, A. Taking Preferences Seriously: A positive liberal theory of international politics, 1997, International Organisations, 51, 4, Autumn, pp. 513–53.

[86]   Moravcsik (1997).

[87]   Ibid.

[88]   Wu (1997), p. 662.

[89]   Netanel (2000).

is distinct and disassociated with the real world. A form of self-governance has been seen to be a better option for regulation. The organic and evolutionary growth of the Internet's own law-making institutions and legal system is what is considered to be the most logical according to separatists. On the other hand, there is an argument that every action that occurs in cyberspace or the internet has a real world effect and when these effects are criminal or harmful, then the person perpetrating them should be punishable by real world laws. This inclusionist view sees that real world laws must be applicable to cyberspace and the virtual worlds. The two spaces cannot be separated in real terms for they are one and the same; they are driven by humans and affect humans. The common element is the human being who creates and uses and develops this technology. Although both provide arguments, which have merits and demerits, it is the argument promulgated by the inclusionists which is taken up by the author and assimilated for the purposes of investigating economic crime in virtual worlds. Virtual worlds as seen above are contained within the many ISPs of computer networks. In other words, they are another layer removed from the real world. Yet they have real world effects. The inclusionist view would see jurisdiction lie with the real world. At present, there is no unanimous agreement on cyberspace internationally and many countries have little regulation of the internet, whilst others have extensive control and regulation over the use of the internet. In the next section, we shall look at what devices can be used to control access to information which states and countries deem to be inappropriate for their citizens. The chapter will then move on to examine the legitimacy of control of the internet and whether regulation of the internet is in line with the rule of law. However, the reader must keep in mind that this is from an inclusionist point of view, where regulation of the virtual worlds must first come from the countries themselves and eventually emanate from an international agreement.

TECHNOLOGICAL ENFORCEMENTS

One way in which governments can control the access of their people to the internet and the knowledge within is through technological enforcements and barriers. Reidenberg, as we have seen earlier in this chapter, demonstrates the logical assumption that through the use of technological developments the government can use advances in technology to control and maintain legal enforcement. Technological barriers are just this. By having a technological barrier to all or some of the internet, governments can control or limit what people can see and use on the internet and if a breach occurs, then they have jurisdiction over their people. Many countries use this method of limitation as a way of maintaining jurisdiction. Within the UK the government has introduced the Digital Economy Bill 2011.[90] The Bill is a response to the Digital Britain White Paper[91] and the technological advancements of recent years. One of the most controversial elements of the Bill aims to prevent illegal downloading and copyright infringement. The Bill states:

> Internet service providers would have to cooperate with copyright owners to help curb illegal sharing or downloading of material, initially using a system of notification letters to users associated with repeated infringement. Copyright owners would be able to apply to a court to identify individuals suspected of more serious breaches thus aiding legal action using the current enforcement system. If these changes prove ineffective at reducing online piracy, the Bill would allow for the introduction of technical measures, including internet disconnection, to be used as a last resort against the most serious offenders.

This would ensure that ISP providers are responsible for what is happening throughout their networks. This would be regulated by OfCom, the independent regulator and competition authority for the UK communication industries.[92] Although the government is enacting a technological border to inhibit and prevent illegal downloading and copyright infringement, similarities can be drawn and assimilated for the purposes of virtual economic crime. The Bill demonstrates the government intention to limit or prevent use of the internet by criminals through restrictions on their ISP. As economic crime is a criminal offence, a technological border could be imposed to prevent identified criminals from gaining access to the internet. However, through the use of internet cafés and free wi-fi space, people can gain free access to the internet in most communal places. However, with careful thought on all aspects of the crime, technological borders could allow jurisdictional issues to be ratified in accordance with the rule of law. Reidenberg states that 'for democratic societies, adherence to the rule of law means that the use of any technological enforcement instrument necessitates carefully prescribed authorisation criteria'.[93] Furthermore, the instrument chosen must be the 'least intrusive to accomplish rule enforcement'.[94] To ensure this, Reidenberg advises that four factors must be considered: (1) a state must weigh the magnitude of any threat to public order; (2) the urgency of

---

[90]   House of Commons, Digital Economy Bill, Bill 89, 2009–10, 29 March 2010.
[91]   Cm 7650, June 2009.
[92]   For more, visit: http://www.ofcom.org.uk/.
[93]   Reidenberg (2005), p. 1964.
[94]   Ibid.

the threat must be considered; (3) the state must evaluate the effectiveness of the tool used, and (4) the state must consider the ultimate enforcement goal.[95] Therefore if we consider these in relation to the threat of economic crime and money laundering, we can see that hypothetically speaking the government would regard economic crime and money laundering to be a great threat against public order. This is due to the causal link between money laundering and terrorist financing.[96] The urgency of the threat within the UK is present, real and highly likely and has been labelled severe by the Home Office.[97] Therefore if there is a causal link between virtual money laundering and economic crime and terrorist financing and the likelihood of a terrorist attack occurring, then we can see there is a need for technological barriers being in place even after stage two of the test. In the UK there is no tool currently in use to block terrorist financing through virtual economic crime, but should there be, then it must also meet stage three of the test, being able to evaluate the effectiveness of the tool. In other words, it must not prohibit any freedom of a person unless it is strictly necessary to directly prohibit economic crime. In other words, it must still adhere to basic human rights, but it must prevent what it sets out to prevent. Such a tool must therefore be carefully designed and built into any technological blocking system. Should the UK, or any other country, use this method of enforcement, then they must design the tool with the end enforcement goal in mind. The end goal is to prevent virtual money laundering and economic crime from occurring. A system must therefore be designed to prevent this. The end goal is not to prevent terrorist financing, since although there is a direct causal link to terrorist activities, economic crime is one step removed. The state must be careful to keep this consideration in mind so as to not to lose sight of the end goal. Terrorist financing is such an emotive subject that the end goal may be lost without careful and considered planning. Therefore, while any technological barriers must be implemented as a reaction to the problem, there must be a well-thought-out and joined-up strategy. Many considerations need to be taken into account, which have been highlighted already in this chapter. However, it is worth re-stating them here once more. Consideration needs to be given as to whether each individual state applies jurisdiction and monitors and controls the situation within its

---

[95]   Ibid.

[96]   Ryder (2011).

[97]   Home Office, 'Counter Terrorism', http://www.homeoffice.gov.uk/counter-terrorism/current-threat-level/, accessed 28 February 2011.

own boundaries or whether there is an internationally agreed upon plan to combat economic crime globally.

Although the UK does not have an economic crime barrier in place, the UK can and does use the Regulation of Investigatory Powers Act 2000 (RIPA). RIPA requires that when public authorities – such as the police or government departments – need to use covert techniques to obtain private information about someone, they do it in a way that is necessary, proportionate, and compatible with human rights.[98] RIPA's guidelines and codes apply to actions such as:

- intercepting communications, such as the content of telephone calls, emails or letters;
- acquiring communications data – the 'who, when and where' of communications, such as a telephone bill or subscriber details;
- conducting covert surveillance, either in private premises or vehicles (intrusive surveillance) or in public places (directed surveillance);
- the use of covert human intelligence sources, such as informants or undercover officers;
- access to electronic data protected by encryption or passwords.

Therefore in one way it could be said that the UK does play an important role in trying to combat economic crime. What is problematic for the crime agencies is that little is known about economic crime in virtual worlds and how to catch the criminals. Technology inhibits control in this instance. In other countries, for example the US, and in Interpol, work is being done to monitor the situation and to provide technological solutions.

RULE OF LAW AND VIRTUAL WORLD JURISDICTIONS

From the two previous sections we can see that there is rigorous debate as to whether the internet and cyberspace can be regulated and if so, who it can be regulated by. Extrapolating further from these debates leads to an analysis of whether, if there were law present in cyberspace, it would be compliant with the rule of law and democratic procedures. For example,

---

[98]   Home Office, 'Regulation of Investigatory Powers Act', http://www.home-office.gov.uk/counter-terrorism/regulation-investigatory-powers/, accessed 28 February 2011.

if we regulate the internet, who has the right to govern? Proceeding from a self-governance and separatist viewpoint, regulation would be evolving from the people that are governed by it. Democracy would be with the people. However, if we take an inclusionist point of view and the view proffered above, in the first instance we would see power lying in the hands of central government in each country or zone and later being held by an international committee on cyber regulation. For any legal system in cyberspace to be legitimate, we must ask those questions which are asked in the real world, such as: 'who rules the Internet, in whose interest, by which mechanisms and for which purposes?'[99] Weber and Grosz propose a new method by which internet governance could be perceived so as to legitimise their actions. Presently there is a move afoot to move from the traditional international and political understanding of legitimacy towards a multi-stakeholder governance, but it has been questioned whether this would provide sufficient legitimacy. Weber and Groz state that the internet, being cross-jurisdictional, is the perfect platform for democratic governance. The Geneva Declaration of Principles, adopted by the World Summit on the Information Society (WSIS) 2003, noted: 'the international management of the internet should be multilateral, transparent, and democratic, with the full involvement of governments, the private sector, civil society and international organisation'.[100]

Although this utopian view of the Internet and its governance provides a form of legitimacy and democratic procedures, it is impractical in practice. To ensure that all states agree on matters relating to the internet would be impossible given countries' and states' differing views on core subjects. For example in China, Facebook[101] is banned and technological barriers block people's access to the site, whereas in most parts of the world, Facebook is widely used by many people in society and is freely available to all. As long as the digital divide persists, global participation is a very ambitious objective.[102] To legitimise the regulation of authority means that there is a right for the person or persons in charge to make these regulations. In other words, there must be a democracy. For a democratic election to occur all participatory states must have the same access to vote and have the same information available to them so they can make an informed choice. In countries which are either curtailed in freedom of

---

[99] Weber and Grosz (2007).
[100] The Geneva Declaration of Principles, adopted by the World Summit on the Information Society (WSIS) 2003, para. 48, http://www.itu.int/wsis/docs/geneva/official/dop.html, accessed 3 March 2011.
[101] Social Media Networking Site, www.facebook.com.
[102] Weber and Grosz (2009).

information or in developing countries which do not have the technological infrastructure to allow this to occur, this democratic procedure would be nearly impossible to achieve. Therefore to ensure a legitimate regulation which spanned all countries would at this stage in history be impractical. However, should this be possible, democracy and the rule of law must not be forgotten in the legitimising of internet regulation. As Reidenberg states, 'jurisdiction fits within a border struggle over the respect for the rule of law in the information society. In effect, jurisdiction over activities on the Internet has become one of the main battlegrounds for the struggle to establish the rule of law in information society'.[103]

As iterated in Chapter 3, the rule of law suggested by Lord Bingham is that all persons and authorities within the state, whether public or private, should be bound by and entitled to the benefit of laws publicly and prospectively promulgated and publicly administered in the courts.[104] In general therefore it means that no one is above the law and that the state's citizens are bound by the rules and that if they break them, they shall be tried fairly by a fair legal system. This system of legitimising the legal system is not new but the manner in which is applied to the internet has provoked much debate on the subject.[105] Lord Bingham has clarified the rule of law through seven points:

1. That law must be accessible and so far as possible intelligible, clear and predictable.

As outlined above, presently this cannot happen for either political or technological reasons since not everyone in the world has the ability to use the internet or has access to a legal system which would govern the use of such technology.

2. That questions of legal right and liability should ordinarily be resolved by application of the law and not the exercise of discretion.

The second of Lord Bingham's pronouncements also poses problems with the application of a legal system to those people whose countries and government provide a stricter control over access to information than others. There is no universal openness of information in the present day.

---

[103] Reidenberg (1998).
[104] Lord Bingham Text Transcript, Law Society for Hereford and Worcester, Tuesday 15 April 2010.
[105] For more debate on the rule of law and the internet, see Reidenberg (2005); Kohl (2002); Chik (2010).

3.   That the laws of the land should apply equally to all, save to the extent that objective differences justify differentiation.

Again to ensure that there is universal coverage of laws to everyone would be impossible in today's world as each government holds its own views as to what is acceptable for its people. The freedom that the internet provides is often inhibited.

4.   That means must be provided for resolving, without prohibitive cost or inordinate delay, bona fide civil disputes which the parties themselves are unable to resolve.

Presently, disputes are resolved using either choice of law, private or public international law. There is no agreement as to what is best and most applicable for the internet.[106]

5.   That ministers and public officers at all levels must exercise the powers conferred on them reasonably, in good faith, for the purpose for which the powers were conferred and without exceeding the limits of such powers.

Lord Bingham's fifth point about expanding the rule of law can also not be fulfilled when looking at the regulation and exercise of power over the internet. There is presently no democracy in place to be exercised over the internet; rather it is for democratically elected states to ensure regulation. This is one step removed from direct regulation.

6.   That adjudicative procedures provided by the state should be fair. The rule of law would seem to require no less.

Once more although internet disputes are resolved within the courts of participating countries, there is no united adjudicative procedure for any dispute or criminal act.

7.   That the existing principle of the rule of law requires compliance by the state with its obligations in international law, the law which whether deriving from treaty or international custom and practice governs the conduct of nations.

The seventh principle as stated by the late Lord Bingham opens the rule of law to the wider application of international law. If, as Lord Bingham

---

[106]   Wang (2011).

states, there must be adherence to international laws, then laws relating to the internet and cyberspace must also be adhered to. Therefore if we take the inclusionist view that presently each country has to control and regulate its own use of the internet, then each country must, under the rule of law, adhere to those principles offered by other countries. This is the beginning of the creation of a universal regulation for the internet.

Kohl accepts that there is a legal system operating within cyberspace, albeit in a piecemeal way, and that the legal system is applicable to the rule of law. Kohl points out that in any legal system there is a maxim which states 'ignorance of the law is no defence'. This must apply even in cyberspace and provides an incentive for users of the internet to make themselves aware of their legal obligations whilst in cyberspace. Kohl uses Raz's definition of the rule of law 'as a political ideal, according to which people should obey the law and be ruled by it'.[107] Raz further opines that the law of any system must be clear and precise and that it must not be secret or hidden.[108] In many ways, his view is the same as Lord Bingham's and both cause problems for users of the internet because of the lack of transparency surrounding internet sites as to which jurisdiction is applicable for individual sites. Although laws must not be hidden, because of the cross-jurisdictional issues associated with internet sites, a person may not be aware that they have stepped out of one jurisdiction that they are aware of and into another. The possibility of breaching laws that people do not know exists is therefore probable. As iterated above, given that ignorance is no defence, then it can be foreseen that the internet is going to pose more legal questions in the future as use and technology develop.

SUMMARY

This chapter began with the British Advisory Fraud Panel describing virtual worlds as 'a parallel universe with almost no external rule of law, no enforced banking regulations or compliance, no policing and no government oversight'.[109] Throughout this chapter we have proved this not to be the case. There are rules and laws within the virtual world and within the internet. Cases have been decided using real world principles

---

107   Raz (1977), pp. 195, 196.
108   Ibid.
109   Fraud Advisory Panel (2009).

to solve in-world disputes. However, what is clear is that to regulate the virtual world is a complex matter, for in any virtual world, there are many networks and ISPs which can cross many jurisdictional borders. Locating the true jurisdiction of any virtual world is time consuming and extremely complex. There are many virtual worlds contained on even more networks and although law is present within cyberspace, virtual worlds are relatively law free. Indeed, they are almost completely banking law free. Therefore economic crime and money laundering occur. It is not as if the authorities are not aware of the problem; rather they are working to solve it. However, to tackle economic crime in virtual worlds is complex. Many questions need to be answered and many of these cannot be answered or solved by one or even a couple of countries cooperating. The internet has the capability of being global. Constraints, such as technology or political will, prevent full take-up of the technology, but that capability exists. For there to be a regulation which would encompass all countries, there would have to be an agreement by all countries as to what the law is, who is in control, what the adjudicative procedure should be and what would be a suitable punishment. In reality, views on this are very much personal to each individual country. To gain an agreement of all countries would take many years. This chapter has therefore asked various questions and examined the academic debate surrounding them. The chapter has asked: who can govern the internet? How is the internet different from the virtual world? Who holds the democratic authority to decide what is right and wrong within the virtual worlds? Can you implement laws within the internet and thus virtual worlds? Can virtual world laws be part of the real world legal system, and if so from what legal system, or are they separate from the real world? How can you impose laws onto a virtual world which crosses borders and jurisdictions? Where can people who have committed a wrong in a virtual world be held accountable? Through an examination of the debate between separatists and inclusionists on what regulation in a virtual world would be like, as well as analysing the rule of law and jurisdiction of the internet and virtual worlds, these questions have been explored. Many also remain without a final solution. Technology, like law, moves rapidly and presently they are out of sync with each other over regulating not only economic crime but general behaviour on the internet and in virtual worlds. There has been much debate about the legal system of the internet, but little has been constructed around virtual worlds. This chapter, and indeed this book, aims to use the law and legal thinking in place surrounding the internet and apply it to the virtual world phenomenon. Judge Posner, speaking in Second Life as an avatar, said that he believed customs would evolve into laws in virtual worlds. He states, 'The way law historically develops is from custom. I can imagine customs emerging from interactions among avatars, and then Linden codifying the customs, as laws, that seem to best regulate the virtual world . . . eventually there will be an international law of virtual worlds'.[110]

---

[110] Posner (2006).

7.   Recommendations and conclusion

INTRODUCTION

Virtual economic crime is an interesting phenomenon. Throughout human history we have seen how technology advances our lives and also lets criminals devise new ingenious ways of breaking the laws that society have agreed on. Virtual worlds are just one new opportunity for those wishing to break the law, but the manner in which virtual worlds could be regulated is very uncertain. Little regulation is in place to control and monitor the goings-on in virtual worlds, enabling criminals to take advantage of these loopholes in the law and commit financial crime. As we already know, financial crime can have devastating effects. For example, financial crime can be the starting point of funding terrorist activity.

Within this book an examination of virtual economic crime and in particular of money laundering within Second Life has taken place. Each chapter has added its own twist and turn to the multifaceted aspects of virtual economic crime. In the second chapter, the history and evolution of the virtual world, Second Life, was discussed. The aim of the chapter was to explain and highlight how virtual worlds, although based on the internet, have evolved and grown in similar ways to how real societies have evolved and developed. The point of this was to explain that although the ethos of these worlds is to create a second life outside the realms of the laws and physics of the real world, the human psyche is ingrained in the structure and organisation of virtual worlds. For example, even though the avatar created by a resident in Second Life can fly, they also dress themselves in clothes and can have normal everyday items such as trainers, cars. They can go to the shops, banks and do business. The virtual world is 'virtual' in the sense that it is intangible and not because it is outside the realms of the human social construct. Chapter 2 therefore sets the scene for the general discussion throughout the book which develops the argument that if virtual worlds are not truly virtual and if what occurs in the virtual world can have a real effect on the real world, then these virtual worlds should be regulated to ensure that human rights, beliefs and general laws are upheld and not breached.

Chapter 3 examines the movement of money and the philosophy behind virtual economies. The concepts of virtual economies and the virtual marketplace are discussed in order to outline the need for regulation by demonstrating the economic effects on the real world by the virtual economy within these virtual worlds. Second Life is once again used as an example of virtual economies and virtual businesses. The chapter also highlights examples of virtual economic crimes, virtual crises and virtual bank runs. This is used to promulgate the argument that the virtual world in terms of economic development and evolution is not so different from the real world. The chapter also deals with the bifurcation of opinion as to whether the virtual economies of virtual worlds do indeed have a real world impact. Academics and industry are divided as to whether the economic impact of virtual worlds are significant enough to really affect the real world. This interesting debate is a constant theme throughout the book, whereby there is a strong division between whether people accept the virtual worlds as having an impact and effect on the real world. This division of opinion is another obstacle when it comes to effectively tackling financial crime within the virtual worlds. The chapter argues that in order to create effective regulation there needs to be cohesive agreement as to how to tackle virtual financial crime. If this is not achieved, then virtual financial criminals will continue to get away with crimes. However, this cannot be done until the furore surrounding the true nature of virtual worlds is settled. The chapter also highlights the impossibility of deterring, catching and prosecuting financial criminals, given the lack of certainty surrounding jurisdictions over the crime committed.

In order to try to settle the argument surrounding the nature of virtual economies, Chapter 4 examines the history and development of money. The essence of this chapter is to explain that even the real world currency was once considered to be virtual or un-real. For example, when bartering was the main economic system, if a time traveller had gone back and asked to pay for a bag of grain with a debit card, this would not have been considered a real or legal method of currency. Thus the history of money is discussed to demonstrate not only the evolution of money but also how society adapts to different methods of payment and economic systems. To this end, it is hoped that the reader will gain an understanding that human perceptions as to what constitutes the real and the virtual is a great influence on the true regulation of virtual economies. The chapter also considers the rules and regulations of real world banking and finance in order to demonstrate how money in virtual worlds needs to be regulated. In the real world, given the latest economic crisis of 2007–8, financial regulation is important to maintain equilibrium and growth within a society. For Second Life to maintain its pattern of development, or indeed for any other virtual worlds, there needs to be an effective legal system in place.

Chapter 5 examines virtual money and explains how virtual money laundering and financial crime occur within virtual worlds. It looks at the technical difficulties in combating virtual crime. The chapter also looks at different case studies of instances where financial crime has occurred in the virtual world and how law enforcement agencies are trying to combat it. The chapter concludes by looking at how real world money laundering and financial crime legislative provisions do not consider virtual economic crime. The chapter consider various countries, selected either because virtual economic crime is thought to take place there or because criminals come from such countries or else they are the main driving force in combating virtual economic crime. The countries in question are Korea, China, Hong Kong, the USA and the UK. The chapter concludes that there is little domestic legislation in these countries that actually tries to tackle virtual financial crime; such activity merely comes under normal financial crime acts. In addition, international virtual financial crime acts are also non-existent. The EU Convention on Cyber Crime is considered later in this concluding chapter.

Chapter 6 is an exploration of the laws and regulations surrounding virtual worlds and virtual economies. An interesting discussion takes place on the views of the inclusionists and the separatists as to whether virtual laws should be derived from real world laws or whether, as the separatists argue, virtual worlds laws should either be separate from the real world, since the virtual world has nothing to do with the real world, or there should be no laws at all. The chapter begins with an examination of the 1996 Declaration of Independence by Barlow, which states that the internet is a world separate from the real and that the real world has no sovereignty over the internet. As mentioned in earlier chapters, this argument really impedes the movement towards a consensus on a joined-up policy towards combating virtual financial crime. The chapter moves on to discuss the complexity of regulating the internet, which has many layers of differing connections in many different jurisdictions. The regulation of the internet is not a simple matter. It appears that technology and the law has moved out of sync with each other and the law is struggling to keep pace with the ever changing and evolving technology. However, what can be deduced is that criminals are using the internet and virtual worlds to find new ways of laundering money and committing financial crimes.

THE FIGHT AGAINST VIRTUAL ECONOMIC CRIME

Throughout this book the nature of virtual economic crime has been explored and in Chapter 6 an examination of the legal position was

outlined. In this section, an examination of the conventions and protocols surrounding cyber crime in general will be carried out. The reason
for doing this here is because these conventions and protocols discuss
the wider remit of cyber crime and not the particular crime of virtual
financial crime. Therefore it is important to discuss these in order to for-
mulate recommendations as to how to create a convention or protocol
which could encompass virtual financial crime, which is the aim of this
chapter.

In early 2011, the UK government decided to opt into the new EU
Directive on Attacks against Information Systems. The government in the
UK, as well as in other countries, such as the US, China and Australia, to
name but a few, are taking seriously the need to tackle cyber crime. The
Directive will allow the police forces of Member States who opt into the
Directive to work more closely with each other. It will also set minimum
rules which will be applicable across the EU, sending out a message to
criminals that there are no soft countries on this topic. The EU Directive
will replace the 2005 Framework Decision and will require countries to
criminalise the international interception of non-public transmissions of
computer data from an information system.[1]

This announcement came only a year after the UK, US, Canada and
the EU failed to reach an agreement in general terms with Russia, China
and a number of other developing countries in order to create a global
treaty on cyber crime under the auspices of the United Nations (UN).
The disagreement over the global treaty was largely due to the issues of
sovereignty and concerns for human rights. The EU and US also held the
position that a new treaty was not needed given the Budapest Convention
on Cyber Crime which is already in place and has been signed and ratified
by 46 countries since it was drafted by the Council of Europe in 2001. The
Budapest Convention will be discussed later in this chapter. Furthermore,
the US and the UK believed that any UN or global treaty would take too
long to agree on.

Contrary to the ideology of the US, UK and other EU Member
States, Australia is taking rather a hard line on tackling cyber crime.
Peter Coroneous, co-founder of the International Internet Industry
Association and head of Australia's internet body, believes that if cyber
crime as an agenda item was brought to meetings such as those of the
G20, then it would accelerate the adoption of a global consensus on cyber

---

[1]   BBC News, 'UK Decides to Opt in to EU-wide Cyber Security Plan', 3
February 2011, http://www.bbc.co.uk/news/uk-politics-12354931, accessed 27 July
2011.

crime.[2] Australia is already putting in place security plans to prevent cyber hacking and has announced a cyber defence strategy. The UK, as well as the rest of the world, should take note of these measures taken by Australia because it was reported in 2011 that cyber crime costs have now risen to £27bn a year in the UK. Given the financial situation presently experienced in the UK, this is a cost which must be tackled, for it will only grow over time.

UNITED NATIONS CONVENTION AGAINST TRANSNATIONAL ORGANISED CRIME AND THE PROTOCOLS 2000

It has already been established that the link between cyber crime, money laundering, financial crime and organised crime is a verifiable fact. Cyber crime conventions and regulations have therefore stemmed from the basic preambles of combating organised crime. This 2000 convention is the first that can be used to highlight the important of cross-border cooperation. However, the convention does not refer to cyber crime or internet crime and certainly does not refer to virtual world economic crime. The Kofi Annan statement in the foreword that 'if crime crosses borders, so must law enforcement. If the rule of law is undermined not only in one country, but in many, then those who defend it cannot limit themselves to purely national means'.[3] This sentiment is still pertinent several years later and is still not being accepted by all countries of the world.

Article 4 outlines the recognition and protection of countries' sovereignty within their national boundaries of laws and regulations. This acknowledgement of the importance of sovereignty depicts the battle that regulators and policy makers have faced ever since. The convention also outlines the criminalisation of participating in organised crime and creates benchmark standards on prosecutions and penalties for these criminal acts. However, it is outdated and not applicable to today's cyber crimes, but if it was needed, then its provisions are broad enough to be interpreted to encompass various aspects of cyber crime, even though it is not openly specified within the convention.

---

[2] Reuters, 'World Leaders Should Put Cyber Security on Agenda: Internet Body', 2011, http://www.reuters.com/article/2011/06/14/us-cyber-internet-idUS TRE75D1AS20110614, accessed 17 July 2011.

[3] United Nations Convention against Transnational Organised Crime and the Protocols 2000, p. iii.

THE BUDAPEST CONVENTION 2001

The Budapest Convention on Cyber Crime was signed in 2001 and allows police to cross national borders, without the consent of local authorities, in order to access servers. However, the network system providers need to give permission to the police to access their servers. Not all countries have agreed to these measures, among them Russia and China and other developing countries, because of concerns over human rights and privacy issues. This is an interesting division of opinion given that countries such as China have a known record of preventing open use of the internet by their own people.

Though the Budapest Convention is known as the cyber crime convention, it does not specially mention virtual economic crime or virtual worlds. This convention is now ten years out of date. It too promotes the importance of mutual assistance, international cooperation and adopting a common criminal policy. It also states that it 'must be mindful to ensure a proper balance between the interest of law enforcement and respect for fundamental human rights'. This is a balance which has been part of the regulators' mindset for the last decade. It could be said that it has been an obstacle when devising an effective policy to fight cyber crime and in particular virtual economic crime. The need to protect basic human rights can also be used as an argument in favour of enacting a more joined-up cyber crime convention, given that people's rights online are also being breached by criminals and that there is a lack of regulation designed to protect those basic rights. Human rights is an interesting principle which must undoubtedly be balanced when creating any laws, but its principles must be seen in both lights and the primary objective of protecting people must be at the forefront of the agenda. The convention is therefore outdated and not appropriate for combating virtual economic crime, but its principles on cooperation and mutual assistance go a long way to building a path for a convention which would encompass these elements. The convention is, however, the regulation in force which has the broadest reach, even today.

FINANCIAL ACTION TASK FORCE (FATF) 2003–4, 40 RECOMMENDATIONS

The FATF's 40 recommendations and nine special recommendations deal with regulating and internationalising cooperation in relation to money laundering and terrorist financing. When conducting a content analysis search for the words 'cyber crime', neither the FATF 2003–4

40 Recommendations nor its guidance report mentions this criminal act. When doing the same for internet crime, only two hits appears and these are in relation to casino-related money laundering crimes, where casinos cannot be placed online. Although these recommendations are comprehensive and do set out effective standards for combating money laundering and terrorist financing, they do not encompass the new trend in virtual economic crime which can lead to terrorist financing and also encompasses money laundering. These recommendations are now six years out of date and need to be updated to allow for new developments in financial crime.

FINANCIAL ACTION TASK FORCE – MONEY LAUNDERING AND TERRORIST FINANCING VULNERABILITIES OF COMMERCIAL WEBSITES AND INTERNET PAYMENT SYSTEMS 2008

This report in 2008 is the first document which outlines the risk the inter-net poses in terms of money laundering and terrorist financing. When conducting a content analysis search, the word 'internet' appears 259 times, the word 'cyber' appears once on page 7 in relation to cyber cafes and the anonymity issues of detection. The word 'virtual' appears three times – twice on page 13 in relation to virtual precious metals being sold through payment systems and once again on page 18 in relation to the internet being a virtual fence for selling counterfeit products. The report goes some way to tackling the ideas of the correlation between the inter-net and money laundering and terrorist financing, but even some three years ago the problems of virtual money laundering and virtual economic crime were not present in regulators' minds. This is a reason for concern because whether or not policy makers and regulators were thinking about virtual economic crime, the criminals would still have been using these avenues for criminal pursuits. The report does acknowledge that the internet does pose a high risk of money laundering and terrorist financing due to such things as anonymity, non-face-to-face registrations, limited human intervention, yet it fails to take the small leap to encompass virtual economic crimes. Also for the first time, the report acknowledges that the risks associated with money laundering and terrorist financing also apply to commercial transactions on the internet. Furthermore, the report opines that in order to regulate against money laundering and ter-rorist financing correctly, regulations cannot be hampered by differing countries' legislative procedures and thus an international standard is required.

UK'S CYBER CRIMES STRATEGY 2010

This is one of the most up-to-date policy statements on combating cyber crimes in the UK. Other policy statements relate to those cyber crimes that are outside the remit of the book. On a content analysis search of the document, virtual was mentioned in relation to the virtual criminal networks five times. It made no further mention of virtual economic crimes nor of virtual money laundering. Indeed it made no mention at all of money laundering or terrorist financing. It did, however, put forward the notion that cyber crime can only be tackled with a joined-up approach and agencies such as the Serious Organised Crime Association (SOCA), Office of Cyber Security (OCS), the Police Central E-crimes Unit (PCeU), United National, Internet Governance Forum, the Global Virtual Task Force and the Association of Chief Police Officers (ACPO), to name but a few of the pertinent agencies. What is enlightening is that the stance of the government is that if an activity is illegal offline, then it shall be illegal online too. This is the right ethos to be moving forward with. The report also fails to acknowledge the presence of virtual economic crime being a substantial threat to the economy, thus demonstrating the importance on improving awareness on the subject.

TWELFTH UNITED NATIONS CONGRESS ON CRIME PREVENTION AND CRIMINAL JUSTICE 2010

This report by the UN demonstrates how important the detection and prevention of cyber crime is. It states clearly that there has been no effort to harmonise national legislation to create a global convention on cyber crime. The report outlines how cyber crime is continually growing in terms of occurrences and also in the methods by which crimes are being committed. Like many of its counterparts, it states that there needs to be cross-border cooperation to ensure a standardised set of rules for combating cyber crime. Unlike the other reports discussed, this report notes the use of restricting cross-border information flows throughout the use of ISP restrictions. This is mainly used for the protection of minors against paedophilia. However, care must be taken over the use of restrictions because of the implications this may have for affecting people's human rights under the European Convention on Human Rights.

When conducting a content analysis search of the report, it was found that cyber crime appeared 54 times, none of which related to economic or financial cyber crime. Money laundering and financial crime appear once each. Once again, it appears to be strange to ignore such a large aspect of economic cyber crime in such a report. The report did, however, remark on the need to train law enforcement agencies in the detection of cyber crime and commented upon the cyber crime tool kit that was created by European Funding.[4]

CONCLUDING REMARKS

Despite the publication of rules and regulation in this area, it is the courts that have to keep pace with the evolution of technology and its legal basis. Financial criminal acts which span jurisdictions were once considered to be no one else's business but that of the country in which the crime took place. The restrictive approach adopted by the common law in the late nineteenth and early twentieth centuries typifies this. Take the *SS Lotus* case, PCIJ (Ser. A) No. 10 (1927), where it was determined that a country 'may not exercise its power in any form in the territory of any other state'. Furthermore, Lord Halsbury stated in *Macleod v A-G for New South Wales* [1891] AC 455 (at 458) that 'all crime is local'. However, during the twentieth century a new principle called the Comity principle relaxed these rules and allowed countries to punish individuals outside of their territorial boundaries. The principle was developed by Lord Diplock in the case of *DPP v Treacy* [1971] AC 537. Lord Diplock was highly critical of the territorial principle and now the Comity principle has become the prevailing test for criminal jurisdiction.

This ability to punish financial crimes outside jurisdiction is helpful when looking for a way to punish virtual financial crimes, which, by their very nature, are outside a specific jurisdiction. What is required is for regulators, governments, politicians, law makers, law enforcement agencies and academics to come together to create a unified law which allows cross-border jurisdiction specifically related to virtual financial crimes. In the above discussion on current policy papers, it is clear that virtual financial crime is the forgotten cyber crime of the twenty-first century. Its absence from this report is telling. There are several reasons for this, but it is not because virtual financial crime is not occurring, for throughout this book it has been demonstrated that it is an ever present threat. Indeed law enforcement agencies have shown their concerns over this growing threat. The reason for the lack of discussion of virtual financial crime is because it is a difficult concept and there are many complex and unresolved aspects

---

[4] For more information, please see: Cybercrime toolkit, http://www.itu.int/ITU-D/cyb/cybersecurity/docs/itu-toolkit-cybercrime-legislation.pdf, accessed 10 July 2011.

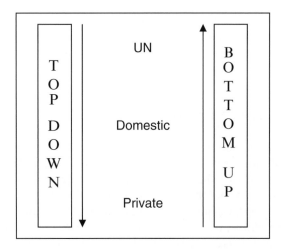

Figure 7.1   Threefold approach to creating a unified virtual financial crime law

that are interlinked with it. For example, as has been shown in previous chapters, there is discourse as to whether virtual financial crime even exists or not. There is further discourse as to whether the real world law has a place or governance within the virtual world. There are discussions over jurisdiction issues, as well as the problem of how to regulate and control a virtual economy. Various things must happen for virtual financial crime to be taken seriously.

1.   There must be more awareness of virtual financial crime.
2.   Training must be provided for law enforcement agencies and law makers as to the intricacies of the crime.
3.   There must be a sufficient software tool which will help detect and deter financial criminals from using virtual worlds to commit crime.
4.   ISPs must take responsibility for their part in monitoring and also preventing virtual financial crime. They must also have the necessary tools and legal backing to block the flow of information across borders.
5.   There must be a joined-up global convention on cyber crime which must have a specific section on virtual financial crime.
6.   More research must be conducted into virtual financial crime so that the above can happen.

The approach must therefore be threefold, and it must be top down and bottom up (see Figure 7.1).

This book is just the beginning of research into this area of law. It is hoped it will promote awareness in the area and allow policy makers a chance to create a new law on virtual financial crime. What this book has demonstrated is that there is a real and ever present threat of virtual financial crime. It is costing the economies of the world billions of dollars each year and criminals are being allowed to exploit legal loopholes to commit financial crime. Just because something is not what we are used to does not mean that it does not exist or is any less real. Virtual financial crime is a real international crime and not a game to be played. Furthermore, it needs a real international convention to combat it.

Bibliography

2009 e-commerce Survey of Business datasets, http://www.statistics.gov.
uk/downloads/theme_economy/ecommerce-2009/dataset-links2009.pdf,
accessed 18 January 2011.

Akdenzi, Y. (2001), 'Yahoo', *Electronic Business Law Reports*, 1(3), 110–
120, http://www.cyber-rights.org/documents/yahoo_ya.pdf, accessed 23
February 2011.

Alcock, A. (1998), 'Financial Services: A Regulatory Monster', *Journal of
Business Law*, July, 371.

Aragandona, A. (2009), 'Can Corporate Social Responsibility Help us
Understand the Credit Crisis', University of Navarra, IESE Business
School, http://papers.ssrn.com/sol3/papers.cfm?abstract_id=1392762,
accessed 26 May 2011.

Arora A. (1988), 'The Banking Act 1987: Part 1', *The Company Lawyer*,
9(1), 8–13.

Bank of England Website, www.bankofengland.org.uk, 5 December 2011,
p.43.

Barlow, J.P. (1996), 'A Declaration of the Independence of Cyberspace',
8 February, Davos, https://projects.eff.org/~barlow/Declaration-Final.
html, accessed 8 February 2011.

Bartle, R. (2004), *Designing Virtual Worlds*, Indianapolis: New Riders
Press, 3–21.

BBC News, 'UK Decides to Opt in to EU-wide Cyber Security Plan',
3 February 2011, http://www.bbc.co.uk/news/uk-politics-12354931,
accessed 27 July 2011.

BBC News, 'Robots to Get their own Internet', 9 February 2011, http://
www.bbc.co.uk/news/technology-12400647, accessed 9 February 2011.

BBC News, 'Credit Crunch Timeline', 7 August 2009, http://news.bbc.
co.uk/1/hi/business/7521250.stm.

BBC News, 'FSA Failed over Northern Rock', 26 January 2008, http://
news.bbc.co.uk/1/hi/business/7209500.stm.

BBC News, 'Rock Report Prompts Reform Calls', 26 January 2008, http://
news.bbc.co.uk/1/hi/business/7210897.stm, accessed 20 February 2009.

BBC News, 'Rush on Northern Rock Continues', 15 September 2007,
http://news.bbc.co.uk/1/hi/business/6996136.stm.

BBC News, 'Sub Prime Crisis Sours US Dream', 5 April 2007, http://news. bbc.co.uk/1/hi/business/6528387.stm.

BBC News, 'UK Net Use Grows Despite Digital Inequalities', 11 November 2010, http://www.bbc.co.uk/news/technology-11734910, accessed 18 January 2011.

BBC News, 'Key US Mortgage Lender Collapses', 13 July 2008, http:// news.bbc.co.uk/1/hi/business/7503109.stm.

BBC News, 'US Moves to Bolster Firms', 14 July 2008, http://news.bbc. co.uk/1/hi/business/7504122.stm.

BBC News, '$200bn Fed Move over Credit Fears', 7 March 2008, http:// news.bbc.co.uk/1/hi/business/7284101.stm.

BBC News, 'Billions Stolen in Online Robbery', 3 July 2009, http://news. bbc.co.uk/2/hi/technology/8132547.stm, accessed 26 April 2010.

BBC News, 'France Bans Internet Nazi Auctions', 23 May 2000, http://news. bbc.co.uk/1/hi/world/europe/760782.stm, accessed 23 February 2011.

BBC News, 'B&B Nationalisation Confirmed', 29 September 2008, http:// news.bbc.co.uk/1/hi/business/7641193.stm.

BBC News, 'Bank of England Plan to Help Out UK Banks', 21 April 2008, http://news.bbc.co.uk/1/hi/business/7351506.stm.

BBC News, 'Banking Act comes into Effect', 21 February 2009, http:// news.bbc.co.uk/1/hi/business/7902350.stm, retrieved 21 February 2009.

BBC News, 'Barclays Plan £4.5bn Fundraising', 25 June 2008, http://news. bbc.co.uk/1/hi/world/7472666.stm.

BBC News, 'Bradford and Bingley Announces Losses', 22 August 2008, http://news.bbc.co.uk/1/hi/business/7587360.stm.

BBC News, 'Brown: Banks Should Be "Servants"', 22 February 2009, http://news.bbc.co.uk/1/hi/uk/7903985.stm, retrieved 22 February 2009.

BBC News, 'Citigroup's $9.8bn Sub-prime Loss', 15 January 2008, http:// news.bbc.co.uk/1/hi/business/7188909.stm.

BBC News, 'Credit Crunch Could Cost $1 Trillion', 8 April 2008, http:// news.bbc.co.uk/1/hi/business/7336744.stm.

BBC News, 'Deal Agreed for Euro Bank Fortis', 29 September 2008, http://news.bbc.co.uk/1/hi/business/7641132.stm.

BBC News, 'FBI Hold 406 People on Mortgage Fraud', 19 June 2008, http://news.bbc.co.uk/1/hi/business/7464298.stm.

BBC News, 'Bear Stearns Ex-manager Charged', 19 June 2008, http:// news.bbc.co.uk/1/hi/business/7463713.stm.

BBC News, 'Fed Slashes Rates in Shock Move', 22 January 2008, http:// news.bbc.co.uk/1/hi/business/7202645.stm.

BBC News, 'Global Shares Tumble on US Fears', 22 January 2008, http:// news.bbc.co.uk/1/hi/business/7199552.stm.

ापर

BBC News, 'Home Repossessions Rise to 27,000', 8 February 2008, http://news.bbc.co.uk/1/hi/business/7234254.stm.

BBC News, 'Leap in Companies Administration', 2 May 2008, http://news.bbc.co.uk/1/hi/business/7380531.stm.

BBC News, 'Lehman Bros Files for Bankruptcy', 16 September 2008, http://news.bbc.co.uk/1/hi/business/7615931.stm.

BBC News, 'Lloyds TSB Seals £12bn HBOS Deal', 17 September 2008, http://news.bbc.co.uk/1/hi/business/7622180.stm.

BBC News, 'RBS Sets out £12bn Rights Issue', 22 April 2008, http://news.bbc.co.uk/1/hi/business/7359940.stm.

BBC News, 'Stamp Duty Axed below £175,000', 2 September 2008, http://news.bbc.co.uk/1/hi/uk_politics/7592852.stm.

BBC News, 'UBS Launches $15.5bn Cash Call', 22 May 2008, http://news.bbc.co.uk/1/hi/business/7414167.stm.

BBC News, 'US Government Rescue Insurer AIG', 17 September 2008, http://news.bbc.co.uk/1/hi/business/7620127.stm.

BBC News, 'US Takes over Key Mortgage Firms', 7 September 2008, http://news.bbc.co.uk/1/hi/business/7602992.stm.

BBC News, 'Warning as HSBC Profits fall 28%', 4 August 2008, http://news.bbc.co.uk/1/hi/business/7540404.stm.

BBC News, 'China Boom "Cushions World Slump"', 9 January 2008, http://news.bbc.co.uk/1/hi/business/7177397.stm.

Benkler, Y. (2006), *The Wealth of Networks*, New York and London: Yale University Press.

Bond, R. (2009), 'Business Trends in Virtual Worlds and Social Networks – an Overview of the Legal and Regulatory Issues Relating to Intellectual Property and Money Transactions', *Entertainment Law Review*, 20(4), 121–8.

Brenner, S.W. (2001), 'Is there Such a Thing as a Virtual Crime', *California Criminal Law Review*, 4(1), 105–11.

Bugeja, M. (2010), 'Avatar Rape', *Inside Higher Ed*, 25 February, http://www.insidehighered.com/views/2010/02/25/bugeja, accessed 29 April 2010.

Butler-Borror, V., 'The Business Benefits of Second Life', Its all Virtual, http://allvirtual.wordpress.com/2010/03/23/business-benefits-of-second-life/, accessed 4 May 2010.

Castronova, E. (2001), 'Virtual Worlds: A First Hand Account of Market and Society on the Cyberian Frontier', CESifo Working Papers, No. 618, December.

Castronova, E. (2002), 'On Virtual Economies', CESifo Working Papers, No. 752, July.

Chambers, C.L. (2004), 'Financial Education and Banking Regulation in the United Kingdom: A template Analysis', Bournemouth University.

Chambers, C.L. (2009), 'The Turner Review: A Verbose Attempt at Curbing the Cycle', *Business Law Review*, May, 158–60.

Chambers, C.L. (2010a), *Financial Exclusion and Banking Regulation in the UK: A Template Analysis*, Saarbrücken, Germany: Lambert Academic Publishing.

Chambers, C.L. (2010b), 'Banking on Reform in 2010: Is Regulatory Change ever enough and will 2010 and the General Election Hold the Answers for the Financial Services Industry?' *The Law Teacher*, July, 44(2), 218.

Chambers, C.L. (2010), 'The Banking Act 2009: A Historical Piece of Legislation or a Relic of our Time; Only History can Tell?' *International Journal of Liability and Scientific Enquiry*, January (online).

Chambers, C.L. and Shufflebottom, M. (2010a), 'Innovation in Inclusion: A Financial M-learning Game Part 1', *The Law Teacher*, March, 44(1), 17–31.

Chambers, C.L. and Shufflebottom, M. (2010b), 'Innovation in Inclusion: A Financial M-learning Game Part 2', *The Law Teacher*, July, 44(2), 117.

Chik, W.B. (2010), 'Customary Internet-ional Law: Creating a Body of Customary Law for Cyberspace, Part 1: Developing Rules for Transitioning Custom into Law', *Computer Law & Security Report*, 26, 3.

Coins to QQ at Web 2.0, 19 February 2008, http://www.forbes.com/2010/01/04/virtual-economy-gaming-technology-breakthroughs-levchin.html, accessed 23 April 2010.

Collins English Dictionary.

Computer Weekly, 'PayPal Launches Multi-pronged Attack on E-crime', 17 March 2008, http://www.computerweekly.com/Articles/2008/03/17/229884/paypal-launches-multi-pronged-attack-on-e-crime.htm, accessed 21 July 2010.

Consumer Affairs Directorate (2001), 'Report by the Task Force on Tackling Over-indebtedness', Consumer Affairs Directorate, p. 7.

Cox, R. (2009), 'A Virtual Bank with Real Woes', *The New York Times*, 15 June, http://www.nytimes.com/2009/06/15/business/15views.html, accessed 29 January 2010.

Cranston, R. (1997), *Principles of Banking Law*, Oxford: Clarendon Press.

Current Law Statutes (1998), Vol. 1, London: Sweet & Maxwell.

Cybercrime toolkit, http://www.itu.int/ITU-D/cyb/cybersecurity/docs/itu-toolkit-cybercrime-legislation.pdf, accessed 10 July 2011.

Dale, R. (1995), 'Bank Crisis Management: The Case of the United Kingdom', *Journal of International Banking Law*, 10(8), 326–32.

Davies, G. (2002), 'History of Money, From Ancient Times to the Present day', Cardiff: University of Wales Press.

Department of Trade and Industry (1985), Cm 9432.

Desguin, H. (2008), 'Money Laundering through Virtual Games'. Strategic assessment, Florida. Department of Law Enforcement, Office of Statewide Intelligence, October.

DGC Magazine, 'China Bans Gold Farming & Limits Virtual Currency', 21 November 2009, http://www.dgcmagazine.com/dp/content/china-bans-gold-farming-limits-virtual-currency.htm, accessed 27 May 2010.

Di Nicola, A. and Scartezzini, A. (2000), 'When Economic Crime Becomes Organised: The Role of Information Technologies. A Case Study', *Journal of the Institute of Criminology*, University of Sydney Faculty of Law, 11(3).

Dibbell, J. (1993), 'A Rape in Cyberspace', *Village Voice*, XXXVIII(51), December.

Dibbell J. (1998), *My Tiny Life Crime and Passion in a Virtual World*, New York: Holt paperbacks.

Edu Games Blog (2008), 'A Run on Virtual Banks in SL', 23 January, http://edugamesblog.worldpress.com/2008/01/23/a-run-on-virtual-banks-in-sl/, accessed 29 January 2010.

Einzig, P. (1966), *Primitive Money in its Ethological, Historical and Economic Aspects*, 2nd edition, Oxford: Pergamon Press.

Electronic Frontier Foundation, 'President Lula and the Cyber Crime Bill', 17 July 2009, http://www.eff.org/deeplinks/2009/07/lula-and-cybercrime, accessed 15 July 2010.

Ellinger, E.P. and Lomnicka, E. (1996), *Modern Banking Law*, Oxford: Clarendon Press.

Ellinger, E.P., Lomnicka, E., and Hooley R. (2006), *Ellinger's Modern Banking Law*, Oxford: Oxford University Press.

Engage Digital, 'OpenLife grid to adopt virtual currency', 13 January 2009, http://www.engagedigital.com/blog/2009/01/13/openlife-grid-to-adopt-virtual-currency-2/, accessed 6 May 2011.

Engle, C. and Keller, K.H. (2002), 'Global Networks and Local Values: A Comparative Look at Germany and the United States', Washington, National Research Council.

European Central Bank, http://www.ecb.int/home/html/index.en.html.

Faber, D.A. (1996), 'Stretching the Margins: The Geographic Nexus in Environmental Law', Stanford Law Review, 48, 1247.

Financial Action Task Force (2006), 'Report on New Payment Methods', October, http://www.fatf-gafi.org/dataoecd/30/47/37627240.pdf, accessed 16 July 2010.

Financial Services Authority, 'Financial Risk Outlook 2008'.

Financial Services Authority, 'Electronic Money Regulations', 1 May 2011, http://www.fsa.gov.uk/Pages/About/What/International/emoney/index.shtml, accessed 1 June 2011.

Finextra, 'PayPal found in Breach of Australia's Anti-money Laundering Laws', 23 November 2009, http://www.finextra.com/news/fullstory.aspx?newsitemid=20781, accessed 21 July 2010.

Forbes (2008), 'Coins to QQ at Web 2.0', 19 February, http://www.forbes.com/2010/01/04/virtual-economy-gaming-technology-breakthroughs-levchin.html, accessed 23 April 2010.

Fraud Advisory Panel (2009), 'Cyber Crime: Social Networking and Virtual Worlds', Issue 4, October, http://www.fraudadvisorypanel.org/new/pdf_show.php?id=119, accessed 15 July 2010.

Froomkin, A.M., 'International and National Regulation of the Internet', University of Miami School of Law, froomkin@law.miami.edu, submitted 8 December 2003, http://law.tm/docs/International-regulation.pdf, accessed 28 February 2011.

Galbraith, J.K. (1975), *Money: Whence it Came, Where it Went*, London: André Deutsch.

Gardiner, B. (2007), 'Bank Failure in Second Life Leads to Calls for Regulation', *Wired*, 15 July, http://www.wired.com/gaming/virtual-worlds/news/2007/08/virtual_bank, accessed 7 May 2010.

Goldsmith, J. and Wu, T. (2006), *Who Controls the Internet? Illusions of a Borderless World*, New York: Oxford University Press.

Gray, J. (2009), 'Northern Rock Shareholders' Challenge to Basis of Compensation in Nationalisation Considered in High Court and Court of Appeal', *Journal of Financial Regulation and Compliance*, 17(4), 467–75.

Griffiths, J. (1986), 'What is Legal Pluralism?', *Journal of Legal Pluralism and Unofficial Law*, 1–56.

Hall, M. (2008), 'The Sub-prime Crisis, The Credit Squeeze and Northern Rock: The Lessons to be Learned', *Journal of Financial Regulation and Financial Regulation and Compliance*, 16(1), 19–34.

Havranek, M. (2000), 'The Bank of England and Bank Failures', *Insolvency Lawyer*, 2(4), 73–80.

Hayek, F. A. (1978), *Denationalisation of Money – The Argument Refined*, London: Institute of Economic Affairs.

Hecks, R. (2008), 'Current Analysis and Future Research Agenda on "Gold Farming": Real World Production in Developing Countries for the Virtual Economies of Online Games', Development Informatics Groups, University of Manchester, UK.

HM Treasury, 'Government Introduces Financial Services Bill', 19 November 2009, http://www.hm-treasury.gov.uk/press_108_09.htm, accessed 22 March 2010.

HM Treasury, Newsroom and Speeches, 'New Banking Act Comes into Effect', 23 February 2009, http://www.hm-treasury.gov.uk/press_16_09.htm, retrieved 23 February 2009.

Home Office, Counter Terrorism, http://www.homeoffice.gov.uk/counter-terrorism/current-threat-level/, accessed 28 February 2011.

Home Office, 'Regulation of Investigatory Powers Act', http://www.homeoffice.gov.uk/counter-terrorism/regulation-investigatory-powers/, accessed 28 February 2011.

House of Commons, Financial Services and Markets Bill No. 121, 1998–9, p.23.

House of Commons Treasury Committee, 'The Run on the Rock, Fifth Report of session', volume 1, London, 2008.

House of Commons, Research Paper, Financial Services Bill, Bill No. 6, 2009–10, 27 November 2009.

House of Commons, Digital Economy Bill, Bill No. 89, 2009–10, 29 March 2010.

House of Lords Science and Technology Committee (2007), p.10, http://www.publications.parliament.uk/pa/ld200607/ldselect/ldsctech/166/16602.htmhttp://www.indiabroadband.net/india-broadband-telecom-news/11682-india-register-500-growth-broadband-services-within-5-years.html, accessed 15 July 2010.

Inside Social Games, 8 December 2008, http://www.insidesocialgames.com/2008/12/08/top-25-facebook-games-for-november-24-2008/, accessed 19 October 2011.

International Herald Tribune, Global Edition of New York Times, 'CEO of Germany's Landesbank Sachsen Says He will Resign', 23 August 2007, http://www.iht.com/articles/ap/2007/08/23/business/EU-FIN-COM-Germany-SachsenLB-CEO-Resigns.php.

Interpol, 'Cybercrime Fact Sheet', 2008, COM/FS/2008-07/FHT-02.

Interpol, 'Robert Hodgins', http://www.interpol.int/public/Data/Wanted/Notices/Data/2010/56/2010_7456.asp, accessed 1 June 2011.

Interpol, 'Virtual Money', 27 May 2010, http://interpol.int/Public/TechnologyCrime/CrimePrev/VirtualMoney.asp, accessed 27 May 2010.

Jang, J. (2008), 'The Current Situation and Countermeasures to Cybercrime and Cyber Terror in the Republic of Korea', Department of Police Science, Korea National Police University, Republic of Korea, http://www.unafei.or.jp/english/pdf/PDF_rms/no79/09-1_P46-56.pdf, accessed 21 July 2010.

Jin, G. (2006), 'Chinese Gold Farmers in the Game World', *Consumers, Commodities & Consumption*, 7(2), May, https://netfiles.uiuc.edu/dtcook/www/CCCnewsletter/7-2/jin.htm, accessed 26 May 2011.

Johnson, D. R. (2007), 'The Life of the Law Online', New York Law School Law Review, 51, 956.

Johnson, D. R. and Post, D. G. (1996), 'Law and Borders: The Rise of the Law in Cyberspace', *Stanford Law Review*, 48, 1367–74.

Jones, R. 'The Internet, Legal Regulation and Legal Pluralism', British and Irish Legal Education and Technology Conference, 27–28 March 1998, Dublin, http://www.bileta.ac.uk/Document%20Library/1/The%20Internet,%20Legal%20Regulation%20and%20Legal%20Pluralism.pdf, accessed 1 March 2011.

Kempson, E. and Whyley, C. (1998), 'Access to Current Accounts', A report to the British Bankers Association, Bristol, Personal Finance Research Centre, University of Bristol.

Kerr, O. S. (2003), 'Problems of Perspective', Georgetown Law Journal, 91, 357.

Kock, N. (2008), 'E-collaboration and E-commerce in Virtual Worlds: The Potential of Second Life and World of War Craft', *International Journal of E-collaboration*, 4(3).

Kohl, U. (2002), 'The Rule of Law, Jurisdiction and the Internet', *International Journal of Law and Information Technology*, 12(3).

Korolov, M. (2010), 'Resilience during Virtual Disasters', *Hypergrid Business*, 29 April, http://www.hypergridbusiness.com/2010/04/resilience-during-virtual-disasters/, accessed 7 May 2010.

Lastowka, G. and Hunter, D. (2004), 'Virtual Crimes', *New York Law School Review*, 49, 293.

Leapman, B. (2007), 'Second Life World may be Haven for terrorists', *The Telegraph*, 13 May, http://www.telegraph.co.uk/news/uknews/1551423/Second-Life-world-may-be-haven-for-terrorists.htm, accessed 11 May 2010.

Lessig, L. (1995–6), 'The Zones of Cyberspace', *Stanford Law Review*, 48, 1403–13.

Lessig, L. (1998), 'The Laws of Cyberspace', Draft 3, presented at Taiwan Net '98 conference, in Taipei, March 1998, http://www.lessig.org/content/articles/works/laws_cyberspace.pdf, accessed 21 February 2011.

Lessig, L. (1999), *Code and other Laws of Cyberspace*, New York: Basic Books.

Lessig, L. (2001a), *The Future of Ideas: The Fate of the Commons in a Connected World*, New York: Random House.

Lessig, L. (2001b), 'The Law of the Horse: What Cyberlaw Might Teach', in Jerry Kang, *Communications Law and Policy: Cases and Materials*, New York: Aspen Law and Business.

Lessig, L. (2003), 'The Place of Cyberlaw', in Austin Sarat (ed.), *The Place of Law*, Ann Arbor, MI: University of Michigan Press.

Lessig, L., Zittrain, J., Nesson, C. R., Fisher, W. W. and Benkler, Y. (2002), *Internet Law*, New York: Foundation Press.

Levi, M. (2010), 'Combating the Financing of Terrorism: A History and Assessment of the Control of "Threat Finance"', *British Journal of Criminology*, 650.

Levi, M., Flemming, M. H. and Hopkins, M. (2007), 'The Nature, Extent and Economic Impact of Fraud in the UK', Report for the Association of Chief Police Officers' Economic Crime Portfolio, February.

Ligue contre le racisme et l'antisémitisme et Union des étudiants juifs de France c. Yahoo! Inc. et Société Yahoo! France (*LICRA v. Yahoo!*) 2000.

Linden Labs (2008), 'New Policy Regarding In-World Banks', 8 January, http://blogs.secondlife.com/community/features/blog/2008/01/01/new-policy-regarding-in-world-banks.htm, accessed 15 March 2010.

Linn, C. J. (2008), 'Regulating the Cross-border Movement of Prepaid Cards', *Journal of Money Laundering Control*, 146.

Lomnicka, E. (1999), 'Reforming U.K. Financial Services Regulation: The Creation of a Single Regulator', *Journal of Business Law*, September, 480–892.

Lord Bingham Text Transcript, Law Society for Hereford and Worcester, Tuesday 15 April 2010.

Lynn, V. (2007), 'Virtual Rape is Traumatic, but Is it a Crime?', *Wired*, 5 April, http://www.wired.com/culture/lifestyle/commentary/sexdrive/2007/05/sexdrive_0504, accessed 29 April 2010.

MacKinnon, R. (2007) 'Virtual Rape', *Journal of Computer Mediated Communications*, October 2(4).

MacNeil, I. (1999), 'The Future for Financial Services Regulation: The Financial Services and Markets Bill', *Modern Law Review*, 62(5), 725–43.

Mark, 'World's First Virtual Currency Banking Licences Issued at Entropia Universe', *Money World*, ed. Doug Hanna, 8 May 2007, b5 Media, 17 July 2007, http://www.digitalmoneyworld.com/worlds-first-virtual-currency-banking-licenses-issued-at-entropia-universe, accessed 21 July 2010.

Marshall, J. and Herrod, N. (2009), 'Lehman Brothers Insolvency – Client Assets', *Law and Financial Markets Review*, 3(2), 145–7.

Matonis, J. (1995), 'Digital Cash and Monetary Freedom', Libertarian Alliance Monetary Freedom, http://www.libertarian.co.uk/lapubs/econn/econn063.pdf, accessed 21 July 2010.

McCreevy, C. European Commissioner for the Internal Market and Services, 7th Annual European Financial Services Conference, Financial Markets and Economic Recovery, 27 January 2009, Brussels. See: http://www.forum-europe.com/7th_Annual_European_Financial, retrieved 24 February 2009.

McKnight, A. (2009), 'The Banking Act 2009', *Law and Financial Markets Review*, 3(4), 325–32.

Miller, C. and Stone, B. (2009), 'Virtual Goods Start Bringing Real Paydays', *New York Times*, 6 November.

Monroe, B. (2007), 'Virtual Worlds Clear and Present Danger for Money Laundering', 26 April, Fortent, http://inform.fortent.com/FortentWeb/NewsSummaryHomeGuest.htm?GUID={fd2fl878-4980-887e-157ceff6a3ba}, accessed 11 May 2010.

Moravcsik, A. (1997), 'Taking Preferences Seriously: A Positive Liberal Theory of International Politics', *International Organization*, 51, 513–53.

Nardo, M. (2011), 'Economic Crime and Illegal Markets Integration: A Platform for Analysis', *Journal of Financial Crime*, 47.

National Fraud Authority, 'Annual Fraud Indicators', January 2011.

Netanel, N. W. (2000), 'Cyberspace Self-Governance: A Sceptical View from Liberal Democratic Theory', *California Law Review*, 88, (March), 395.

OECD, http://www.oecd.org/dsti/sti/it/index.htm, accessed 28 February 2011.

Office for National Statistics, internet, access, http://www.statistics.gov.uk/cci/nugget.asp?id=8, accessed 18 January 2011.

Open University Computer Laboratories (2000), 'An Electronic Purse, Specification, Refinement and Proof', http://www-users.cs.york.ac.uk/susan/bib/ss/z/prg126.pdf, accessed 15 July 2010.

Orsingher, R. (1967), *Banks of the World*, London: Macmillian.

PatrickPretty.com, '5 Convicted to Date in Money Laundering Case Involving Colombian Drug Operation that Used the Same Debit Card as AdSurfDaily Autosurf', 17 April 2010, http://www.patrickpretty.com/2010/04/17/update-5-convictions-to-date-in-money-laundering-cases-involving-colombian-drug-operation-that-used-same-debit-card-as-adsurfdaily/, accessed 1 June 2011.

PayPal, 'PayPal Anti-money Laundering and Counter Terrorist-financing Statement', 11 May 2009, https://cms.paypal.com/us/cgi-bin/?&cmd=_render-content&content_ID=ua/AML_full, accessed 21 July 2010.

Point Topic, http://point-topic.com/dslanalysis.php, accessed 15 July 2010.

Posner, R. A. (2006), 'The Second Life of Judge Posner', *New World Notes*, 11 December, http://nwn.blogs.com/nwn/2006/12/the_second life.html, accessed 20 July 2011.

Princeton Education, www.wordnetweb.princeton.edu/perl/webwn, accessed 29 April 2010.

Raz, J. (1977), 'The Rule of Law and its Virtue', *Law Quarterly Review*, 93, 195–211.

Read Write Web, http://www.readwriteweb.com/, accessed 1 October 2011.

Reidenberg, J. R. (1998), 'Lex Informatica: The Formulation of Information Policy Rules through Technology', *Texas Law Review*, 76, 554–5.

Reidenberg, J. R. (2005), 'Technology and Internet Jurisdiction', *University of Pennsylvania Law Review*, 153, 1951–74.

Research Paper, 08/77, Banking Bill, Bill 147 of 2007–08, 10 October 2008.

Reuters Video, 'Sudden Exit for UBS CEO', 6 July 2007, http://www.reuters.com/news/video?videoId=59280.

Reuters, 'World Leaders Should Put Cyber Security on Agenda: Internet Body', 2011, http://www.reuters.com/article/2011/06/14/us-cyber-internet-idUSTRE75D1AS20110614, accessed 17 July 2011.

Reuters (2006), 'Ginko Financial – Pyramid or Pioneer?', 15 October, http://secondlife.reuters.com/stories/2006/10/15/ginko-financial-pioneer-or-pyramid/, accessed 7 May 2010.

Robbins, S. and Bell, M. (2007), *Second Life for Dummies*, New York: Wiley Publishing.

Ryder, N. (2001), 'Two Plus Two Equals Financial Education – the Financial Services Authority and Consumer Education', *Law Teacher*, 35(2), 216–32.

Ryder, N. (2008), 'The Financial Services Authority, the Reduction of Financial Crime and the Money Launderer – A Game of Cat and Mouse', *Cambridge Law Journal*, 67(3), 635–53.

Ryder, N. (2011), *Financial Crime in the 21st Century*, Cheltenham, UK and Northampton, MA, USA: Edward Elgar.

Rymaszewski, M., Au, W. J., Ondrejka, C., Platel, R., Van Gorden, S., Cezanne, J., Cezenne, P., Batson-Cunningham, B., Krotoski, A., Trollop, C., and Rossingnol, J. (2008), *Second Life: The Official Guide*, 2nd edition, Indianapolis, IN: Wiley Publishing.

Schultz, T. (2008), 'Carving up the Internet, Jurisdiction, Legal Order and the Private/Public International law Interface', *The European Journal of International Law*, 19(4), 799–840.

Second Life, 'Business Opportunities', http://secondlife.com/whatis/businesses.php, accessed 4 May 2010.

Semuels, A. (2008), 'Virtual Bank's Second Life Scheme Raises Real Concerns', 22 January, http://articles.latimes.com/2008/jan/22/business/fi-secondlife22, accessed 26 April 2010.

Shea, V. (1994), *Netiquette*, San Francisco: Albion Books, http://www.albion.com/bookNetiquette/0963702513p4.html, accessed 16 February 2011.

Sidel, R. (2008), 'Cheer up Ben: Your Economy Isn't As Bad as This One', *The Wall Street Journal*, 23 January, http://online.wsj.com/article/SB120104351064608025.html, accessed 15 March 2010.

Singh, D. (2007), *Banking Regulation of UK and US Financial Markets*, Aldershot: Ashgate.

Singh, D. and LaBrosse, J. (2010), 'Northern Rock, Depositors and Deposit Insurance Coverage: Some Critical Reflections', *Journal of Business Law*, 2, 55–84.

Sipress, A. (2006), 'Where Real Money Meets Virtual Reality, the Jury is Still Out', *Washington Post*, 26 December, http://www.washington-post.com/wp-dyn/content/article/2006/12/25/AR2006122500635.html, accessed 29 January 2010.

Si-Soo, P. (2010), 'Korea Supreme Court Rules Virtual Currency Convertible to Real Cash', *The Korea Times*, 10 January, http://kore-atimes.co.kr/www/nation/2010/01/116_58775.html, accessed 24 June 2010.

SL Bar Association Website, http://www.slba.info/credentials.hmtl, accessed 20 October 2011.

SL Index, www.secondlife.com/my.index/market.php, accessed 12 September 2011.

Slentre, SLEentrepreneur Profile, Swafette Firefly, Owner and Founder of SF Designs, 6 January 2010, http://www.slentre.com/slentrepreneur-profile-swaffette-firefly-owner-and-founder-sf-designs/, accessed 5 May 2010.

Social Media Networking Site, www.facebook.com.

Software Interrupted (2009), 'US Inches Closes to Taxation of Virtual Goods', 9 January, http://news.cnet.com/8301-13846_3-10138800-62.html, accessed 6 May 2011.

Solomon, M. (2010), 'Why Virtual Economics Matter', *Journal of Virtual World Research*, February, 2(4), 3–14.

Sullivan, K. (2008), 'Virtual Money Laundering and Fraud', 'Anti-money Laundering Training', www.AMLtrainer.com, accessed 12 May 2010.

Sutter, J. D. 'China Restricts Virtual Economies', 1 July 2009, CNN News, http://edition.cnn.com/2009/TECH/07/01/china.virtual.currency/index.html, accessed 27 May 2010.

Technology (2008), 'Credit Crunch Hits Second Life', 30 December, http://www.stuff.co.nz.technology/777892, accessed 15 March 2010.

The Economist, 'Barbarians at the Vault', 15 May 2008, http://www.economist.com/opinion/PrinterFriendly.cfm?story_id=11376185, retrieved 18 February 2009

The Economist, 'Greed & Mash; and Fear', 22 January 2009.

The Financial Times, 21 May 1997.

The Geneva Declaration of Principles, adopted by the World Summit on the Information Society (WSIS) 2003, para. 48, http://www.itu.int/wsis/docs/geneva/official/dop.html, accessed 3 March 2011.

The Guardian, 'A Financial Crisis Unmatched since the Great Depression, Say Analysts', 18 March 2008, http://www.guardian.co.uk/business/2008/mar/18/creditcrunch.marketturmoil1.

The Guardian, 'Panic Selling Shuts £2bn Fund', 18 January 2008, http://www.guardian.co.uk/money/2008/jan/18/property.moneyinvestments.

The Independent, 'Merrill Lynch CEO Poised to Step Down amid Spiralling Losses', 29 October 2008, http://www.independent.co.uk/news/business/news/merrill-lynch-ceo-poised-to-step-down-amid-spiralling-losses-398246.html.

The Wall Street Journal, (2009), 'China Cracks Down on Virtual Currency for Real', 29 June, http://blogs.wsj.com/chinarealtime/2009/06/29/china-cracks-down-on-virtual-currency-for-real/, accessed 21 July 2010.

Times Online, 'The Credit Crunch Explained', 14 August 2008, http://www.timesonline.co.uk/tol/money/reader_guides/article4530072.ece.

Tomasic, R. (2008a), 'Corporate Rescue, Governance and Risk-taking in Northern Rock: Part 1', *Company Lawyer*, 29(10), 297–303.

Tomasic, R. (2008), 'Corporate Rescue, Governance and Risk Taking in Northern Rock: Part 2', *Company Lawyer*, 29(11), 330–37.

Tomasic, R. (2008b), 'The Rescue of Northern Rock: Nationalisation in the Shadow of Insolvency', *Corporate Rescue and Insolvency Journal*, 1(4), 2.

TPA, CM 7308, 30 January 2008, available at: www.hm-treasury.gov.uk/media/3/5/banking_stability_pu477.pdf, retrieved 1 February 2008.

TPA, Cm 7436, 1 July 2008, available at: www.bankofengland.co.uk/publications/other/financialstabilitydepositorprotection080701.pdf, retrieved 10 July 2008.

TPA, Cm 7459, 22 July 2008, available at: www.offical-documents.gov.uk/document/cm74/7459/7459.pdf, retrieved 23 July 2008.

Treasury Select Committee, 'The Mis-selling of Personal Pensions', 12 November 1998, HC 712-II 1997-8.

Treasury Select Committee, Memorandum submitted by the Department of Trade and Industry and HM Treasury, April 2002, http://www.publications.parliament.uk/pa/cm200102/cmselect/cmtreasy/758/2070216.htm.

Treasury Select Committee, 'Run on the Rock', House of Commons, 2008, Fifth Report of Session 2007–08, Vol. 1. p. 3.

United Nations Convention against Transnational Organised Crime and the Protocols 2000.

US Department of Justice National Drug Intelligence Center (NDIC) (2006), 'Prepaid Stored Value Cards: A Potential Alternative to Traditional Money Laundering Methods', No. 2006-R0803-001.

US Department of Justice National Drug Intelligence Center (NDIC), (2008), 'Money Laundering in Digital Currencies', No. 2008-R0709-003, June, p. 1.

US Federal Reserves, http://www.federalreserve.gov/.

Van den Bergh, G. C. J. J. (1992), 'Legal Pluralism in Roman Law', in C. Verga (ed.), *Comparative Legal Cultures*, New York: New York University Press, 451–4.

Virtual World News (2008), 'Virtual Currency, Real Money Laundering', Future Crimes, October, http://www.virtualworldnews.com/2008/10/group-laundered-38m-in-virtual-currencies-in-18-months.html, accessed 27 May 2010.

Virtual World News (2009), 'OpenLife Grid to Adopt Virtual Currency', 13 January, http://www.virtualworldsnews.com/2009/01/openlife-grid-to-adopt-virtual-currency.html, accessed 29 April 2010.

Walker, G. (2010), 'Financial Services Bill', *Financial Regulation Intelligence*, 8–16 February.

Wang, F. F. (2008), 'Obstacles and Solutions to Internet Jurisdiction: A Comparative Analysis of the EU and US Laws', *Journal of International Commercial Law and Technology*, 3(4), 233–41.

Wang, F. F. (2011), *Internet Jurisdiction and Choice of Law: Legal Practices in the EU, US and China*, Cambridge: Cambridge University Press.

Wang, Y. and Mainwaring, S. (2008), 'Human Currency Interaction – Learning from Virtual Currency Use in China', CHI, Florence, Italy, http://www.isr.uci.edu/~yangwang/papers/CHI08-AuthorCopy.pdf, accessed 4 May 2010.

Weber, R. H. and Grosz, M. (2007), 'Internet Governance – from vague Ideas to Realistic Implementation', *Medialex*, 3, 119–35.

Weber, R. H. and Grosz, M. (2009), 'Legitimate Governing of the Internet', *International Journal of Private Law*, 2(3), 316–30.

Wicks, Sir Nigel, Chairman Euroclear, 7th Annual European Financial Services Conference, Financial Markets and Economic Recovery, 27 January 2009, Brussels.

Wu, T. S. (1997), 'Cyberspace Sovereignty? – The Internet and the International System', *Harvard Law Review*, 10(3), summer, 647–66.

Yamaguchi, H. (2004), 'An Analysis of Virtual Currencies in Online Games', The Japanese Centre for International Finance, Social Science Research Institute, International Christian University.

Yoon, U.-G. (2004), 'Real Money Trading in MMORPG Items from a Legal and Policy Perspective', Social Science Research Network, 13 December, http://papers.ssrn.com/sol3/papers.cfm?abstract_id=1113327, accessed 26 May 2011.

Zippo Mfr. Co. v. Zippo Dot Com, Inc., 952 F. Supp. 1119 (W.D. Pa. 1997).

Zittrain, J. (2003a), 'Be Careful What you Ask For: Reconciling a Global Internet and Local Law', in A. Thierer and C. W. Crews (eds), *Who*

Rules the Net? Internet Governance and Jurisdiction, Washington, DC: Cato Institute.

Zittrain, J. (2003b), 'Internet Points of Control', *Boston College Law Review*, 44, 653–88.

Glossary

Avatar	online creation of a person. User's persona created online for virtual worlds
BCCI	Bank of Credit and Commerce International
BOE	Bank of England
CML	Council for Mortgage Lenders
CSR	corporate social responsibility
Digital currencies	electronic money used within an online game/ platform
E-gold	a company which traded gold on an immediate basis, traded illegally and was prosecuted for illegal activities
Economic cyber crime	any form of economic crime such as fraud, money laundering, theft which is performed via the internet. Used interchangeably with virtual economic crime and virtual financial crime
EULA	End User Licence Agreement
FAP	Fraud Advisory Panel
FSA	Financial Services Authority
FSMA	Financial Services and Markets Act
GDCA	Global Digital Currency Association
Gold farming	creation of wealth by people creating goods and services to be sold online in games
Illicit crime	criminal activity related to drug trafficking, human trafficking and financial crime
ISK	interstellar credits
ISP	Internet Service Provider
m-accounts	mobile accounts
MMO	Massively Multiplayer
Money laundering	the process of making illegally gained money to appear to be legal
NFA	National Fraud Authority
OECD	Organisation for Economic Co-operation and Development

Phishing	a means of attempting to acquire sensitive information such as usernames, passwords and credit card details over the internet
Residents	people who are using the virtual worlds
RIPA	Regulation of Investigatory Powers Act 2000
RMT	real money trading
Second Life	virtual world allowing people to create an avatar within the world
SL	Second Life
Spamming	sending unsolicited bulk electronic messages indiscriminately
TOS	Terms of Service
TOU	Terms of User
UNCITRAL	United Nations Commission on International Trade Law
Users	people who are using the virtual worlds
UUI	Universal Unique Identifier
Virtual economic crime	any form of economic crime such as fraud, money laundering, theft which is performed via the internet. Used interchangeably with economic cyber crime and virtual financial crime
Virtual economy	emerging economy where real money can be used to purchase virtual money during 'play' in an online game/platform
Virtual financial crime	any form of economic crime such as fraud, money laundering, theft which is performed via the internet. Used interchangeably with virtual economic crime and economic cyber crime
Virtual goods	goods/services which are created in an online game/platform which can be bought and sold with virtual money in game
Virtual money	currency used within an online game/platform
Virtual money laundering	the process of making illegally gained money appear to be legal through the internet
Virtual world	meaning any online game/platform which allows people to build and create a virtual life
World of Warcraft	virtual world allowing people to create an avatar within the world
WSIS	World Summit on the Information Society
WWIIOL	World War II Online

Index

DATE DUE
